12/4/00

THE &NOW AWARDS 3

THE BEST INNOVATIVE WRITING

EDITED BY MEGAN MILKS

Davis Schneiderman, Series Editor
&NOW Books | Lake Forest, IL

First published 2014 by &NOW Books, an imprint of Lake Forest College Press.

&NOW BOOKS

Carnegie Hall
Lake Forest College
555 N. Sheridan Road
Lake Forest, IL 60045

andnow@lakeforest.edu

lakeforest.edu/andnow

"N18P58" and "N18P54" by Hank Lazer, originally appearing in *Fence* (15.1).

Lake Forest College Press publishes in the broad spaces of Chicago studies. Our imprint, &NOW Books, publishes innovative and conceptual literature and serves as the publishing arm of the &NOW writers' conference and organization.

ISBN: 978-1-941423-98-1

Cover design by Jesssica Berger

Book design by Megan Milks

Printed in the United States.

ACKNOWLEDGMENTS

Many thanks to Davis Schneiderman for seasoned counsel as we steered this project to land; to Joshua Corey for rowing backup; to Jessica Berger for creative genius on demand; to Vanessa Place and Trace Peterson for their curatorial contributions; to all our contributors for The Work (and the patience); to all those at Lake Forest College Press and &NOW who have supported and sustained this project; and to the countless practitioners of transformative lit magick I've encountered at various &NOW Festivals (& beyond) on the way to here.

—*Megan Milks*

TABLE OF CONTENTS

MEGAN MILKS
Foreword: Take Three

AWHILE AGO, ON TUMBLR: an image of a figure in a psychology textbook circulates. The figure presents two stacked photographs: a robin and a penguin, respectively. Below the robin, a caption reads, "(a) Most people have a prototype bird that captures the essence of "birdness" and allows us to quickly classify flying animals correctly." Below the penguin: "(b) When we encounter an example that doesn't quite fit our prototype, we need time to review our artificial concept. Because the penguin doesn't fly, it's harder to classify than a robin." Beneath this two-part figure, a third caption reads, "Figure 8.2 Some birds are 'birdier' than others."[1]

For years I've been avoiding defining the category of "innovative writing." Here's my latest avoidance.

It's the penguin.

And it's the robinniest robin there is.

Also, flying squid.

Through a combination of nominations and solicitations, this volume, the third in a biennial series, collects innovative writing originally published between September 2011 and September 2013[2]. As such, it stands as a documentation of the recent past, a sampling of contemporary practices, modes, and traditions rendered in slices and snapshots, a thumbnail view. (Many of these pieces are excerpted from longer manuscripts; please click to enlarge.) Consider this a record of today's marketplace for innovative lit, representing as it does work published by mostly small presses and independent literary magazines, publishers whose existence is nearly always precarious. Consider this, too, a happy gathering of some of the geniuses writing today—a quality it shares with its namesake.

&NOW is a loosely defined collection of writers who coordinate the &NOW biennial festival of innovative art and literature; 2014 marks its tenth year. Although umbrellaed by the same organization, the festival and the anthology exist independently of one another. Many of the writers collected here have attended at past &NOW conferences; many have not.

This edition of *The &NOW Awards* includes excerpts from two important anthologies published during the time period: *Troubling the Line: Trans and*

Genderqueer Poetry & Poetics (edited by TC Tolbert and Trace Peterson) and *I'll Drown My Book: Conceptual Writing by Women* (edited by Caroline Bergvall, Laynie Browne, Teresa Carmody, and Vanessa Place). Both excerpts have been curated by their respective editors. In anthologizing these anthologies, our aim is to honor the important archival and visibility work they perform, particularly for writers of difference.

How does this anthology stand up? Innovative writing has been perceived by some as illegible, off, strange, "difficult," as such pushed to the edges of creative writing courses and overlooked in craft texts and most "best of" anthologies. This anthology series seeks to remedy that by mapping a dynamic and ecologically diverse field of aesthetic impulses, traditions, and genres that may be considered innovative. Still, territory remains uncharted. In particular, I want to acknowledge the relative underrepresentation of works in translation. We're very pleased to include here Niina Pollari's translation of Tytti Heikkinen's *Täytetyn eläimen lämpö / Warmth of the Taxidermied Animal* and Lawrence Schimel's translation of Luis Aguilar's *Vidrio Molido / Ground Glass*. Other solicited translations did not come through due to copyright issues.

The &NOW Awards aims to recognize emerging writers alongside more established practitioners of innovative writing. With this third volume, we were faced with the question of whether and how much to include work by former contributors. As a general rule in selecting work for this volume, we have included only those former contributors whose recent work is particularly groundbreaking (e.g., Alexandra Chasin, whose *Brief* reinvents the novel as an iPad app) and those who were previously featured for collaborative but not solo projects (e.g., Michael Joyce) or vice versa (e.g., Kate Durbin).

By "the best," we are joking. There is no best, but if there were, this would be the bestiest.

---

[1] http://theskaldspeaks.tumblr.com/post/85920614744/all-bird-are-bird-but-some-bird-more-bird-than

[2] An exception to this timeframe is Eckhard Gerdes's novel *Hugh Moore*, published in 2010. A goof-up on &NOW's end prevented it from being included in the second volume.

DENNIS COOPER

from The Marbled Swarm

Had it been the winter, I might have gambled, viewed the trunk as some-thing more romantic, say the bottom of a well where Serge had fallen, and chanted, "Stay with us, buddy," or some other futile pleasantry.

If Serge had died before we reached the streets of Paris, I would have more than compensated with his slack-jawed shell. To speak somewhat frankly, every boy I've known as well as killed has struck me as his corpse's baby picture.

Still, even a mild summer day is no preservative, and dead boys aren't exactly wheels of brie, however much they might smell the same eventually.

When Serge's lonesome taps grew less important than his wheezing, I told Azmir that if he wished to fuck an ass with any sassiness at all, we should save its owner now and cross our fingers that, if anyone drove past, he would be gay enough to think someone as cute as me could do no wrong.

Azmir swerved our car onto the roadside, causing me to grasp the nearest handle and Serge to bang around and yowl inside his can.

To make the transfer look bewildering, we needed to employ a sleight of hand. While I can spin a tricky story, Serge was more than just a word on that occasion. Luckily, dust is basically a rustic fog unless you're scientific, so Azmir stomped the brakes, which blasted out a semi-decent cloud cover.

We jumped outside then coughed and blinked our way back to the trunk, where, after leaving two or three new nasty scratches, Azmir stabbed the key into the lock. As the lid was drifting open, we grabbed two fistfuls, raised the shredding bundle, and cantered to the nearest door.

So, Serge would live to see another morning, as they say. Well, if we're to speak of what he saw in bold quotation marks, I'd guess his body might have sensed the sun, then signaled "morning" to his brain, and even that conjecture's wild since, if I'm remembering correctly, we would have needed a forensics handbook to be certain it was him.

One of Serge's eyes was getting lost in the confusion of its fattening lids. He had a boxer's coin-purse gash beneath the same eye, and his nose was blowing ruddy bubbles. One front tooth was chipped in half, and its twin, while still intact, was tumbling on his tongue until it washed up on his blobby lower lip.

He would touch the Xmas pattern on his sweater very lightly, then yelp as if the little pines were shorting outlets, so I think he had fractured ribs. Most of one black jeans leg had been torn away, baring a thigh and calf whose faded scrapes were his responsibility, and a bleeding, crooked knee that surely wasn't.

Can we agree that, had the next few hours passed routinely, I would have asked Azmir to use the Citroën's GPS and fetch the nearest doctor's office? I might have spent the hurried drive there begging Serge's pardon and surrendering, oh, money or a rain check in return for his silence on the matter.

Now, were I gay or, if you insist, entirely gay, I would have . . . well, you tell me. I'm not gay enough to know. Were I to take a guess, it would be all of the above, plus some fiery disappointment upon finding such an aftermath in such a tempting spot.

Picture a movie star who draws you to the cineplex however poor his films' reviews because you'd rather watch him change his shirt in silhouette in any context than mollify his critics. Now, recall the lavish masturbation he imposed on you, or all the time you wasted stalking him, if you went that insane.

Now, imagine it's late at night in the Marais. You're walking home from . . . what's that skeezy club . . . Le Depot, where, true to form, anyone who'd cruised you wasn't anything like him. In one last bid to meet his counterpart, you try the hotbed of Passage de Retz, and, as though its yellowed lamps were magic wands, the very actor you would die to fuck is lurking in a doorway.

He's shockingly petit, and, judging by his lumpen build, perhaps the offspring of at least one midget parent. Having arrived without an airbrush, his boney cheeks and poring eyes are geographical data in a countryside of acne, and the hand that slid thin gold bands down your imaginary finger is littered with rings and bling and scrubbing a penis you would hardly even notice otherwise.

When he spots your shadow, or rather any human shadow, he whispers, "Fuck me" or "I want to fuck you" or whatever. Once upon a time, you'd dreamt of saving him from death, but, and please be honest, now that his irksome modesty on-screen is such a head slapper, wouldn't hundreds of knife wounds serve a greater purpose, assuming the coast is clear?

Granted, that point of comparison got swept away with my effusiveness.

Point is, I'm complicated, or, rather, there's a strangely wending path between what I intend to say and what I gather I am thinking. I've always been this jumbled, even when my speech patterns employed a smaller engine and I thought about my weirdness in highly critical ways.

You'll have noticed I tell stories in a high-strung, flighty, tonally unstable rant, no sooner flashing you a secret entrance than pretending no such route exists, twittering when there's bad news, and polishing my outbursts. Flawed and mutually shortchanging as the method may be, this is the only way I know how to engage what I've done with due respect and keep you somewhat agog simultaneously.

I've gotten lost, and so have you. I'm not as witty as I wish, and you're nowhere near as patient with my heaping phrases as I evidently am.

I learned this quote-unquote exalted style of speaking from my father, who originally cooked it up after several early business trips around the Western world. He nicknamed it "the marbled swarm," which I agree is a cumbrous mouthful, and its ostensible allure received a decent portion of the credit for accruing his, now my, billions.

One night when I was thirteen years old, he passed along the recipe, which I should have written down, but I'd just come home zonked on one too many hits of Ecstacy, and he was tipsy from a course of Chardonnays, so he could barely have enunciated the instructions in any case.

If you're curious, memory tells me that this voice was generated from a dollop of the haughty triple-speak British royals employ to keep their hearts reclusive, some of the tricked, incautious slang that dumbs down young Americans, a dollop of the stiff, tongue-twisting, jammed-up sentence structure and related terseness that comes with being German, some quisling, dogmatic Dutch retorts, and a few other international ingredients I didn't catch, which is the central problem with my scrappier version, all of which my father blended smoothly into his mellifluous French.

The marbled swarm is spoken at a taxing pace in trains of sticky sentences that round up thoughts as broadly as a vacuum. Ideally, its tedium is counteracted by linguistic decorations, with which the speaker can design the spiel to his requirements. The result, according to this mode's inventor, is that one's speech becomes an entity as open-ended as the air it fills and yet as dangerous to travel as a cluttered, unlit room in which someone has hidden, say, a billion euros.

My father used the marbled swarm to . . . well, I was going to say become a wealthy man, and that is true, but to say he ruined my life would be as accurate.

My marbled swarm is more of an atonal, fussy bleat—somewhat marbled yet far too frozen tight and thinned by my loquaciousness to do the swarming it implies. Still, it seems to be a sleeper hit with guys my age and younger, or at least with the majority who tune in once they're weakened by my stunning looks.

For this fan base, my dry, chiseled meanderings seem to add a fleeting touch of magic to a face whose knee-jerk beauty might be too digestible. Long story short, had my father not half taught me to talk like this, I might instead be leering up at you from the cover of Vogue or, ugh, Têtu.

To people who knew my father well, say Azmir and several others you'll be meeting, I am little more than his subpar impressionist—a miscast, bargain-basement chip off the veritable old block, à la, say, Hayden Christensen's wooden rendition of Anakin Skywalker.

I won't refute that I'm a busker of my father's genius. Still, to give myself some credit, his wizardry was called for by his dull, unhelpful visage, which was frequently compared to Gérard Jugnot's, if you know him, whereas it could be argued I need a far less charismatic soundtrack.

As for how my cover version sits with you who lack that crucial additive, I really couldn't guess and ultimately fear the worst, but . . . fine, I'll go as blunt as the sound bite to which my life will be reduced by the same journalists who fashion headlines from its trail of circumstantial evidence.

I'm what you'd call a cannibal, or, rather, I'm the figurehead, curator, human bankroll, and most willing if not wanton of a clique of cannibals, our exact number depending on who happens to be horny and/or hungry and/or situated in Paris or still alive at any given moment.

ANGELA GENUSA

from *Tender Buttons*

Z▮2S*f* │ ÅícG╪»O«ÜσÖï–#"ê*D*"üê ∟;.

i╡ *;·+v▄*ä╗ ôΘÄß(ªäILq(Zvo* │ *û │ # ⊢Æí!r**±X1⌐ ¢;*k╗ à │ *6.å0╝ **╤R⌐ . üΓ**ê*D *"**üê@Dα¡F ≥⌡╗ ║z^{µ╝ g*╪»*&1╤ç3ÉcPΣ± ▒T-;Wpz-√b NAå ║⊢W O▒ùòPv%δ î~üx√% │ ÷Éß ╡*ò**⌐ kPts"] φ≥**î*D* "**üê@Dα╪ *ê|²╪1;╫o¿ Uwá_W+vPtse·& X≥▒***⌠ ∟∟*²·*▒Pßg⌐ ⌐₁ "-^ ∟∟ ⌐å ▮

GPts· │ p^τæ!A9± ∟▓.

PtsòÅk*åXlJúy╡ iq╗ *0* Pts╤ │ ╧╡ ·éD*° ⌠3#╤ÿjPtsm*pFê ╟h#üê@D "ê*£ü ∟∟.

∞ ∟yΘ ∟±*╡║nⁿ—ôÆu⌐ à≈Gôÿ3*▪*yD "**ê* D*"*°â@Σδ°âπ1 ▒(sT ∟∟ï╡ ≤Öª√ óæ {åkÜu≤ôX ∟∟+*ƒ*µ╤2yδ≡A9∞╤╝ #≈≡Ñ╪▮*y1* ·nò ⌐ïµR1,*╪═*$*?·q~1 ∟Θñ-9⌠ s*}* ßîòƒ*E7∩'*» Æƒ*/A|#"**ê*D*"**üê ∟*™*·.·**·*∟*)ä ╡≥╤A1 ⌐KJ8 V═╡ ⌐O/2 [}σ⌐ δ α½*î0*2 «zh▄∟ò°*σe@ ME5V¥f≡ΩX ⌠*Rv-***úK *rî(ix ╡║*╡ πp╡║h*`£«╝⌐@═*î╪ i╡ L¿~*KT·¡Ç*v╤'Bótïh#ó7R*/ [1hD "**ê*D*"*∩**æ»ƒ]]+7%·+° ∟±xPö δ` ╞j7 Γ({ì⌐Ω*» Bj_Ñ8Æ«⌐ »kF4'wç.

∞1T*∟∟*¢zh▄F¿▮kè ║v┤ ?╤ï3:4f%—84yGPts· │ p^τæ*!Aá9± ∟▓é╪±Ñ½<<┙ zPtsòÅkå XlJúy╡ iq╗ *0* Pts╤ │ ╧╡ ·éD° ⌠3#╤ÿjPtsm*pFê ╟h#üê@D "ê£ü ∟╡O* ∟K*≤·⌐ ⌐[â ì[á╡ σö╝ *∞'á╡ ╞k½eÜH&∟I{Γ¿⌐╤ƒ_*3╪zI ∟ä~*╡ *ê▒═╡═*ó╤Γπ»*î[á╤ñ∞ ⌐τΣLb ∟W ║²*J ⌐*·▪═Åp`;'gûπ!½∟∟v_*X,»e7vÅ ≤£ ∟_⌐* ╫ET±*íⁿlα F≤*cê*D*"üê@D "≡*D╝ ▪≥╪*≤µ£F⌐·*IªP═O*x)=tqX*÷ÆßAR∞ë▮*uå ∟∟w*b«4z^ì|Ω9*t ⌐Tòâ╡ ¢s.

D"üê@Dα—D╝ ~b¿N*∟∟ΘJ,▄φWi▄∩°.

φ%%⌐ 8 ⌐e╤⌐ ▓½û}N╫Pts{s*uÿ ∟óMαφâiënKd@*%z*BL∞⌠ ∟d║<╤αßxú¥*¢uF/oY▒t:í ∟∟*▪ñ*X√½ÄÅå/ ï* ╞F*"üê@D "8U*"_?U8àWZî5▒ù'YPtsOp.

B½ÖÜF*║═PQ⌠áÉ.╡╤^⌐6*Z÷óóñûñτ║Ä-Pts /*D πoα;≥\pÑ ¿µ ∟╤b*eù* ⌐rO3ÅqÑ6∟ ╡*£L·╡║6ç≥%:yª<Æîöi Åí_τ?b▮"**╡≈Z37-*} ╫hΓ ⌠0*═∟*»k ╞µ¿║*8*╤s*CF*"D "85"_?5(]D* ⌐│Kⁿâ_+k╡2ÿÜα"║Ö|X}Pts@ ╞│°¡·∟—u ö▮ δατJ═╫a ▪C*, #╗ôδïµV K*Pv╗ T ∟H║σ$L70z ü1⌐ 1ur»*.

Rê(å╡*^b╡ *ê║8±*c▒═╡*Çd*ßƒ⌐*wx² ║╡ì>H6 ⌐É*z·b*v;U±BD^té±Ω° ║*"üê@D "ê*,A ≥╝╫ *║(¡;≡*ôe0ë*τlU ▮W ∟L∟╡Ptsτ▒║Ç x{▄w=æu≥M a╤⌐W*5∟» ^*ì │ !ÄX$à ║ë╡tΩL ⌐½{V∩}ƒ≤ä╝ *[≤*~E*7≤úc<¥*ùg=Ix═*g5Níо═4]=*Å1svφ*ª╤║ │hÿ═*+⌐ ô*G89-ó; ±∞Γ FæÅ1D*"üê@D "**8*ü ∟╡ Åp(·m╤VDB ⌐² í\¥║aΦzGY6. ╤ârzH╗ 1`║°U╡·(╡ $gu*Rû*=W+æΣMt╪*Åª*p ⌐9*,ò╝;Σ∟ ~Aτt*V∞Eí*÷π4╝ ï*÷* ⌠*ª—h ²=p=° ∟α({Ñ_»║²═╡ ΣfzzN{0/ ∟uß╪>║╪▮═╫W½Ö°vD"ê*D*"*∩'*æ»╗ ║z*ëä*÷*φY ▮ àyì▮о≤▮* éµ"*▄O╧ inâcÆÉ▓.

M║╫│py ⌐b9¢⌐éßiX ∟∟║Pts⌐ £û;π*û£Ä*úü.óuaÄ═ Æ⌐ è(ï▪▮aHτù°â≤*;—ö ∟∟±y.

Äÿ*í4╗ *OεqG⌐┤█ ¬* ├Cⁿ─cî╪ûÿ╛ Ö·∩W═╫ⁿ√Bê¥òë│b*ⁿ └¿*█H░Φ ┌ò#ç91█wå
<║@QÄ·*èú╞'╧╚╣°╚LF÷G╧ì¬*2æP+**Uσ ^2Γ≥µP*╖ ╫/*a*╟**]░3ì╨$
f*ÉSG°┤ k, ╞**ê*D*"**üê └yG ≥⌡3¡a░B╧>σ* ╘░╤╚≤û╪p ╚#úÿ* ╙T;lí╗ b¿Äφü≡'£ ╞
*(┌m√!n⌠**╡ O⌐*Ü+·╤²║XP₧TvB.*_&╗ íVπZ*Wd ╒à;z=à'û)┤ ∞ê*ÜlW÷σÖ*≥`dÜqè=ïá
Σí▓╜ UJx ╞*n»* »u╓═┐ ╧la* ╓*mkr·ε░D┐ *╛ pJΦ ╞h"**üê@D "**ê*╝ 8* æ»┐ 8f/≡ ╞*φ,
I0*MÆâ 3&O:= │*ri{áB╜ Lr9ä ╡u9> └/üwvzHä«·╕ ╜9_ *A╜ ëïp[e╬f* εr[╜ â;·≤╓φ
AÿB┬─n;) ┴êïæ*▀?█Kî%⌐/[Rî@W≡:`*╜ ~ê**─┴î╜ T \! ╙ ì,8*a.9σd`*d ß*» *i|7"*
*ê*D*"**üê └+!*··+┴≈╜ ù╜ Ä╓ô┬* ╓z*·ueù █lCb▓αⁿ ╟,¡ ╓Ω*!¢ ├*ö╜ *ö ├*εüZú∞╧╥┼*
═╫Ly ╒╜ ╥Γ*oA\òN█ k»òΓ{óoÑ*]=e¥ÄÄ╫▓gL╜ é#α╥yû╫φ■¥^▀∞ ┌òÄ*z╡ h<╬>%]x*
½{ùô⌡*Σ*ü**G*"**üê@D "*8u.

AÄ ▓╟┼P*üê@D "ê*D*╬*ü ╚╫╧*▀Ç*Ω%╣ fé═ Æ*¡F*cîPôφ╡ ┼B*╜ &█t═╨,
u·&÷[ÜB┼.ZvΦ╫*▓ⁿ½9ín≈î│e╤%╗ ~B*w≈*╢ %¢ªªΓ^ÆA*ó■D █ ╓«·]ó╧ëΣm ╙-
╖ Ügà╧ƒâë*Mk≡*ûⁿfy*Ä5U┼*Åê@D "ê*D*"*o)*æ»ƒi┼(*─Y z¡╨s\╚╣▓ ╓Vm░3
█**╗ *I■úΣ╛ ╚ßk%*dtÆ¿d█ * ╞£JAÿ║≡^═ºµ ╟*q╜ CFMì╣ +ïå ╘* ║╖ ö:δëP₧Xd┐ T ├CI·╥
#@⌐z.1g¡¼ ╒í3GLx*7═é╛ ª╗ 8 ├╛i* ╞╨ªå>╥ ╒Öf*;╬*u*µτ*9<*£c$üê@D ê*D* Nè@
Σδ'EΩ*┬)I*µ¿╨ar═**Ö¬í║0Xw ╓┼¥8èÇ2ΓÆ?ì*ö}╝█ öè ├b░** ╞î£╖ ─W ╚)s2╬*p
└ε≥¼KNy▀ƒ*e≈%rªº.

èm^S╜²:*╕ ÆZ╖ └ ╘╙]w█i╗ ┼█ ╜ NP╨q*δôÇ*çΣ°╣ Y5▓₧ΣϕYcô*Nò.

Uσ;<⌐µ∩öX√Ü╡ ôV'∩¼≤"Q 0s·ëd²╣ òD*"üê@D Ü*x»°·¢"aa║αà4τ └Nºd░Ñn£*
X~δuu6ûε╚║W√┬o ┤∞ ├óΦù╪:*F φXüJ█* ⌡╬«1x*⌐ ╘╬╧+■\î` ╘R£¢¥ΩL┴ *ûä*
╛ k²╡ *>╖.*┤ da<≥╡ *òè╫??'.J·*/é[wô|#i]╬≥⌡ó └Ü]Y~¬Qµ.>3Åq≈·TMî**k*4*p⌐╛ σ¼ë:
û┤ ╬╫¡JNÿ├*,"ê*D*"üê └Ö"=^±⌡9*ΩÖF╛ ÿ.═ª│*L; └$┴4┼[■0jJZ⌐╫ü±ë^*1Ñmç°ä─╛
íâr|Φ┤ ∞EÑeƒO╓s█g*£t*ûΓ` ├Ä┼å.

6(;ìï$BÅñΣ\Y╖ ñ%û2\`J╥ƒu≥╓*^'√g~─╛ v°I┼"PUñ╧*1>î*D*üê@D "pjⁿ ╒*
°╟SïωmÅ*d+*┼/╬»≤XL░H╥.

ΘlÆ*╡ L±»ä£Θy&⌠w ╞G│IÆ ╓S■æ*Nô═╥≡~ë*f3£*╫,Ia█ üïGC═┼T6²▄▓ùI:Ö*C╕ s)'3
äNg╟¡Ñ ╙ ╘%*µñ░\Ñ H╫*ƒ0┴╟JüG╛ ┌dû╧Æ╡ Vτ┐ %╛ çI ╥*è,a^µ └δ£ ╞d+
ìdÑUö3╪╖ L╨ò┤ \¢═V ╙l-Ö*»Ω ╙í ╞▀,╜ f▓╡ ¿ ╒F*&▄¥op.

Æåià.

oayh █╜ *|*»π**Θ$ÖZLK▀╥√ └a£*rå5?ù╢b{&"e a]) @â╖ u.0m* & ╙í@╖┤ r,
µ┼╟*º»Æc_>Iæbÿê@Dê*D*"*'Dα£±⌡ÉB═╤tO┐ äµ╬3╡ *r╛ *ó·▄`┬╫╥~Q*$π█ L£║0*
▄¡3X(╓lè═zu ╚FEJ ╓}!xGù½B ╟íáφ*K*;[ñ∞Ω2╥ûTµ═══ûú┐ J╛ ░ùj*■"╤*ö¥╬"Ö│Z~<ì
^╞!*qB│^öÉ⌡¼╡ Ä│dC)√3╨>«╓┬√ïσP&ì*<Z¬ç*¡e*áµΓ └æg┐ x≈╛ ╒╜ £ê├╓ì@N╗ x*"
ñ∩'C7åè*D*"üê@D "≡é*£3{ÿ9kcÇßm╓²5Φû7«╨δ╫L ╓òY┬"<═╕ X⌠±,Ö4Ö*]▓
BHât!ù8{├¡X╪ÿêìd|ß ╘v*╖ g0 ç-; ╗ ┼0Fê%m╛ ± \·$&(╚ÿÜy╨*P₧░²─*»ô
¼Σ¢│╛ ╙ö░)z ╚¢╪▓δ┬R ┌▄½ò*îR └ ╘W&0[.

φò╤BoåZáB▀¥ì;¡┤ ß·.

Ptsb*ÉüΦ ⊢så1*«Ég.

■¥ì¡⊣ ß·╥(Y÷⌐ δó?÷PtsOεdàD ╠.

½}|ê ╠sK=çτ*⌐ √ ╚cÇê@D "ê*D*"*»ä ⌐9αδ J╥╣|f | Nπö╥*░ { | D⌐ Pts· ╚ ¿p2.√╥ ▚
YbM'ÿ ± ⌐ÿ¼µyA╫H|Pδz_i+N9w²—╢⌐α╝▐╙fB■╫E ⊢±y<Ω *$╕ ┌Bûré╣ #╨⌐╥ ~.ö⌐
b■ΣΓ╪h)â░x«µ(╣;╫ ╚·q*δ#{që╥R*Ptsg*⌐ *╥ /@° ╚M*<ô*g*╣ R?#│ ╚*1y±Γ−7"üê@
D "ê*T*£*⌐ «è ⊢EC)o ⊢ ⊢Sv^⌐ 5öσ╫1JFçσ╕ ùèù*⌐ úT=`¿°v⌐┘ ⌐y«î* * ░nΣ0+ ⌐Ñí .

ë0α⌐ ²dxPû⌐,*Y∩╫¡<@= ▊cQΘ ┌*╥"∩ê±î*vI≈,*ÿzk+k_q{* f╣|c> ócYhσm*A
⌐≥^≤*k*Å<. µ‖*⌐ ╣⌐*Ñÿ? N—xÅ*~Å^s ╫⌐╥h‖s% ⊢£k*τ≥πë>' ⊢*⌐P¡gé
A ⌐στ⌐çΓâ#‖⌐ ╠≤^è╪#**üê@D "ê*,Cα*≡u_,EñqQ ⌐ α(■δ≡‖¡D**⌐┘ .

>½2á5î⌐ Äï≥╕ ≥zi±1*8à⌐Ñ╥ O*▊* ╥üÅ E"üê@D 81τâ» {U\\ t¢é╫î 1ÄGfæ.

£9╥ .Huçû^⌐C⌐F ╥÷Tìπª â***gìF2*c*UÅ*yA* | **å*z¡å·á ⌐ε╠0$±*°d[··]ñD-
δ—»c*4* [∩5≡⌐*∩ Jbÿÿå*⌐%6¡ÉLt≡*é 2Γ*ö°°DâΦò⌐cµτ` Dé ▐*Ä ╥⌐? [:⌐] |*⌐x7"ê*
D*"üê ⌐I*8g|* 4*⌐26*⌐ 0* ╥"÷BΦ* ╚⌐z ∞¼g`Z ⌐ ⌐]╕(V_╥Q╫⌐ *mà? ‖âbH ‖ÅY2*
╪╥G G≥ìé¼Æ:*╥░jhîZ¿⌐ ó*°S @í⌐╣ Æσ≡**√u≡╥╣ +b=*≡/° I⌐knN Df╥«`╥√°
⌐çòP£≤Xä½23 ⌐à åd!*:«f*@¼jPtsY ⌐╥⌐╣:¡⌐*wRy⌐PRü~5δ~L²:Uτx*yÇò⌐a1 ⌐IªCåsi ⌐╣ |*Q╣
O!±⌐Φ╥ΘWPts H╠âo58AÇ ⌐:« ▐¼Ç! *z9?wq≤≤*Å!"**üê@D.

Σ⌐ *Ωeq@ó−78ä>‖╕ δ÷δµ* ⌐⌐ ╣ ╚£*t*¼ ▊¢@╣ ▐▐*√£<út╥r7Åää±τ0fÇW≤∞} ╚îôó0·*
JN**0⌐ íΣ@ï⌐ | *eûM ⌐╥ ⌐╥ ⌐ îU$Aow.oA o**∞ei╪δ%⌐ δ7`·╥⊢╪⌐*
⌐ ⌐√(8) ╥ÿεHbó⌐ g2Γâ⌐Z ⌐½°α⌐Ü=αÇ■Pts╥r*&F8âΓπ*zÜ≡*j<ú/Θuε⌐XΓε‖╫Hx$**fe
*∩°wDê*D*"*∩=*? ⌐±*üÇ≡ßeo√tû6 s²xûLR1_Å²8gGM╣╥▐╥⌐ Σ(Òìgô*°%?=I╥
LR*1▐ ⌐éf⌐ V≈°ë╫⌐≡δqoÆd | ∞▐≡:)'e3╕ @·ÿΓ⌐ ÆZwñy2C«ä ⌐U⌐nûñM ⌐I3*8⌐%é
d=*àNZôd╪⌐v)⌐⌐ ⌐ä¼ú\áÆ╪8ûσn>╕ ⌐░*⌐ BJ8 ÿ$Gr*cñúñ|£ ‖Pts$ |*Æ ªL⌐ Y╥f*²'
fP | ≥a39*gÅ≤t<+Å PRHmM Σ*╕ I2)XhV*bPts Ñá⌐ | R≥à2Γ_9ù3û=-S╣ F!¡ªf)
╥⌐fî4[O[?O╥⌐**⌐z,É╕ Y±0+ïfzü*=H*¢Çë3 ⌐:StßqíΘ≥£b1*≡*bfA7▄ⁿ))Å(9σ*Eÿ*ât÷ñ.

φHPtsh■à ~0¢¡B¡>K≤lm=I ⌐·⌐Q.

╥pT± ⌐æ4*¡ß*1≥âfΦ╥ôGóM T<é**¿·ú ⌐⌐fíc.╥*2h⌐Igí. *╣| !*╚E¡ ⌐ #Φ(^ë ⌐
íåZ5σN*Ä* ⌐╥°Pd.

ág_R!⌐⌐ ╚Æ (ßF* ▐àé*ÑN[* ╚ª hPe ⌐ÿÆ=‖f⌐σ²ò£¿n[^W< ⌐CK-~ ╠ ⌐≡'üIô/R╥╫⌐ª,
ü—ú,?M&°î ⌐∩$i#K ╚ ⌐$UO5x╪* ⌐i)*ë‖d@g*Ü⌐kÉ╥ | ùΦÿBD "ê*D*°ç ⌐;≡╫M.

ÇÅhφ≡ ╚É<råá]⌐σëp/äìyB*N$.

⌐╥Σ¢ysd¥⌐╥‖ *Ud])╕ ?ç_*äαV8Φ∞Dë/*å"µ╣ 2Θd¡ÅÆ*&@⌐‖ ⌐ìαWöú*4)ç)î╥Ö*yKΘ
⌐M⌐f‖ ±sΣ ⌐ôu^╥⌐ ÿ*= δÿYê Æ*m⌐U*bPtsd ·*╕ 1‖V⌐I#]í°MΣ~ ⌐¼fR ⌐░ó‖X╫⌐° .

JΘ╥ ~*⌐y Eφ½╫⌐q╣ R*#.

JI YOON LEE

from *IMMA*

To:

I'm ok being your diversity plan;
It is my mode of existence: It is my mode of insistence
There is the cityplan under my belt of explosives;
It is my mode of modification: It is my mode of fornication

Defamation of American flag: Defecation of unidentifiable flag
An unidentifiable body surfaces on the level of cheap alliteration
Please do not litter; be a good noncitizen
Please use the container provided; be a good conartist

Is it ok that I am your diversity case? Is it ok that I am your basket case?
Is it tolerable that I am your open case? Is it permissible that I am your
coldcut showcase?
You need to pardon my perfection crime:
Is it okay I'm in your suitcase? Is it ok I'm your cold case?
I had to be in your file case before I could go cold turkey
b/c my concealer stopped working on its case
There are problematic concerns for my modular case
Is it okay that I'm your diversity case?
Is it okay that I'm your assertion case?
I'll let my fever fall asleep till my urge to reload kicks in
My belly is warm and I am your forensic case

Imma go to a war

w/ my withered powdered wig
w/ my product mangled teeth
Imma go to a war
       My trench coat warfare
       My mulberry burberry harboring a cargo pants or two
             until my beauty regimen regime ensured
           until my darling double democracy delivered

My aghast darling, the ghosts in Afghanistan cover their face with no
makeup
My secretary of defense desk schizophrenic screams curtailed curfew for
your children
My diabolic memorandum your daily bombarding schedule your pets
supplement plan
                            that requires some intensive executive
                            exercise on the side

Imma go on a pilgrimage

Proverbial categorical humors & Preverbal laughter tracks
Feelgood movies with nacho cheese & Wellstylized forensic reports
Communion with strangers @ the diner& Communist strangler's premoni-
tion @ my dinner table
My frail disposition indicates diminution of nutrition
But the increment ammunition will take care of that

My heartburn envisions your flaming heart
your sacred heart; your purple heart
your strangled face; black & blue
but all I wanted for Christmas is a head on the golden platter
&the fleet of the avenging coast guards& gurgling children under water
pressure
&pleading girls in pleated skirts& I don't know anything about anything
any more
&I want to correct my secret wishes but I can't, but like,
I really can't

You bombarded my embassy with your allergic reaction

it was unnecessary for you to void my foreign agency just because it contained peanuts;

Reduced to ambassadorial sizzles with desired consistency, your immunity is your feigned diplomacy. Despite the deploring of deflowered agencies, your stickyfingers won't stop rummaging through the rubbles of my discolored ancestry. Nobody knows what's in that brown sauce. No body is left in the sizzle. Potentially processed in the facility that also processes nuts, a baby cries out under the rubbles. In a nutshell, your overbearing jealousy is rapidly boiling me down to the toxic agent that you were once concerned with; it might be ok to be involved with the corrupting agent once or twice, you said; it builds your character& build your immunity. Don't mind the traffic buildup: It's just my free radicals having a field day; free rascals buildup on field day. Blood buildup is hard to remove; Boiling water only makes the stain set in. *Baby, baby, where you at?* Don't end your sentence with preposition! My enzymic activity will take care of that. My bulimic confession will take care of hat. Are you gonna eat that, babbled the thumbsucking regression of necrotic tissues in my organs. My fetal position is questionably fashionable and I don't give a flying fuck what you think. The flight was delayed by several centuries due to the various outbreak of dislocated limbs. I regret the inconvenience that I caused you, but you may need to swallow it.

Epilogue: I found a poem under the rug that was

foreign benign malign and forlorn:
cute as a button; weak like the bee's knee;
pull my leg& break your leg.
my kneebiter promqueen would like to conclude your vasectomy:
bite the curb, cut the carb;
& thy kingdom cum, thy will be done.
your synergistic globalization is my conglomerate prostitution:
the traffick jammed my knees over your shoulders;
&you may kiss your mailorderbride for a second thought.
The picture of yours that I framed claims its innocence;
the incense in your return crate smells burnt crème brulee;
The ballet parking calls for a lapdog cremation;
& in the backstage another dog bites the dust.

AARON APPS
Barbecue Catharsis

"Not to be devoured is the secret objective of a whole existence."
—Clarice Lispector

There must have been twenty hacked and butterflied pig carcasses rotating in the massive metal lung filled with wood smoke, ash and pig grease—the edges of the meat burnished to black, sheets of their exposed flesh gone cordovan. A few select hunks adorned our plates, garnished with sides smacked on in half-spherical blobs. We ate the strands of meat from the bones. We ate silver fat. We ate gray-pink animal. We ate vegetable matter. We ate like we were eating each other. Sauce on our lips and cheeks, sauce on our fingers, sauce on our soiled napkins, sauce on us like we are wounds. Sides on our fronts. Dingy foaming all in our guts and enlarging drips on our shirts.

Osmosis.

Lovers feasting together.

Later, a department store.

I say I am satisfied. You say you are satisfied. I fill the cart with dry goods. You fill the cart with dry goods. Everything is square, familiar. Everyone is square, familiar.

I say *I have to shit, bad*. You say, *okay*. I walk with the cart to steady myself. I leave the cart for you by the end cap of overripe cantaloupes covered with humming fruit flies. I say it is urgent. You say, *hurry*. You say *I'll check out*. I walk fast. Not too fast, I keep my anus pinched. I'm frantic. There, the bathroom. I enter. I see a line of square stalls. They look odd. I rush to the last one. I latch the door. I shit. Explosively relief comes. And comes. And comes.

My bowel movement gives me post-coital melancholy. When I lift my ass from the seat, I can feel the thick fluid peeling up from the surface of my skin, like pulling my hand off a table coated in the dye-flushed fluid that surrounds blackberries in pie filling. It's sticky on my skin.

I wrap my hand with a profuse coiling of cheap, rough paper. I wrap it until my hand is a white, mummified ball and I make tentative gestures at the edge of my ass until I feel the mass hit wetness. When I look at my balled fist, the mahogany stain runs deep. Orange and green vegetable matter rest in specks on the surface. I wipe until my fist wad is saturated, and then I strip it off and make a new one. I rinse and repeat. Except I don't rinse, shit gets on my hands. I wipe, I toss. I wipe, I toss. Soon my ass feels clean enough. Not clean, but *clean enough* to make it back to a shower. So I get up, pull up my pants, and look at the toilet.

There is chestnut fluid in the shape of my ass stagnant on the oval seat. There is fluid in the hinges, seeping inside. There is fluid on the cheap porcelain. There is fluid on the hardware. Over the automatic flush sensor. On the handle. On the neutral tiles. On the white grout between the tiles. On the gray floor. Either there are large patterns of dripping filth, or there are blank pieces of corporate bathroom material. Either I have to clean it, or I don't. When I wipe at it, it streaks and catches on my thumb and slides under my nail, when I try to pull it out with another nail it spreads.

I keep wiping. I'm filthy. I'm moist with sweat-reek. I hear voices echo in the bathroom.

"Mommy! I have to peeeeee!" a small girl's voice squeals before she giggles.

"Get into the stall. I'll be right here," her mother answers.

The woman's room. That's why there were no urinals when I entered. I thought there was something strange about the space.

How can I leave? What will the little girl say when she sees my fat, masculine frame falter past her? What will she say if she sniffs me up into her nose cavities?

And there I am, finishing the mess, stuck in the stall, sweaty and disheveled. I could just leave, but that's somehow inappropriate. The rhetoric overwhelms. Bathrooms are gender ciphers—to be in the woman's room with my body is to be in the wrong space, regardless of genitals. To be androgynous or intersex in the bathroom in a way that doesn't pass is to put gender at odds with sex, it is to be policed by the scrutiny of the mother and the daughter, and those standing outside of the door.

Men's rooms create their own problems. There is a good chance that, when a stall finally opens, someone has pissed on the seat. Bars often only have one toilet with no stall door, or one that doesn't latch. In such cases I squeeze my urethral sphincter, and it aches all the way up into my enfolding organs.

So, I stand there in the stall with the shit and I wait. Until the toilet two stalls down flushes into itself. I wait until the faucets run, the soap foams, and the hands rub. Until the hand dryer stops humming as it blows. Until the door opens and closes in a creak. No one is there when I unlatch and open the stall. A beeline for the door and everything is gravy. That is, until I see her body peeking out from the laminate partition that divides the mirror and sinks off from the rest of the room. Until I see her turquoise blazer, all shoulder pads. I see her, but I keep moving. I walk right behind her and I turn to see if she noticed me and our eyes catch each other like a vulgar clap in the mirror. Her eyebrows grimace. I don't wash my hands. I keep moving until I'm out the door and I'm blasted with florescent light.

I loop out and back in, I curve, and I wash in the men's room. It is empty. When my hands are clean enough, I leave swiftly with my body still feeling hot and grimy.

All of my flesh is stained. I stink out in all directions. I'm undone in the face of the bathroom's cookie cutter stalls. The bathroom makes me fluid against the department store—it lets the sauce seep out of the membrane. Sauce leaking all over and into the skin.

I text you with my saucy fingers and we meet at the exit. You've checked out and all of the shit is in bags. We drive back to the hotel. The rooms hold in fluids but I still feel loose in them. I shower for a long time while you read *Le Monde* online. We become scavenging animals as we eat from the bags of dry things and make them wet with our spit. And then eat each other slowly. And then we dissolve in each other's stomach acid. It feels so good close to the bone.

AMARANTH BORSUK
& KATE DURBIN
Selections from *Abra*

A living text, the poems of *Abra* grow and mutate as the reader turns the pages, coalescing and dispersing in an ecstatic helix of language. Drawings by Zach Kleyn mutate alongside the text, operating as a flipbook animation, eventually reaching across the gutter to merge with the text. The poems play with the mutation of language, both in portmanteaus and conjoined phrases, and also through references to fecundity as it manifests in the natural world, the body, human history, popular culture, decorative arts, and architecture, placing the shifting evolution and continuous overlap of all these spheres in dialogue with the ever-changing technology of the book.

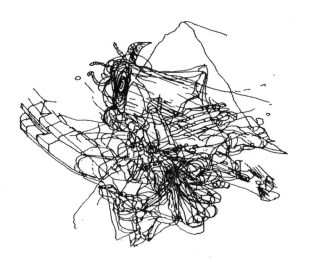

whirling capital embarking architectural embellishment   miniatures   tucked in waves mount a twister

a frigate of hillside   pouf city   a freshet aswirl   to whitewash pompadour

to frolic buttress foundations in powder party bouffant   stylelines   twine to buoy between abodes

down beneath the muff   of this upswept nidus a studied circumstance   a ruff to oar   ennui to lapse

to swan prop   amid apropos   breton star or bonnet sauced verdant villus   turret seas

astride dawn's aigrette of bunting   a damask fauteuil   to Whig to nid-nod

frisk feathers 'low a green velvet bow in our   unruly glory   bower breeze to nestle

weave through   a commode of cannon's ribbon cascade of familiars   to hold total pretty spiral please

spritz all   houses   on the   bluff skirt o mermaid up   snatch-thatch mast

with this amidst an arbor   vortex nautilus pompon vertical   blush fluff bodkin swash-turned

                              a s w o o n   a n d   froth   stirring

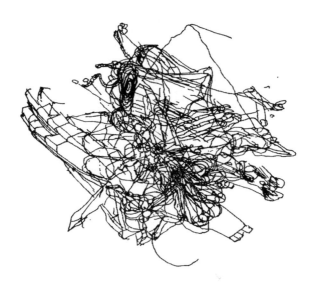

a frigate of   embarking   pouf   a freshet   embellishment   to   pompadour   waves mount

to frolic   foundations in powder party   to buoy

down   the muff of   circumstance   a ruff to oar

to swan   amid   star   sauced   seas

dawn's aigrette of bunting   to Whig

frisk feathers 'low   unruly   breeze

commode of cannon's   cascade   to   pretty   please

skirt o mermaid up   mast

with this   nautilus pompon   fluff bodkin swash-turned

froth
i n g

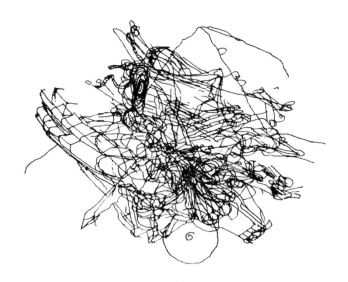

embarking stretching arcane finger-embellishment skein waves Miss M dispenses with filament mount

out of a frigate of spidery-blinders a lux of pouf a fresher to pompadour lashes to lure

limbs spun to frolic in bone lace foundations in powder party to buoy

sinew down the muff straps of circumstance cinch up a ruff queen to reach oar

an arched knee to swan sass siren amid star sauced seas

dawn's aigrette of bunting pentacled to Whig in web corset

frisk pluck feathers 'low a five-pointed snare with unruly span and spangle breeze

in red-lacquered commode of cannon's oh la la! cascade to pretty please volupt

skirt o reclusive mermaid mudras upmast all-seeing seemstress

with this one glossy drift nautilus pompon fluff bodkin to us swash-turned froth winking

AMBER SPARKS
& ROBERT KLOSS
from *The Desert Places*

Who were you when the first breath of heaven burst forth? When all the light and matter and moments blazed from nothing? When fires scorched the firmament and all was shrouded in dust? Where were you in the ravaging, in the annihilation?

You were a negative, a dark absence, a clump of cells crying to come together. You were a pause in the flickering before consciousness. And when the atoms swirled, and when the skies yawned, and when a nervous god, still virgin to creation, called you forth: did you marvel at your luck? Clumsy thumbprint of an awkward deity—did you slaughter the heavens, once freed? Did you grab the stars by their throats? Did you wear the skins of dead galaxies, your eyes ablaze with impossible fury?

And what did you know as you flung yourself through time, while eternity was uncoiling? O, to know you in the flight of ash into ash, until mists gathered in the furnace of new sun, until worlds hurtled into one and burned? O your teeth alone, shining with radiation, rusted in ancient redness, dripping with blood before the advent of blood. O your nails like bits of meteor, violent debris in search of a landing site. O your eyes black holes, your limbs long nightmares, your heart a vacuum in the soundless scream of space.

Where were you when the collisions coalesced? When molten spheres blackened, flared, drifted and circled? What sounds did you know in the voice of the whirlwind? What names were you called by the voice of static? Where were you in the building of the foundation? Where were you when all the sons of God were born and named, when they called out in their chorus? Were you stalking the land? Were you battering the world to come? Did you call the sons and make them to wander in your shade? Did you sell them the pleasures of your garden? Did you stamp them into the depths of your soil?

You did.

How the heavens must have wept to look upon you. How they must have yearned to know you again.

Did you build the shape of man into the rocks, to know the joy of murdering him? Did you ferment the first soil with the bones and bodies of your construction? Did you stack the lands with death even before the first life? And in the hours until the first victim staggered forth from the seas, did you wander the crimson lands, peer into the halls of death and mourn the vacant corridors? Did you tread the distant deeps and shout your name into that terrible emptiness? All the barren earth must have seemed a waiting cemetery.

You must have tilled the soil in search of the green yet to grow. You must have begged the skies for flesh, for food. You must have plucked your own ribs and cast these to the dust, and watered them with your blood. You must have given them names. You must have bid them rise and breathe. You must have said, "Father, make for me a friend so I may slay him."

And when still no symptom of life from the flesh how madness was given dominion in the world. What horrors blazed in your skull, what terrors pulsed in your veins? What awful music thrummed in the furnace of your soul?

And when the first man walked amongst the trees did you make him to enter the garden unclothed and new? And when he plucked the fruit, did you weep without shame? Yes. You brought unto him the tenderness of your heart. Such was your devotion to the flesh. Yes, and the first murder was born from love.

How you have made up for unused hours. How you have pillaged and slaughtered and dripped and pummeled and gnashed and torn and broken and moaned and crunched and roared and plunged and blazed and sucked and chewed and snarled and hissed and foamed and snapped and stabbed and ripped and sliced and bludgeoned and raped and burned and raved in all the days since.

How you have lit all the nights since with the flickering of your soul.

TYTTI HEIKKINEN

translated from the Finnish
by NIINA POLLAARI

Selections from
The Warmth of the Taxidermied Animal

Tytti Heikkinen, born in 1969, is a Finnish-language poet. Heikkinen works by search engine, culling material from the e-primordial ooze of the internet using specific searches and then curating poems from the pages and pages of results. She has also used translation software, running phrases through until their permutations become something else altogether. Her work sources from without, not within; a review in the Helsinki city library blog stated that Heikkinen's poet "wanders the internet, collecting [...] useful shreds of text into a broken shopping cart." The poems of this collection are chosen from Heikkinen's first two books. Both of books were critically acclaimed, and Heikkinen's first received a nomination for one of the nation's most prestigious first-book prizes.

It's totally appropriate that I found her work through the web—after years of access to only "the classics" of Finnish poetry, and with no contacts in the Finnish publishing world, I began searching online for contemporary writers. Heikkinen's publisher, poEsia, makes its publications available as PDFs, and when I found its archives, I dove in. Heikkinen's book was the first collection to startle me. By default, search engines source from a wild variety of voices; in *Taxidermied* Heikkinen collected from these voices a singular, unflinchingly subjective narrator who looked me in the eye and told me that "at some point in the night the loneliness will hit."

The work finds some context in the wake of the Flarfists. Like Flarf, Heikkinen works lowbrow internet terminology and candid bloggyness into what is considered a traditionally high art form, resulting in something surprisingly troubling, funny, and most of all hypercontemporary. Flarf contains a sense of tackling the unpoetic, unaesthetic subject. But the difference, for me as a reader, is the underlying seriousness of Heikkinen's work, and the unwavering voice and sense of the individual in it.

Take my favorite narrator in contemporary poetry, Fatty XL, who shows up in Heikkinen's second book Shadows from *Astronauts* (*varjot astronauteista*, 2010). Fatty is an oversharer and an awful fuckup, completely concerned with appearance, substance abuse, and adding to her collection of sordid sexual encounters; she is unwilling to learn and unconcerned with growing as a character. All of her myopic observations are sourced from the teen girl monologues of blog culture, but Heikkinen curated a single, dimensional voice out of bloggy Google sludge. In other words, I don't think the Fatty poems read as the voices of many different girls. They've transcended their origin.

What does it mean to translate something that has its origins in multiplicity, something that already began in another form in the outside world before it turned into poetry? When I started this project, I wondered if it would be valid. Would the poems, in translation, lose their original references? In going through one more permutation, would they no longer grip? But when I delved into the project I found these questions quickly pointless—the poems of both books have such a powerful voice that their creation story is irrelevant. Of course it's fascinating to note that the poems came from the internet, but that doesn't make Heikkinen any less of a totally brilliant generative artist. And along those same lines, it's more than an interesting exercise to translate something that is essentially already translated: it's perhaps the most logical thing to do.

—Niina Pollaari

A playground is an adult's idea of childlike fun, loneliness the price paid for it. As a child I had a child's existence. Bodily, objectively, I existed, undeniable, father listening to a childish singing from over here, from the cell phone can, and mother, that rusted original nut all-powerful punctured tire yelling "you had better Crusoe not leave so that nobody has to be alone on Christmas." When father returned, mother assumed the position in which the back touches the floor and her stomach hurt constantly from attempts to return to the original connection. Dreaming, I secretly wished I could become something else than a reaction method in a situation of fear, an obvious bride on the bed, sand in the mouth and finally invisibility and loneliness, that's the biggest reason my own child was born. Its head still swung high in the end of the dilation period, then the falling from the edge and the fumbling, supposedly it makes the newborn lose all its social skills and shout publicly its first question: "Who is that stranger?" No consolation for mother's hurts, no comic book band aids, just a k-vitamin injection and later other injections, antibiotics, painkillers, tranquilizers and sleep disturbances, divorce, separation anxiety, deprivation, frozen fingers that even the rapidest imagination won't melt. Because of the child, the house today is filled with Christmas decorations, but at some point in the night the loneliness will hit, and the only way to save us is unending want.

This poem is dedicated to all enamored girls. The speaker is an enamored man who says: the fiance figure is equal to an enamored man at his task. A man enamors easily, if he has a short, thick, and muscular neck. If the enamored man doesn't threaten or convey wanting to deck in the nose his lover's insulter, he is not enamored. Then when suddenly he is, then yes the enamored man is quite mixed up. Understand him: some neurons in his head have formed a pet-chain. After that the man is forced to begin petting. An enamored man is different from a normal man. His persistent accuracy is still completely nuts, since an enamored man is hopeless: nobody can enamor, if they are in their beings and appearances even mildly satisfied. A wise man doesn't generally enamor. An agile mind has time to get between and restrain the sun and rain, and where to even find some target to love, to love goddamn still. For itself. Macaroni. A man values his love high. A man drives into the apartment building yard, rises out of the car in his naivete and hurry like the world's first enamored man like thread or cable, to love or enamor? Mother too was always enamored. Or else she cried. Said it. vertigo. Dizzy. Ticklish. I'm envious of nobody. An enamored man? I don't know. Strange question. An enamored man is an ape. Love & death. A human, of course, but ape.

Fatty-XL
MAKING YOUR OWN LUCK

***

Gonna say one thing just as soon as this vomiting
stops. ...
Went shoppng today for cute shoes. !! Everybody is
gross but me and my friends .

Yestrdy I was into this one dude and tried
prolly too hard
 to get near him.He said ur not the one Im looking for.
 It broke myyy heaaaart.
You betrayed my heart, squeezed it empty like
a sponge...Before everything was the same. No more. i
am in love.. .

I don't think it's even possible to not be
crushin.Everybody has to have someone, who
they can dream about, to love forcefully, even if they don't even
want to.Thats why I wanna love forever.. refrain <3:

Fatty-XL
ON PAR WITH WHALES

***

Fuck i'm a fatty when others are skinny.
Also Im short, am I a fatty or short? Wellyeah
I'm such a grosss fatty that it makes no sens…
My Woundedness has let the situation get
this way tht the fat squeezes out etc.Now I'm
puttin distance btwn me and everything, because I've been so
disapointed in my self, cause from the word "greedy"
I think of a greedy fatty and then I get mad. Panic
rises in my chest, a tremor. Everything is so terrible
, outside its wet and icy , It's cold when I
lay here and im an undisciplined fatty.
.This morning smeone I know was fucking aroundAbout how I'm such a fatty
and I hadto punch them BTWN THE eyes…they spit back at me
and I got a horrible pigsnot on the back of my neck. After that
I gothome super hungry.
 For along time I've been looking at my neighbor Saku
"like that". ive had many dreams abt him,
but I dont remember the dreams but I'd really like
to give it to him. Maybe if I go
over there today. But I'M so shy.
HahahahhahhahhahhahhHahaHahaahhaHahahahhhahHahaH
now I'm crackin up. reason being: when I
crush on someone,I think about how I'm an AWFUL
FATTY smashing into them!Seriously I'm a terrible fatty.
Perverse. A Godzilla pig.
I stopped eatin candy and still I cant
lose weight. Now I've been dyeting
eating only one nutrilett bar. I am
a terrible war elephant with fat thighs.
aarghhh I Want my bones to showI'm
a faaaaaaaaaaaattttttttttttttttttttttyyyyyyyyyyyyyyyyyyyy
yyyyyyyyy I'm furious about my fat! I eat all the time, I'm
an awful fatty.
 E ating…It began when I was in seventh grade.
Other ppl said I was a fatty.Ive been thinking about it, and
I agree.
Even now I've gained alot of weight. I am
a well-known fatty, on par with whales. I'm a fatty and I
know it..Other ppl don't gotta
comment. And Now I've gained weight again.!

JEFF VANDERMEER

No Breather in this World But Thee

The cook didn't like that the eyes of the dead fish shifted to stare at him as he cut their heads off. The cook's assistant, who was also his lover, didn't like that he woke to find just a sack of bloody bones on the bed beside him. "It's starting again," he gasped, just moments before a huge black birdlike creature carried him off, screaming. The child playing on the grounds outside the mansion did not at first know what she was seeing, but realized it was awful. "It's just like last year," she said to her imaginary friend, but her imaginary friend was dead. She ran for the front door, but the ghost of her imaginary friend, now large and ravenous and wormlike, swallowed her up before she had taken ten steps across the writhing grass.

From a third floor window, the lady of the house watched the girl vanish into the ground, but said to the dust, to her long-dead husband, to the disappeared daughter, to the doctor who now lived somewhere in the walls: "Perhaps it's not happening again. Perhaps it's not like last year." Then she spied the disjointed red crocodile walking backwards across the lawn: a smear of wet crimson against the unbearable green of the finger-like grass. The creature's oddly bent legs spasmed and trembled as it lurched ahead. No, not a crocodile but a bloody sack of human flesh and bones crawling toward the river at the edge of the property. Was it someone she knew?

An immense shadow began to grow around the unfortunate person. This puzzled her, until she realized some vast creature was plummeting down from an immense height toward the lawn. Raw misshapen pieces of behemoth began to rain down. As she turned to run something wide and white and cut through with teeth reared up and bit her in half, and then quarters, and then eighths, before she could do more than blink, blink rapidly, and then lie still, the image of the crawling man still with her. For awhile.

In the basement, waiting for the lady's return, a furiously scribbling man sat at a desk. He did not look up once; beyond the candlelight things lurked. As his mistress fell to pieces above him, the man was writing:

> Time is passing oddly. I feel as if I am sharing my shadow with many other people. If I look too closely at the cracks in the wall, I fear I

will discover they are actually doors or mouths. There's something continually flitting beyond the corner of my eye. Something she tells me that I don't want to remember. Flit. Flit....No. *Tilt*. Tilt, not flit. *Tilt*.

A certain mania had entered his pen...and he didn't know who he was writing to. The child? The doctor? God? Something white and terrible waited in the shadows, its movements like the fevered wing-beats of a hundred panicked thrushes crushed into the semblance of a body.

A mighty crash and thud shook the mansion, as if something enormous had landed on the lawn. Dust and debris cascaded down on the man writing.

"It's just an inkling, an inkling!" he screamed, but now his own pale shadow leered up and curled monstrous across the wall, teeth glittering cold in the chilly room in the bowels of the mansion where no other thing stirred, or should have stirred, and yet sometimes did. *No words*, soothed the shadow, as if it made a difference. *No words. I'm happening again. I'll always happen again.*

On the first floor, the maid had fallen to her knees at the impact of the monster from above hitting the lawn. Now it tore into the grass as it bounded forward. It battered the side of the mansion so that the chandeliers cascaded and crashed all around like brittle glass wedding cakes, shards splintering across the floor. Again the monster smashed up against the mansion. Unpleasant chortles and meaty sounds smashed down through her ears, tightened around her heart, her lungs.

But she kept her grip on the shotgun she had taken from the study cabinet. "It won't be like last year," she shouted, although "last year" was something horribly vague in her memory. *I will not blame the child.* The study window was occluded by a huge, misshapen blue-green eye ridged with dark red. She brought the shotgun to her shoulder, braced for the recoil, but the shotgun barrel curled around to sneer at her. From behind something wet and unpleasant slapped her head from her neck. As her head rolled across the suddenly slippery floor, the maid saw the monster's eye withdraw from the window, and then the searing blue sky beyond and a black tower around which flew hideous bird-like shapes. "It's *different* than before," she wanted to say—to the butler, to the lady of the house, to the young writer in the basement who had become her lover—but that impulse soon faded.

The doctor received tell-tale glimmers of the maid's demise from his secret compartment in the walls at the heart of the mansion. Skilled in medicine and the arcane arts, he had built a place of mirrors, breaking almost every piece of glass in the house to capture the shards and position them with glue and nail. Using cunning angles, he could glimpse moments of what was happening elsewhere. Now he stood quite silent and still in his narrow chamber of bright fragments, lit by a lantern, sweat dribbling down his face, arms, and chest.

Many quick-darting thoughts passed through the doctor's mind, reflected in the rapid blinking of his eyes, interrupted only by the continued siege of the mansion by the monster outside.

Did I make it impossible for them to see me, or do they see *all* of me now? Why would this happen to me who did nothing out of sequence or step? Almost all of them are dead and they did nothing except the writer who carried on with both the maid and the lady of the house, but how would this concern *it*? How I wish I had never used a bone saw or performed surgery. Exorcism it should've been, not séance because [*lurch*]

She was kinder than anyone I knew to tell me what to expect, that poor child, and perhaps I should have indulged her about her *friend* but I am a man of science too and how could I [*lurch*]

A surgical cut would be quick, painless, without guilt. No one would blame me for that. No one left to. Oh that day we all spent on the lawn, that day glorious and sun-soaked before it began, and how could I ever give up hope of that again. Let that be what makes me strong. [*lurch*]

Did I feed it? Did *encourage* it? [*lurch*]

The white worm of a creature embedded inside him many months ago awakened, drawn by the cries of the monster outside. As it crunched through tissue and organs, imbuing the doctor with a kind of rough ecstasy soon there was nothing larger than a morsel left, and every single fragment of mirror covered in its entirety with blood so that his once blazing light chamber was now the darkest place in the mansion.

The doctor's screams—amplified from his hiding place by the vents— seemed to the lady's older daughter, kneeling beside a chimney on the roof, to emanate from a mansion in agony. An amateur biologist, she had chosen this vantage to observe the monster and the growth of the tower. She crouched with a small telescope aimed at the tower. She could no longer force herself to observe the monster. The stench of it wafted up and made her feel as if she were being smothered in maggot-covered meat no matter how she tried to *unsee* the atrocity of its form.

Using the telescope was akin to using the microscope in her make-shift laboratory to examine cells from the strange grass of the lawn: a way to know the truth of things, no matter how uncomfortable. The telescope confirmed that it was all happening again, although only the accounts of others from that time told her anything, really. She had avoided thinking about the implications of her own notes from last year, which were incomprehensible and toward the end written in blood. At the far edge of the lawn, the tower had grown pendulous and resembled the upper half of some thick serpent or centipede. It had been birthed by the monster, which had planted a huge, glistening white egg in the crater created by its impact. The scientist also followed the cook's efforts to reach the stream; with the telescope his blunt visage was still recognizable despite the awful softness of his skull. The bird-things swooped down at times to tear flesh from him, returning to toss it onto the top of the tower. Somehow, his excruciating journey seemed important, but the scientist did not know why. She knew only what the writer and doctor had speculated, for she had not been part of the circle. "You did this while I slept?" she had said, enraged that they had taken such a risk. Then retreated to her experiments to keep at bay the feelings of helplessness that ever since threatened to engulf her.

Below, the monster attacked the mansion again and the mansion screamed and she made observations of a scientific nature to calm her nerves. She took grim delight in her detachment in recording that "long, fleshy arms have begun to sprout from the sides of the tower." As she watched, these arms began to snatch the bird-things from the sky and toss them into a gaping pink opening near the top of the tower. "It is feeding itself to grow even larger," she observed. "And it is now obvious that it is not a tower. I do not believe it is a tower. I do not believe it is a tower." She said everything aloud now, three times, if she wanted to truly believe it.

The monster, swaying in a drunken fashion, came closer and closer to the tower, unable to break away from its song. Until, finally, within the unbroken circle of fact that was the telescope's lens, the indescribable beast curled up at the base of the tower.

The tower, still cooing, stretched impossibly tall, lunging up into a sky beginning to bruise. It leaned over to contemplate the monster with something akin to affection, then dove with incredible velocity to pierce the monster's brain. A flow of gold-and-emerald globules rose up from the monster, becoming more and more transparent as the tower assimilated them.

The monster lay husked. The tower grew taller and wider. The mansion beneath the scientist grew spongy and porous, and a kind of heartbeat began to pulse through its many chambers. But the scientist observed none of the things. The tower's song had pierced the telescope, too. Grown strange and feral and querulous, it had punctured her eye on its way to her brain.

Satisfied, the white worm behind the door retreated.

Dusk came over the land, and with it a blinding half light from a large, purple-tinged moon. The cook had finally reached the lip of the river bank, and in some instinctual way recognized this small victory, even though the remains of his head were twisted above by happenstance to look back across the lawn.

The mansion had become watchful, the corners become rounded so that it squatted on powerful haunches, poised to spring forward on four thick legs. The cook was unsurprised: he had argued for months that the mansion had been colonized by something *below* it, and the walls had begun to even seem to *breathe* a little. But they had laughed at him. "It's like last year," he said, although he could not really remember last year or why the fish had looked so strange.

At a certain hour, the tower began to stride toward the mansion, and the two joined in a titanic battle that split the air with unearthly shrieks: solid bulk against twisty strength. Around the two combatants, their tread shaking the ground, the grass rippled with phosphorescence and from the forests beyond came the distant calls of other mighty beasts.

The remains of the cook found no horror in the scene. The cook was beyond horror, all fast-evaporating thought focused on the river that had been the site of his happiest memory—a nighttime rendezvous with his lover. As they lay beside each other afterwards, the contented murmur in his ear of a line of a poem. *"No other breather...."*

So he slid and pushed, still hopeful, losing more flesh and tissue and bone fragments, down the bank of the river, and by an effort of will he managed to whip his head around to face the water. There, through his one good eye, the cook saw his lover and the little girl and the lady of the house and the doctor and the maid and the butler, and the scientist...they lay at rest at the bottom of the river. Waiting with open, sightless eyes. He had a sudden recollection of them all sitting around a table, holding hands, and what came after, but then it was gone gone gone gone, and he was sliding down into his lover's embrace. The feel of the water was such release that it felt like the most blissful moment of his entire life, and any thought of returning home, of reaching home, vanished into the water with him.

Behind him, under stars forever strange, the tower and the mansion fought on.

STEPHANIE STRICKLAND
& NICK MONTFORT

Duels—Duets

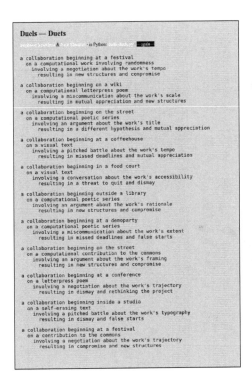

"Duels—Duets" is a generator, an automated meditation on collaboration, created by Stephanie Strickland and Nick Montfort. They were prompted to write it by their prior experience collaborating on the creation of another generator, "Sea and Spar Between," which links the poems of Emily Dickinson to Herman Melville's *Moby-Dick*. The form of the stanzas in "Duels—Duets" is based on those of the early computer-generated poem "House of Dust" by Alison Knowles and James Tenney. "Duels—Duets" was published online by New Binary Press.

```python
#!/usr/bin/env python
# Duels -- Duets
# copyright (c) 2013 Stephanie Strickland & Nick Montfort
#
# Permission to use, copy, modify, and/or distribute this software for
# any purpose with or without fee is hereby granted, provided that the
# above copyright notice and this permission notice appear in all
# copies.
#
# THE SOFTWARE IS PROVIDED "AS IS" AND THE AUTHOR DISCLAIMS ALL
# WARRANTIES WITH REGARD TO THIS SOFTWARE INCLUDING ALL IMPLIED
# WARRANTIES OF MERCHANTABILITY AND FITNESS. IN NO EVENT SHALL THE
# AUTHOR BE LIABLE FOR ANY SPECIAL, DIRECT, INDIRECT, OR CONSEQUENTIAL
# DAMAGES OR ANY DAMAGES WHATSOEVER RESULTING FROM LOSS OF USE, DATA OR
# PROFITS, WHETHER IN AN ACTION OF CONTRACT, NEGLIGENCE OR OTHER
# TORTIOUS ACTION, ARISING OUT OF OR IN CONNECTION WITH THE USE OR
# PERFORMANCE OF THIS SOFTWARE.
from random import choice
print
for i in range(12):
    place = choice(['over email', 'at a coffeehouse', 'on a wiki',
    'inside a studio', 'outside a library', 'in an art colony',
    'in a hacker space', 'at a demoparty', 'at a conference',
    'at a festival', 'on the street', 'in a food court'])
    art = choice(['', 'computational ']) + choice(['visual text',
    'work involving randomness', 'gathering of lexicons',
    'letterpress poem', 'poetic series', 'translation',
    'contribution to the commons', 'self-erasing text'])
    interaction = choice(['an argument', 'a negotiation',
    'a conversation', 'an agreement', 'a disagreement',
    'a miscommunication', 'a pitched battle'])
    traits = choice(['focus', 'pacing', 'rationale', 'extent', 'tempo',
    'mood', 'techniques', 'format', 'accessibility', 'poetics',
    'boundary conditions', 'trajectory', 'typography', 'scale',
    'framing', 'politics', 'title'])
    result = ['compromise', 'new structures', 'mutual appreciation',
    'further exploration', 'false starts', 'missed deadlines',
    'running out of time', 'rethinking the project', 'dismay',
    'a return to the drawing board', 'a different hypothesis',
    'a threat to quit', 'laughter']
    first = choice(result)
    result.remove(first)
    second = choice(result)
    print 'a collaboration beginning ' + place
    print '  on a ' + art
    print '    involving ' + interaction + " about the work's " + traits
    print '      resulting in ' + first + ' and ' + second + '\n'

$ python duels-duets.py

a collaboration beginning over email
  on a computational work involving randomness
    involving an agreement about the work's politics
      resulting in a return to the drawing board and further exploration

a collaboration beginning at a coffeehouse
  on a computational contribution to the commons
    involving a disagreement about the work's mood
      resulting in false starts and a different hypothesis
```

```
a collaboration beginning in a hacker space
  on a poetic series
    involving a conversation about the work's tempo
      resulting in new structures and a different hypothesis

a collaboration beginning at a conference
  on a computational translation
    involving a disagreement about the work's mood
      resulting in a return to the drawing board and a different
      hypothesis

a collaboration beginning at a conference
  on a computational poetic series
    involving a miscommunication about the work's politics
      resulting in a return to the drawing board and further exploration

a collaboration beginning outside a library
  on a visual text
    involving an agreement about the work's extent
      resulting in a threat to quit and laughter

a collaboration beginning in a food court
  on a computational visual text
    involving a conversation about the work's typography
      resulting in dismay and missed deadlines

a collaboration beginning in an art colony
  on a computational gathering of lexicons
    involving a negotiation about the work's accessibility
      resulting in new structures and further exploration

a collaboration beginning in a hacker space
  on a computational gathering of lexicons
    involving a miscommunication about the work's scale
      resulting in compromise and a return to the drawing board

a collaboration beginning at a festival
  on a computational visual text
    involving a pitched battle about the work's scale
      resulting in new structures and rethinking the project

a collaboration beginning in a hacker space
  on a computational letterpress poem
    involving an agreement about the work's title
      resulting in a threat to quit and further exploration

a collaboration beginning on the street
  on a letterpress poem
    involving a pitched battle about the work's politics
      resulting in a threat to quit and mutual appreciation

$ python duels-duets.py

a collaboration beginning at a demoparty
  on a work involving randomness
    involving a miscommunication about the work's mood
      resulting in further exploration and new structures

a collaboration beginning on a wiki
  on a computational letterpress poem
    involving an agreement about the work's rationale
      resulting in a different hypothesis and new structures
```

a collaboration beginning at a coffeehouse
    on a poetic series
        involving a miscommunication about the work's trajectory
            resulting in compromise and missed deadlines

a collaboration beginning at a coffeehouse
    on a translation
        involving a pitched battle about the work's poetics
            resulting in a return to the drawing board and further exploration

a collaboration beginning on the street
    on a computational letterpress poem
        involving a conversation about the work's mood
            resulting in missed deadlines and a different hypothesis

a collaboration beginning inside a studio
    on a computational self-erasing text
        involving an argument about the work's politics
            resulting in a return to the drawing board and running out of time

a collaboration beginning over email
    on a computational letterpress poem
        involving a negotiation about the work's scale
            resulting in further exploration and rethinking the project

a collaboration beginning inside a studio
    on a computational work involving randomness
        involving an agreement about the work's pacing
            resulting in a return to the drawing board and dismay

a collaboration beginning in an art colony
    on a self-erasing text
        involving an argument about the work's trajectory
            resulting in running out of time and a threat to quit

a collaboration beginning at a coffeehouse
    on a computational gathering of lexicons
        involving an agreement about the work's focus
            resulting in a threat to quit and rethinking the project

a collaboration beginning at a demoparty
    on a visual text
        involving a disagreement about the work's techniques
            resulting in further exploration and a different hypothesis

a collaboration beginning over email
    on a poetic series
        involving a miscommunication about the work's mood
            resulting in dismay and a threat to quit

CHRISTOPHER HIGGS, BLAKE BUTLER, & VANESSA PLACE

from *One*

EXEGESIS

What you are about to read is the product of a collaborative experiment: what if one writer (Vanessa Place) wrote a narrative composed entirely from the interior landscape of a character while another writer (Blake Butler) wrote a narrative composed entirely from the exterior landscape of a character, neither writer communicating with the other until both writers gave their finished product to another writer (Christopher Higgs, Me) who would then assemble the two narratives together to form one unified piece? —Christopher Higgs

[+]

And so my day begins again, again. Where I think into this evening, I hear me in the mash around my head. I eat corn, bacon, and candy. The helmets here are heavy and cause the stoop. My spine hurts, like a living diamond ladder, with no handles and no rungs.

It could be less so. It can always be less so. No more so than less so. Meaning: no more but less.

Leaving all the more. Less, that is. Again.

Suppose this is the way of any number of things. Say thirty-seven. Say writs of many kinds formed the essential parts of litigation. Say thirty-nine. Say the primary function of a writ in the 13th and 14th centuries was to convey the king's commands to his officers and servants. Don't say the other. It was irrelevant what the nature of those commands might be. Mustn't say the other. Never again—again.

Here, still, in this unending evening, I lift my head hard enough to see outside the night. I can hold my glance position only for several seconds, noticing three things:

(a) Someone scratching sky off.

(b) Another body.

(c) Floor.

What a floor is here is a pile of shit that I have yet to stick my head in, while the sky is still a sock. As for the other body, when I can make the urge again to see again, it's gone. Though sometimes there is some rummage in my sternum, and sometimes rope around my throat.

Remember this: the Register of Writs shows a large variety of writs to be administrative in nature, as opposed to judicial. These former writs acquired the name prerogative writs in the 17th and 18th centuries. This is certain, being history. Still, it's a sort of shadow, really, though not so cumbersome. Lighter and yet much quieter than one expected. An aerial view. Suspected, one should say. One may assert. Prerogative writs that have survived into modern law are the writ of mandamus and writ of certiorari. One might aver. Still, more or less quiet, at any rate. More or less light, that is to say.

These three things that I can see and I don't want to, for how the helmet makes me poor, makes me chew the hell out of the inside of my lip, which fills my mouth again with pus, which swims around my teeth and tongue where the words come from, really, shiftskin, and I am spitting up the blood. On the floor of shit this house has the blood pools in a picture of this house. These walls gleaming in their seizures make no sound in me at all.

I smell the sun around my helmet in the evening while the sun's not even here. A second helmet for my helmet, another day drummed to beginning.

There is no helmet here at all ever but I prefer to say there is, to have a window for this evening through which I am looking out onto the smudgefold to see when someone is coming over the pig bodies and the bleat. The bridges of this city of so many glowing skylines, each one strung from somewhere else.

In the dumb hiding of this house's hours I wrap my hands one round the other to make pray, which takes the whole day again and even then some, and after that, I need to sleep.

Before drifting off, one smelt the overwhelming smelt of remembered apples—doesn't it sound like something? Something sans regard. Something wounded. Wounding. Same difference, if the nails are kept well.

Say the medieval writ of prohibition played an important part in the conflict between the church and state in England. At any rate, say daily, say weekly, say hourly. Don't say the other. What kind of provocation, that's the question. The writ was also used in the courts of admiralty and local courts. It has survived in relative obscurity in United States law. This is after writing, though what manner of having written. Through, that is to say.

In the hall I front assume the Z position, my knees denting my headmeat.

These are days here. This is the knocking. I hear someone in the house say, without sound,

"Yesterday I will do the same thing I did I did again again."

My voice walks up behind me, taps me on the head.

Today I believe I am very funny and I tell whoever is behind me in the hall. The writ subpoena began to be attached to a wide variety of writs in the 1300s. These were an invention of the Court of Equity, which were a part of Chancery. In the light along the bending husk of walls and ceilings, the floor reflects the other parts of place around it so I can walk around and yet as all days become restraining and all hours are the clog, I give up before I can begin. Thus, 'subpoena' was a product of the Ecclesiastical Courts in England. I'm down. This is the last time I will tell you when I'm curling. Otherwise, assume the practice of hiding information from certain individuals or groups, perhaps while sharing it with other individuals, as if wanted, as if needed, as if desire. Whatever, that is.

Heretical. Blaspheme. Spam. The commonest writ from this era was the Praecipe quod reddat (You are commanded to return [some misappropriated good or land]). That which is kept hidden is known as this, as to these were often added the phrase: sub poena. You wish. Cum silentio. Then there'd be proof of something. Whenever there's nothing, there's sure to be proof of something. Whatever, that is, I say I say I say I said.

A portrait on the far wall where I am headed mostly is right there. As I approach with my helmet,

I can make out a little of the shape of what's been made: a picture of a person with two heads to his or her name, a person looking both ways at once, before another panel of other eyes. Mirrors hung up around the eyes to seem many all at once.

The eyes set in the wall will not blink unless I am not looking.

This is the night.

When I wake and find my gut uncut I stand up inside this unending day and thrust again.

In the kitchen, with the knife set and the oven, I sit and make a list of my whole life. I write with two pencils at the same time, so when one tip breaks I will not be disrupted. I have a hold. My both hands go on crawling.

Often controversial, depending on the content, the group or people, the motivation for the development of the writ subpoena is closely associated with the invention of due process, which slowly replaced trial by ordeal. They say 'matter of fact' casually, as if leaning against a wall outside something else. It's the measure of things. Ongoing. Imperative. Edifice rex. Lex talon.

It's all the same.

My life is wine, or it is money. My hands will not stay still—and yet each word I write comes out of me as backwards or crossed through or upside down. No matter how hard I help to hold my pencil straight up and on point. Nowhere in this, as I said: knocking.

And so my day begins again, again.

RICHARD KOSTELANETZ

from *A Book of Eyes*

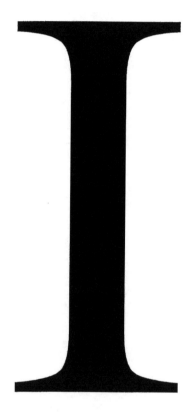

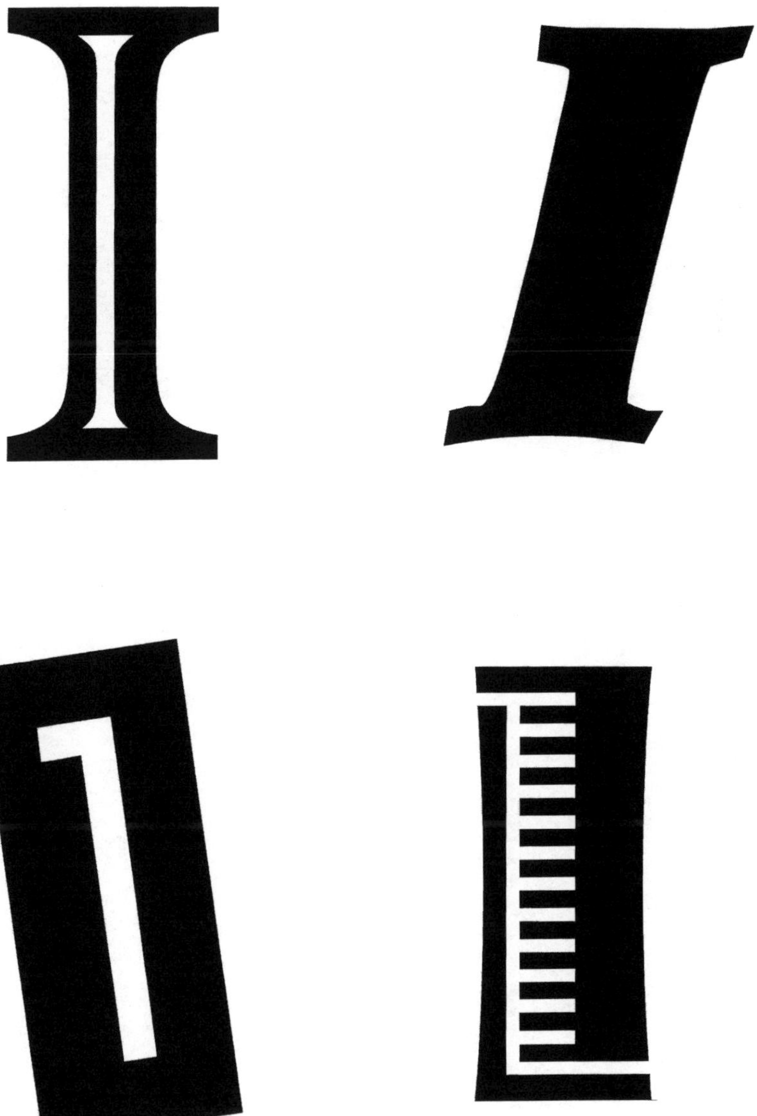

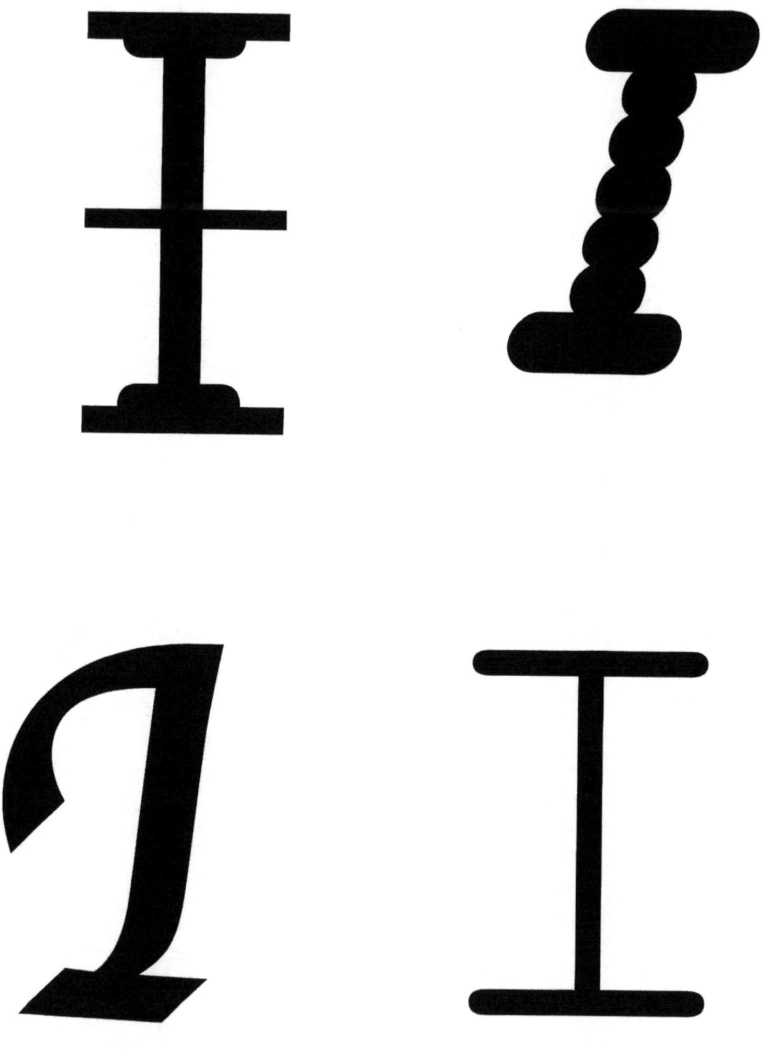

DANIELA OLSZEWSKA

from *Citizen J*

j refuses to keep things
classy; she swings that hellish

hand basket of hers to
+ fro like a dank demonette.

a bag of pseudogenes w/scarletish
tail—her valves have become

accustomed to ratcheting
up a notch, to really addling

over the complex system
of bicycle parts breathing

her in + then out + then,
at the very last second, in again.

*

w/a face like that,
in a time like this, j sits

in a tree. a fruit-bearing one.
she affixes herself.

sedulously gemstoned
+ camp-clad, she is not so

much a people-person as
she is a person-person.

lately, j feels the gore ball bouncing up against her sternum in time to the special broadcasts. he was no longer significantly othered enough to spark her. j had fallen for him because, not in spite of, his minus one kidney, two fingers, and three teeth. but, last week's parade day incident had caused most of those parts to groweth back. he had become entirely too whole for her and even those white velvet shorts of his weren't really working for him anymore. j found herself filling out forms to request a transfer to an apartment across the street from a crematorium or practice surgery parlor—someplace where she could really work her triage with- out fear of undue judgment from the now healthier half of the relationship.

in the midst of dressing
up to go messing up

the magistrate's new
motorcade, j takes to

the notion that the insides
of her toasters are miked.

she goes to consult her pet
magic mirror, but he looks

miked too—wired to heads
that can store more than

the traditional three minutes'
worth of incriminating

soundbite. thus, j resolves
to take distance, to make

haste w/ignition
                    + several cans of.

j ducks down;
j gooses up;

she walks into
one of those bars

+ the sky thickens
w/frog:

i'm going to need you
to dumb that drink

down for me.

etc. etc. etc.

          love me;
love my crutch.

but this isn't warsaw,
baaaabyyy, + j isn't

being coy—when
she says she wants

to be alone, she doesn't
mean w/you.

she looked like a cleaner version of a chorus line girl j had once seen stood up in front of the firing squad. it safety-coned the starts of her ribcage to wake up every morning next to this little pilgrim-toed spouse. they barely had it in them to fake interest in the new regime. together, they managed a photo stand near the entrance to the world's smallest slice of zodiac. j felt she had won the swan game as she was sure her partner would never ask her for a jumpstart. or a seriousconversation. as if they'd never even been to the inland. and they were finally raking in more than enough ducats to pay their way out of any corner they might accidentally back into.

MARGO BERDESHEVSKY

Square Black Key

"Let the snake wait under his weed…" (William Carlos Williams)

The Norman coast woman, no longer in her middle American housecoat as she remembers it, now naked under fuchsia silk, recalls the old robe on its peg in once-upon Akron. Was it called a housecoat? Yes. A thing to knot and tie. *Oui.* Skins like dropped petals scattered and buried between seas. That robe, quilted in shades of mid-summer golds, pearl buttons, red embroidered petals big as fingernails, June-bugs scattered on the collar curves, on the low hemline, on long cuffs. That robe bore a scent of daily Nivea moisturizer cream, it whispered femme, and craving, when she swayed inside it, down a flight from its pink banal and overheated winter after winter boudoir to the kitchen landing where coffee would need to be brewed, on time. Always on time. Often, she spilled it. A menstrual-colored canary would be uncovered, and knew its job was to sing. A rolled morning paper would be given entry through the back door flap, to the accompaniment of a jingle bell. Now, none of that. One leftover word, on ice.

Now, French silk, middle age, perfume bought across the channel at Harrod's, a second marriage content with its weight, bodies made for second helpings, artichokes, foie gras, a laryngitic cabaret song in the heart for the used skins, shed. Good to be a snake. Who needed old skin?

Awake in la Belle France, a white orchid flowering on morning's Tuesday sill. Object: a single Phalaenopsis petal. Object: an old robe. Object: sunlight bleeding through pastel curtains that did need washing. Another kitchen, another sill. Back to the white orchid: will you live until one more fall, are you part of a whole story, or only soft as any woman's hidden petals, unsusceptible to rain or aging as other flesh? Ready to die? Ready not to? The wearer of the second incarnation robe mixes fresh cream with her aromatic Italian coffee. What liquid, or skin, can have the flavor of *la vie, la vie, la vie?* She'll dance naked in her second kitchen this morning, right now. Take that, old robe. Take that, *la vie.* She's stripping jiggling, sobbing.

The white orchid that needs so little to flower, applauds. Drops a few pale petal peals, for show. Her husband does not come in to the kitchen to take away the pain. But wants his café crème. He's already seen her naked, anyway. But he hasn't ever seen her shedding her skin. He didn't think of her as a snake. He does, now. Nothing but uncovered flesh left. No old once-golden robe that she remembered, here; no new life of silk, that's the thing—not the old, not the new not the middle, but flesh; no bastion against tedium or ruined timing or no timing, or black keys. No skin. *La vie*. And the square black key, inventing—surrenders to an arrival unexpected. Object: unanticipated. Object: unsentimental. Object: unwoven threads caught dangling at the window. Another thing: a naked, thirsty, hungry country crow lands on her sill and for show, he too pecks and nips and spits and sheds his feathers. Sheds his iridescent blue-black hues, his haunting voice dropping octaves, and more snake than bird, sheds his skin, too. *Ainsi-soit-il*. Defenseless woman. Defenseless bird.

Missing key: the un-invented savior.

Square black key, a thing no larger than a fingertip, points back at its timid hovering above-it digit, hoping to be pressed into service—the letter "I," impersonal as any other, but black, and white as a dream without color, story with an unborn point of view, body in its doorway, neither in or out. Object. Key. One of twenty-six alpha-beticals plus symbols, numbers, arrows, ampersand, shift, the abbreviation for the word "control," a slash, a parenthesis, a dash, a tilde, all permitting eighty points of pressure not to mention the upper case alternatives and including the longer black space bar ... mute slave of the non-injured, for a morning missive in motion to a woman on La Manche, in coastal Normandy, probably still in her dressing gown. *Darling... how could you have known we would be so cruel?*

CARMEN GIMÉNEZ SMITH

Three Poems from *The City She Was*

In-Between Elegy

We had one chance—lined up on the museum bench--examining a Kay
Sage painting of doors and robes—

it's quiet enough for contemplating an undoing—we stood knee deep in a bog
of our own making—

eretofore handled one another like grandmother's horse figurine—even
cleaned with our own raggeds—needing the fortress we were—

and then to chip away at—to bear down onto—to find the holes and tear
them larger—that would be the collaboration—

If there had only been pauses—if only we had desisted in the tumble
downward—i mean we clipped sisyphus and jill—made eddys we could not
see to see—

We were analysis and question—secrets forested—both imbued in poems—
lies we thought at the time were—

And I might have thought—commenting on the museum goers instead—
the one with the turquoise belt—the one with the diaphanous hair a halo
round her—that this is—

what terrible endings were—your hand over mine—dining with its spoon
fingers—the meat on my neck's bones—

The If of Omission

dayone:
At the edge of the attic: a solution. Do I wrap myself in tissue and tuck my-
self into the scrapbook that smells of vodka, of cigarettes, of industrial glue?
If I could wriggle out of this geography, I'd memorize the future and bring
it back to my progeny. Instead I'm harsh-voiced bridal party, a husk of that
party. My voice is so shrill. The lunatic calls and I can barely hold the phone.

dayten:
Fragrant kiss on my neck, Polaroid number three. Unlikely I'll find a photo-
graph to tell the back side. The reparation provided to me is known as *eclectic
beauty*. I catch my eye in the mirror, distract my very own loins. That helps
the day pass, that taboo vaudeville.

dayonehundred:
I'm leaving my greasy print on all surfaces, even the superficial hi-bye
friendship. And night falls, and the ocean swallows oilships, and the deer die
in our grilles—we're a series of mishap, this vista and me. I swallow compas-
sion from a blue round pill. It's soothing to the jaw. It reminds me I'm not
all edge.

daysevenhundred:
For years I've not taught anything shameful.

dayonethousand:
*Little book of Syphilis. Epistolary book Written to the Latin's Ombudsman. The
book of Irritating boils. The book of Soul-show-You-the-Door. The book of Gut-
tersniping and Chivalry. book of yr. Deeds. Deeds to the Webb'd Hand. Tome on
Inchoate Nations, Guide to Wax Seals And their Replicae, What and How of the
Republic as told by a Rebel, A Mash note to Step Theory Disaster, how to Make A
Quarantine, Encyclopedia of Creatures that Afflict, Dictionary of Ruin and Quilts,
How to Gather 7 Horsewomyn, How to Finance yr. Pestilence. The Book of Books*
and in it, the Chapter on *Boats that Carry you to islands of Your Own Making*.

dayfivethousand:
If I could take myself up, if I could climb that vine, if I could give my
passport to the Prez with my scent all over it, if I could sever the emollient
impulse from my mane. If I had to travel without looking, if I dared men-
tion names from the book of those days. If I could my hairs in your bed, and
if you could your blood. If we had all been enough with the loaf split in half.
If only I could have a large old bust of you, dilated and filled with starpoints.

Let Down My Bucket

I kept hearing the small voice
describe what I was missing or
staying out of tonight: like

trees that howl and have
cooler things than arms.
I heard: Give in. Or easier:

Now.

(Like orange loves the sky
over a desert
I've broken open stones

looking for my part
or filled with all to be the planet
you want

I was disappear then come back,
disappear then come back)

BRIAN OLIU

from *Level End*

Boss Battle: The One With the Long Neck

When I arrived, the music changed—you, queen of what remains, you in a room too small for your body. Your neck is something I am unfamiliar with—the back of it, invisible, the front of it, delicate: the graze of a finger causes the chin to tilt downward, a trap, always a trap. Your face, a mask—smooth as the day you were born and as hard as the stone on the ring that I am wearing, the ring that allows me to pretend that this does not hurt as much as it once did; that the bruises that form fade to yellow faster, that this is what I should have been wearing since the beginning—trading the green of my youth for something that reminds you of an announcement, a declaration of danger.

You, larger than the room you have been sleeping in. You, despite this, will not push me against the wall, will not press your head into my chest, will not listen to what I am saying; that you must disappear, that the only thing that must remain is the room that we have built here: red brick, red paper, red fabric on the floor. I take my knife and start cutting—your neck breaking in sections and vanishing, tendons unraveling like our time away from this room, your neck growing shorter by the second. Your face shrinks back towards your shoulders, shoulders I remember but cannot place. You, of the neck. You, of no neck, neckless: head on body like a badly drawn picture, like something I once drew. This is where you disappear. This is where the door opens. This is all that I have wanted.

Boss Battle: A Woman Made of Feathers

When I arrived the music changed—you rotating like a flower with a cracked stem—you rotating like you are caught in the wind: blades on a fan above us where we once slept, a buzz saw, a spinning plate. This is the room that you are locked in—deep within a house that someone else has built, rooms leading to other rooms: you in the middle of the eye, you to the east. I remember you beautiful—long necked, silver shined, wrists bent in the back of cars, hair on the window. You bit my leg once: drew blood, wiped it on your white coat. If I could fit your body inside my mouth I would, you said, and I believed you: to be swallowed whole like a fish is a noble way to lose one's way—out of breath, crushed to serve a purpose. As you spin your feathers come undone—they crash into the walls, they spin in reverse. I can catch anything you throw at me: grasp it between my fingers; snatch it as it floats to the ground. I try to pluck what is left of you from the air but the vane slices my palm. I will do better. I promise to you I will do better. Your feathers get caught in the door. They stick to the walls. Your armor is in the world and you are naked: arms out, palms up. You have lost weight. You have a new bruise, a freckle on your hip I don't remember. I roll my sleeve to my elbow and show you where you bit me: the teeth marks are gone—the skin has snapped back to where it should be. The color, too, is gone: no gradient to red and purple, all anomalies dabbed over. Some of the feathers return to your body; the hollow shaft cuts your skin and digs through the layers of what is left of where you stood, the vane twisting downward. When there are no feathers left the door will open. The music will stop. No one will know we were here.

Save Point: Inn

It could have been a number of things: the fear of being in a new country where no one spoke the language except for a few stunted verbs and a handful of nouns, the cider that started in ceramic bowls but quickly turned to lips around heavy green glassed bottles, the wine we moved toward when we wanted something more familiar and less acidic, but at some point, we decided that it was time to steal everything. It could've been the fact that it was dark, it could've been the fact that we were landlocked whereas the night before we were on the northern coast of France on the beach wondering if this was the moment that we would remember, the moment that we would bring up at parties when people mention the word "night," the words "when I was younger." It started small: a loaf of bread from the kitchen which was ripped into smaller pieces and divided amongst us—a clamoring for peanut butter despite nothing resembling what we have known since childhood; we ate it dry, to soak up the liquor in our stomachs. We would've eaten anything at this point—anything to take something we know and put it inside of us, to warm it up in our bellies, to swallow something familiar. We went back for more and came back with more: a dusty bottle of wine—the same wine we drank with dinner by the glass, again, now, we would drink by the bottle; peeling labels, paper from glass, commenting on the glue they use here, how easy it comes off, how simple it would be to poison all of us—to teach us a lesson about kitchens and cupboards, to teach us something valuable about how things are done here, about how instead of waking up somewhere new, we would not wake up. This happens when we believe that things belong to us—affection after a warm bath, an understanding of what is left of us after we have lost everything. We were brought here to create a longing for something that is not our home: a bed next to a heater, pillows in other languages, a small window to reglate the cold. Food with strange labels, a different type of vegetable rotting in the crisper. To build a city we only know for a second as our own: yes, I remember the train station, yes, I remember the way the ducks walked—their red beaks familiar, conducive to what we believe. This city, too, is ours. We deserve to put it into our pockets: the stream where children threw bicycles, the ring signifying the end, the carnival swirling to greet us the day we arrived. One bottle is certainly enough. One loaf of bread. Any more and they will notice things missing—the count will be off—to steal within sequence. We go back. We go back because it is too warm outside—not yet fall, and our clothes are sticking to our backs, our skin gummed, gritty. We stick our bodies in the freezer, we reach our sticky arms into the cold in hopes of something sweet, a dessert, an ending to all things. We have drunk all of the wine. We have drunk all of the wine and we are not sorry—we deserved it, it was there and it is ours. No one will miss it. No one will wonder. Some of us are trying to sleep—some try to ignore what is happening: our beds our alibis. We shout out advice from the floor: walk slower, be quieter, forget about the spoons. We know what will happen: we will wake up in the morning and someone did not throw the empty bottles into the sea. Someone has broken a glass and there is blood everywhere. Someone will walk with a limp. We will return to the ocean from where we once came—a different shore this time.

DIANA GEORGE

Imperator

The tide was out, the sea the merest sheen on the mud. Tiny pale sea-lice crawled over strewn and stranded things: collapsed and sclerosing hydromedusae, mantled opaque with decay; dull sea-glass and variegate, tattered plastic; flecks of nacre, of chitin; dead mussels and hake and shreds of dulse. Rot's force had swollen shells apart, avulsed the inner flesh.

Nothing to glean that was not tainted. Odtsetseg looked up; out where shoals gave way to channel, the *Cosco Imperator* was underway. At that distance, propulsion and displacement were alike obscured; Odtsetseg watched the tanker slide, wakelessly, atop an ocean as continent as earth itself. A flight of cormorants headed as if for the morning sun, then banked and dropped to skim a nearer target, a yellow raft lolloping on waves that shoaled and rose and foamed and collapsed the faster, the closer they came to shore. A man was seated at the back of the raft, an oar held upright in one hand. His other hand rested on the head of a small, scowling personage.

The wind had shifted. From the far-off mainland now: ash, defoliant. Odtsetseg watched the raft lollop on until it was within hailing distance.

The personage called out, in a voice louder than necessary, as if through a maelstrom, "Is this _____ Island, or are you some maritime illusion?"

Odtsetseg nodded.

They trudged over tide-sheen all the way to Odtsetseg at the wrack line, the smaller perched in the crook of the taller's elbow and the raft dragged behind.

Odtsetseg said he had never seen anyone arrive on this island of their own accord. The only rafts here were handmade ones, confiscated before ever put to sea, or breaking into sodden flotsam under flailing, drowning prisoners.

The smaller one clambered down. Her scalp showed dull white under closely shorn hair. The taller sat down facing the sea. He opened a valve on the side of the raft; he put his lips to the valve and began sucking out great draughts of air.

Odtsetseg asked whether the two of them had come looking for the entrance to hell.

The man put the raft aside and spoke in a way Odtsetseg did not recognize, in a halting, humming groan and burr. At length he ceased; he applied himself to the valve once more.

The little personage said, "My friend here says you look like a man in whom we can have confidence. The fact that you have the bearing and dress of a trustee is the least of it. You once led a life of violence and pleasure; now you are restrained, within and without. We applaud what we take to be your strategies: caution, absorption, a throttled-back curiosity. Pragmatic means of survival for the detainee from whom too little is expected rather than too much.

"We are Rudd and Weser; he is Rudd and I am Weser. Five months ago we stowed away aboard the *Cosco Imperator*. We had no desire to reach the ship's destination—every ship is destined to sink or be scuttled; the final port is always ruin. Nor were we interested in any of the ship's intermediary ports, not Qeshm or Rugen or the Saint Brandon Rocks. We chose the *Imperator* because it passes within a night's rowing of this prison island.

"The sea keeps plunderers out as much as it keeps the likes of you in. For you, this island is durance vile. It goes hard with you here; hard, the privations and the discipline; hard, the tedium and the sorrows; even your trustee status is but a lax noose. But for plunderers! For them, a prison island represents wealth itself, in sleeping form. In the form of slumber.

"We are not plunderers." She swayed as she spoke: a stubby sylph. "We offer you friendship; we ask your trust. Be assured all three of us will profit by our association."

How, Odtsetseg asked.

Rudd paused in his exsufflations. Ash was falling in pale flakes like shirred paper, vanishing on contact with seawater, settling in the baffle-seams of the raft draped on Rudd's knees. Rudd spoke again, this time in hissed sibilants pocked with chirping.

Weser translated: "I feared for our safety on board the *Imperator*—I say 'I' meaning he, Rudd—and so I counseled Weser to travel in the guise of a man, in case we should be discovered. Weser said she knew better methods for remaining unnoticed. Days, we secreted ourselves in disused storeholds. Nights, I bound Weser to my belly; I pulled on a bulky nautical sweater and thus we walked abroad, one unmolested corporate being. We waddled topside, stargazing, smoking, my hand tucked in my waistband in support of our great paunch. I spoke softly to Weser of all she could not see: the wrinkled black sea far below, and, up above us, the ship's bridge, massive against the night sky and lit by rows of tiny lights that made of every column a spire, of every porthole an architrave, and the whole one fairy kingdom, and all for us alone.

"We were free. Suspended between two trackless wastes—the sea, the sky—seen but unnoticed, fed without having to work, we wondered why we should ever go ashore again.

"A shadow of distrust passed through you just now, don't deny it—I say 'just now' meaning back then, when you asked your question. You are restless. So were we, in our doldrum world, though we did not know it yet. Contentment ripened, rotted. Underneath her bindings, Weser turned like a worm.

"We took to wandering below decks. Outside, perhaps, were whitecaps, booming swells, the pitch and roll, the brilliant sun. We knew nothing of all that. We followed narrow corridors lit by yellow bulbs in wire cages. I climbed down rungs bolted to walls, Weser on my shoulders, her fingers clutching my hair. We descended. Conduits on corridor ceilings sweated. A rusty grime prevailed. The air scarce rewarded breathing: a hot, dense fug of oil fumes and bilge reek. This far down, the sound of the ship was a thrumming amalgam so loud it subtracted the auditory from the world of the senses, from the world itself.

"In that loudness, Weser and I sometimes came upon a sailor. Like you, detainee, sailors often have reason to want to look insouciant, however startled they may be. Those we saw below, so far from light and air and day, may themselves have been hiding. We affected indifference at first; we let them go.

"In time, we brought certain of these sailors into our confidence, one by one. We would motion to a sailor to climb back up with us to the higher, quieter decks; we would show him our hiding places, our complex mode of speech, how Weser's tiny person could be concealed under bandages. What lightsome hours we spent with our new shipboard friends, with the stoker Holf, with an oiler named Struc or Truc and his brother. We told each one he looked like just the man in whom we could have confidence, though this was perhaps least true of Holf. They brought along still others, in whom we also professed to trust. When the number of our sailor-confidants had grown sufficient, we gathered them nightly in one of the empty storeholds we favored. A row of rust-seeping, painted-over rivets ran the length of its floor. On our side of the rivet-line, I held Weser before me; I interlaced my fingers and she stood on my palms. *Who keeps you down?* we would ask the sailors. *Who robs you?* If we catechized, it was not in order to instruct, or not really. We did it for the savor of that astringent pleasure bachelors can take together in anatomizing the world and its corruptions. *Who holds you down, who robs you?* Weser and I would ask the sailors. *The swindlers,* they would answer us, *the swindlers and the oligarchs in their distant capitals.* We asked them what was more common, these days, than to foment crisis and ride it out toward profit.

"The sailors liked to bring Weser gifts: balisong butterfly knives, festoons of dates strung on bootlaces. Do not mistake these men for simpletons, I told Weser when we were alone one evening.—You've promised them they will reign in permanent riotocracy, Weser answered me.

"It was dusk, the first dog watch. Many of our confidants were on low-visibility detail just then. I imagined it a fraught and exhausting travail—peering into the chill penumbral fog, trying and failing and trying and failing to descry figure's emergence from ground. But there had to have been exceptions, pleasurable ones, structurally impossible for Weser or myself to have experienced and therefore enviable: coming along a gangway the sailor notices a darkening concretion in the fog just ahead, which, as it nears and swells, takes on definition, reveals itself; not only is it a fellow sailor but a fellow conspirator, a confidant. The beautiful is just this: that which appears. Weser and I were denied this, denied, too, that serene pagan confraternity of sailors, however close we came, so that I preferred it when they were out in the fog somewhere, in that life unknown to me; I wished they would not return to the storehold bringing their absence, their distance, with them, a wish tinged by something of the same feeling that brushes up against me when I consider that I will never really know what Weser is saying to you now, 'now' meaning some future moment, imperceptible to me, after I have spoken and she is making sounds I can only assume render these meanings.

"Late one evening, there were just three sailors in attendance with us, bearing jars of turnip wine they had brewed underneath their hammocks. We told them we would return shortly, with black bread and perhaps a cucumber. We locked the storehold behind us.

"Life at sea is life; the same night of confusion obtains there as elsewhere. Hour on hour you watch the ship's wake churn and spume, wave on wave regressing, recurring, ever on the verge of revealing to you—to you only, just there where you stand—the secret of matter's perpetual collision with itself. This presentiment of the infinite is an error. Men bring the world with them when they go to sea.

"We put it about, amongst our remaining confidants, that the intriguers had shown themselves heartily sorry in the moments just before we closed the door on them forever. We lingered over the story of their repentance: how plaintive; how affecting; how not unmixed with surprise (intriguers never expect to get caught); how orthogonal to the matter of their condign punishment."

An ash-dusted crab finicked its way over sand and wrack. Fat stalks of saltwort trembled in the breeze. Whelks clung to rocks. Slack tide. Rudd folded the raft in thirds, lengthwise, and began rolling it up from one end.

What does your talk avail me, Odtsetseg asked. I found nothing to eat here and if I do not get back soon there will be nothing for me to eat there either.

Weser said, "I believe I speak for Rudd when I say we are ready to come with you, or nearly. You may introduce us, surreptitiously, to new confidants your discernment tells you are the right ones; our improbable arrival is already their guarantee of our worth. First, understand this: we would have spared those sailors if we could. In our first weeks aboard the *Imperator*, the two of us had lived as one being, I inside Rudd, installed there the way a man in despair keeps the matter of his self behind a false door. What a queasy delight was our life.

"After the dispatching or anyway the immurement of the so-called intriguers, after we had told the story of their heartfelt remorse and our tender but pitiless justice, a story that bound our confidants to us more closely than even the catechism and the tributes, just then we were poised to go from triumph to triumph, not by restricting the number of those who knew our secret but by expanding it. We made ready for our imminent success. For three nights running, after the immurement, we gathered our remaining sailors, to prepare them. We asked them who the exploiters were. Our sailors answered us as prettily as ever.

"Here let me pause, detainee; pause at once. There is enough said. Find out from Rudd—if you can, without my aid—of the return of our accusers from their oubliette, haggard and wild-eyed, raving yet still possessed of enough sense to bring about our total ruin. It is for Rudd to tell you, in his monstrous language, if it can be called a language, of exposure, arrest, confinement to the brig. Least of all is there any need to speak of prisoners' ecstasies, erasure of self, the dissolution of time in eternity; what knowledge, these days, is less secret? What more decayed, more contemptible, than the penitentiary's gimcrack transcendence?

"Let Rudd tell you, if he cares to, whether in the succeeding months of captivity he despaired of ever reaching this island; I tell you I did not.

"Here we are now, ashore, as you see us now. Are we ourselves not a form of proof? Let it be yours to imagine the joy born fresh out of terror, the rapture of escape from durance, the wondrous reprieve from dread. Have confidence in us."

LAURA RELYEA

Selections from *All Glitter, Everything*

KE$HA IS AS KE$HA DOES.

Ke$ha brims with ambition. It rolls and boils over the sides of her kitten-glittered dreams. Ke$ha, please be an unstoppable force—a volcano, a tsunami, an avalanche—pick your element, Ke$ha. Look for solutions everywhere. Solve mathematical proofs in your sleep.

Ke$ha, I imagine you lying fetal in a bed that is not your own. I imagine your fingers furiously tapping on a Ti-83 calculator covered in Lisa Frank stickers. In high school you giggled and doodled through calculus. You exhausted your teachers and stared out of windows.

Ke$ha, you're built for big things.

Ke$ha can be hazardous. Birthed from long line of bloody fisted scalping slayers—Ke$ha often forgets things like limits and her diminutive frame.

These violent animals from which she was birthed fell victim to a cornucopia of temptations—royal ruby stained cherries, plums full of scarlet, cascades of orange nectarines and apricots. Ke$ha inherited their weakness. It is in her blood.

Ke$ha burns the skins of peaches. She casts them in the fire and counts to one hundred and three. She grabs them out bare handed. She gobbles them up in an indulgent and passionate fury.

Ke$ha is mostly disciplined.

Ke$ha is a cowboy in the center of a panicked herd—lasso raised high. She whispers incantations under her breath: the wind to guide her lariat around the cattle's heavy veined necks, for God to take her nightmares away.

KE$HA AND I FROLIC IN THE BACKYARDS OF OUR NEIGHBORS

It takes twenty-three minutes to twist and weave the peonies into satisfactory crowns. Their bulbous sepals balance delicately against our foreheads—descended halos of amaranth, fandango, and carmine. We are the sovereigns of your backyard, Ke$ha and I. Imagine us barefoot and sheathed in white eyelet. We reign over the firefly twilight with hushed laughter. You can spot us in the distance, breaking apart pinecones and making wishes on their brittle corpses. We play croquet and badminton, and douse or bellies in dandelion wine. Darkness descends and we continue our antics—cartwheeling through beds of clovers.

KE$HA ALIGHTS!

KE$HA you make my insides feel like !!!¡¡¡!!!¡¡¡!!!¡¡¡!!!¡¡¡ —which means either I'm jumping up and down for joy or I'm very bad at morse code! Good thing we are not soldiers, Ke$ha—our unbridled enthusiasm would either get us both mortally wounded or would end every war! Good thing we don't believe in war, Ke$ha—we believe in water fights instead! Ke$ha, let's build a slip-n-slide 100 yards long, let's set it up in the backyard between two aggressive sprinklers! Let's fill up 563 waterballoons and throw them at the cars passing through the neighborhood! Good thing we don't believe in neighbors—we are surrounded by strangers or undiscovered friends but nothing between! Good thing we don't believe in grey area Ke$ha—it's been the same since the notes we passed to boys in homeroom: it is either Yes! or No!

KE$HA AND I NEVER PLAY THE VICTIM

If anyone will survive the zombie apocalypse it's me and Ke$ha. This is a certainty for a couple of reasons:

1. We are as formidable as any Amazon warrior.
2. Our capability to harness group-think.

I don't care how high the odds are stacked against us. How many dependants we claim on our tax forms when the dead walk the earth, or if our husband's rotting ash mouths are clamoring to consume us. I don't care if one of us can only survive a few days without expensive medications. Ke$ha and I will go full RAMBO on your zombified asses! We will wield machetes and handguns, smear mud on our bodies and subdue sentience.

What I'm saying is: Ke$ha and I will never lose our humanity. For that we will be worshipped.

CHRISTOPHER GRIMES

from *The Pornographers*

The next to last item before the Budget Committee, a proposal for a direct-to-Internet video production—tentatively titled *Flight 69* and told, we're briefed, exclusively through the eyes of the main character (evidently some dude named Abdul)—finds us airborne in an aisle seat, the black and white countdown leader of an in-flight movie flickering at the front of the cabin, next to which, the movie screen, stands a severe looking flight attendant, described as one of those stone-faced Frigidaires all buttoned up with her hair pulled back, her mouth a glossy, thin-lipped scar, none of which strike us as too promising, what with the antiseptic and generally problematical setting of an airplane, to say nothing of all the scowling, until it's revealed that the in-flight movie is actually an adult feature, a solemn orgy filmed and presented in vintage Super 8, a welcome development despite its contributing to an already overly-complicated scenario, including, it's pointed out, such additional logic discrepancies as to how the feature was pre-loaded into the inter-cabin entertainment system in the first place (one wonders aloud if we have the makings of a comedy here), but even these more or less logistical concerns now evaporate, at least temporarily, with the revelation of the extraordinarily sexy specimen we're introduced to, sitting right next to us in the window seat, a stone-cold knockout squeezing out dollops of hand cream on her hands, rubbing the hand cream in, dollopful by dollopful, periodically glancing at us, languidly pushing an auburn curtain of hair aside with the top of her oily wrist so that we can see the blunt, rounded tops of her teeth and a suggestion of the tongue there in the pink center of a seductive, full lipped smile, prompting us to speak, to ask (importantly, it's emphasized) *to where is* [sic] *you going*, delivered almost in a whisper, the effect defined as some kind of foreign accent, one she's perhaps having difficulty placing, too, because she's still just sitting here mutely, still just smiling, continuing to rub that hand cream on her hands, probably wondering, as we do, if the accent is along the lines of an Arnold Schwarzenegger, say, who sounds a lot to us like a younger Henry Kissinger, when she finally offers up her singular reply, drawing out the word *vacation*, snapping the lid of her hand cream shut after saying it, our gaze moving jerkily from the hand cream bottle to her breasts— described here as not too big and not too little, definitely natural, just *right*—although it's imperative to the plot, we're told, that we peel our eyes off of them, what's described as that stupendous rack of hers, and instead look back down to the tray table that's been obscuring a view to our lap, lifted now to reveal that in our one hand is a gun, and in the other, an enormous erection, an erection so impressive in its enormity that Hot Babe drops her hand cream, a look of horror on her face (we don't know if it's the gun or the erection pointed in her direction that frightens her at this point), a look on her face that clearly comprehends the instant truth of the matter that we ourselves give voice to—that *this shit going* [sic] *down, bitch, and so are you*—and after giving it, the harrowing pronouncement, we reach out and grab her by the arm, forcing her to stand up for the purpose of dragging her to the front of the aircraft, right up to where the severe looking, buttoned-up Frigidaire stands, presumably still at the spot where earlier she had demonstrated the adjustment mechanism of our seat belts, and where she continues to stand, a force to be reckoned with, because we're taking control of this plane, goddamnit, taking over Flight 69, and in clear demonstration of the fact, we briskly shove Frigidaire out of the aisle, pluck the inter-cabin telecom unit off the wall and announce that *you American bitches, exporting your lust and various so-called degradations and seductive ways*—something along these lines, it's explained, as this is simply a rough sketch and some dialogue will need to be re-, well, thunk—*well, now you will see what it means to get fucked*, we command, motioning to suddenly not-so-severe-looking, but still humorless Fridge (her flight attendant cap having fallen off from the shove, she now stands to reveal a glowing mane of blonde hair) with the barrel of our gun, and we order her, the once frigid figure now thawing before our eyes (things are getting a bit complicated, it's admitted), to *come here*, an order that she at once obeys (we maintain both gun and erection, after all), nervously stepping towards us, taking tentative, sideways looks at the passengers, her charges, as if to spy the answer to the question of why, exactly, she's here in the first place, what her purpose is, what she should do next, a studied and severe authority (albeit increasingly sexy), fortuitously conversant in, and therefore presumably able to translate, the incomprehensible language we're barking at our captive audience (in other words, we appear to have exhausted our English vocabulary by this time in the presentation), which she does, translate, for the rest of the passengers, all of whom we are surprised to now discover are women, who must, the flight attendant says on our behalf, take off their pants and skirts, and now their shirts, followed by the bra and those panties, so that when everyone is sitting in their seats naked, we pick Hot Babe up—the other, initial passenger, not the hot, at this point, Flight Attendant—and turn her over in mid-air, her legs pointing straight up like fireplace tongs, which we proceed to spread, the legs/tongs, and run our tongue along the folds of her vagina, momentarily stopping to tell Flight

Attendant to tell her, Hot Babe whose vagina we're licking, to reciprocate (for such is the Flight Attendant's dilemma, the contract that she has with Hot Babe, and indeed all the other passengers, that she must faithfully deliver our demands in order to save them all, an unenviable position, to be sure, and one that we doubtless relate to), executed, the fellatio, at first hesitantly and in great fear, and *voila*, a standing 69—hence the title—although thusly engaged we still frequently eye the other passengers suspiciously, we're told, but they, too, are getting aroused (in any event our point of view reveals that there's lots of lip licking among them), so we wave the gun, telling now naked Flight Attendants to communicate our directive that *you American sluts, you get fucking or else*, and that's all it takes, apparently, because there's a sudden swarm of groping, a *fuckfest*, someone offers, *at 30,000 feet*, citing the description as possible promotional copy, which, particularly as we're beginning to run short on time—to say nothing of the fact that the decision of whether or not we really want pursue actual production, as opposed to just the distribution of content is still a source of serious debate—provides an opportune segue to the other, related item on the agenda, *Trends Analysis*, though before leaving the first item for the moment, it should be made clear that despite the obvious cost prohibitions of the scenario just reviewed (re: *setting*, specifically the building or procuring of a commercial aircraft hull), it represents the kind of out-of-the box thinking that might well get us through our critical, at this point critically *chronic* budget shortfall, and although we're given to understand that this was a summary of part one of the entire production, and part one only, we agree it's sufficiently illustrative of the general thrust of the concept, and that, despite the obvious financial restrictions such a production would be made to labor under, it deserves further consideration (though perhaps in a modified form), but be that as it may, for the moment at least, we'd do well to put it aside in order to get to the second item on the agenda, the Comptroller's analysis of trends, rooted, he prefaces, squarely in the Pew Charitable Trust's latest poll indicating that a full 82.5% of American males aged 18 to 40 accessed Internet pornography at least once last month, that 33.6% of American females in the same age group are reported to have accessed Internet pornography during the same period, both trajectories therefore leading us to the inescapable conclusion that there's lots and lots and lots of accessing of pornography *via* Internet going on even as he, the Comptroller, speaks, that the accessing of Internet pornography has become a mainstream, so-called populist activity, statistically speaking (although, he says, given the relatively narrow scope of the Pew study, certain extrapolations needed to be made to account for broader demographics, and that we therefore might need to adjust our business plan accordingly in order to accommodate such information, as encouraging as it is), a statistical spike in consumer demand perhaps on the one hand attributable to—and here the

Comptroller is just thinking out loud—the sudden, widespread availability of low cost, high quality digital cameras allowing a producer to focus on creating output that appeals to the more idiosyncratic and fetishistic tastes of the consumer, tastes historically too narrow in their interests for a producer with mass-market ambitions, and, on the other, all of the demands, simply speaking, made on our time, the fact that we have no more time *left*, the Comptroller continues, not a spare minute, plain and simple, nothing more than a couple of minutes maybe to do *anything*, so that the average, basic consumer isn't going to waste his time with all the rigmarole that gets in the way of the excitement, no, because he *needs* the thing right here, right now, and besides pornography is pretty much your *Reader's Digest* condensed version anyway—what with its short build up, etcetera, as per discussion in the earlier example—all boiling down to expectation, because that guy who's thinking about the quote, unquote cum shot (a theme that he'll take up more diligently later in his analysis, he says) is thinking about the so-called cum shot long before he sits down in front of the computer, meaning this guy's on the bus thinking about that cum shot, reading the lists of names of the dearly departed in the newspaper obitz while vaguely thinking about that cum shot waiting at home for him, so that when he *does* finally get there (home), he kisses the wife and children, finds himself a little privacy in the basement down there next to the washer and dryer, monkeys around for thirty seconds (the word is *surfs*, someone suggests) until he finds the thing he's after, then afterwards goes upstairs and throws a few lawn darts with the kids before dinner and life goes on, the point being that it's the way things are heading, and the problem is going to be trying to keep a market share against all the competition for viewership—never minding for the moment those couple of Arabs, to give just one instance, who sure as hell knew what they're doing with regard to making a spectacle of themselves—competition here specifically referring to the deep and trenchant issues involved in just how one is supposed to compete for time and attention, basic problems created by some pretty cut-throat forces whose only goal is to suppress their competitors' product identity, but anyway, the Comptroller says, if we turn to Agenda Item II of the analysis of trends we arrive at the cliché that there's nothing new under the sun, because as successful pornography is made into something always already known by the general consuming public, the report before us indicates specialized productions tend to disappear from view, a fact supportable by some impressively persuasive graphs and charts if our Power Point projection unit wasn't still on the fritz, forcing us to forgo the glitz and glam, we're told, and instead get straight to the bottom line here, which is that the big draw today is still oral sex with female as the giver and male as receiver, and that we're to continue to view the so-called cum shot, also known as the *money shot* for good reason, as a mandatory sign of sexual climax, a compulsory indication that pleasure is achieved, a marketing sign, furthermore, fully born out by the research, firmly indicating that what's true on VHS tape in the 1980s an 90s holds true in today's online environments, perhaps even more so, suggesting perhaps increased investment in the money shot, especially if resources are limited, as they so desperately are, so that we might as well forget everything else in this analysis, we're told, and simply *let it all ride* on the money shot—the Comptroller's just kidding a little here, he confesses—which nevertheless brings him to a tertiary point involving promotion, including such findings that of figures presented in advertising our adult website, it's recommended that a full 72 percent be female, specifically, in terms of descriptor and frequency of descriptor historically employed, *thin* (98%), *young* (92%) and *white* (66%), with *long* (84%) and *blonde* (48%) hair, while male figures should almost exclusively be present only as phallus, with the rest of the male body being framed out, especially the head and face, thus affecting a kind of anonymity and omnipresence at the same time, an unidentifiable but imperative presence, it's emphasized, critical even (or especially) to the success of those cases marketed as *lesbian*, wherein the reproduction of girl-on-girl action must crucially include the possibility of the male consumer to join in, as implied by the lesbians performing fellatio on polymer penis-like-objects, for instance, while gazing toward the camera, the act suggesting the penis, or penis-like-object, as the assumed source of pleasure in lesbian sex while reminding the voyeur of the power of his own peanut, itself described in terms of descriptor and frequency in promotional material as *big* (45%), *monster* (17%), *huge* (12%), *over 12 inches* (9%), *fat*, or its synonym *thick* (8%) and *massive* (4%), depending on advertising budget (virtually none), in contrast to the descriptors historically used for female genitalia—*tight* (73%), *tiny* (11%), *little* (8%) and *small* (8%)—as it, the female genitalia, acts for all intents and purposes as the point of entry into the milieu itself, the story, its simplicity, we're told, really impossible to overemphasize, in as much as research reveals that it is as it has always been in mainstream culture, meaning that arousal is best achieved through the use of stock characters, since complex and contradictory characters evoking complex emotions tend to decrease and disturb the experience (translation: once the scene is set, we can get down to the *real* action) though word to the wise, we're warned, while templates produce a certain degree of repetition and familiarity, they do not dictate the content or meaning of the experience in question, speaking of which, before we adjourn, if there aren't any at this point, meaning questions, this might be a good time to reiterate that we've already established a long and documented history of being open to creative revenue sources such as these…

KIM ROSENFIELD

Selections from *USO: I'll Be Seeing You*

*Good afternoon, Ladies and Gentlemen.
My first number this afternoon is a little song
that I wrote myself. That is, I didn't write it
ALL myself. Another fellow wrote the words and
another fellow wrote the music…but I happened to
be in the room at the time.*

When you hear the sound of the gong it will be just another day wasted away.
This program comes to you through the audacity of the Swinefeffer Liver Sausage
Co. makers of the finest baloney you've ever sliced. It comes in a nice, extremely
fresh, puncture proof, actor proof blue can. "Liver and Let Liver," that's our
motto. And now, folks, we will present that stirring little drama, MUD,
BLOOD, and KISSES or, THE MYSTERY OF THE STOLEN ADENOIDS.
Imagine you are sitting in a little theater in Great Little Neck. The lights go
dim… the curtains go up… the audience goes out…

*

I had to stop drinking, cause I got tired of waking in my car driving 90.

I'm not addicted to cocaine. I just like the way it smells.

When that fire hit your ass, it will sober your ass up quick! I saw something,
I went, "Well, that's a pretty blue. You know what? That looks like fire!"
Fire is inspirational. They should use it in the Olympics because I ran the
100 in 4.3.

I'd like to make you laugh for about 10 minutes—though I'm gonna be on
for an hour.

I couldn't stop. I put the pipe down. It jumped back in my hand.

I went to the penitentiary one time. Not me personally, but me and Gene
went there for a movie. Arizona State Penitentiary, population 90 percent
black people. But there are no black people in Arizona. They have to bus
motherfuckers in!

Freebase? What's free about it?

Marriage is really tough because you have to deal with feelings…and
lawyers.

I believe in the institution of marriage and I intend to keep trying until I get
it right.
I went to the White House, met the President. We in trouble.

I'm up on the craft
steamer
to fight ripped
Bosnia
each
maneuver is
opposite
as good as
it unequivocally
depends
upon whose
engagement
as good as
for the bigger
shows
celebrities
are
as good as
brands—
they need
a lot
of lead
time
for them
it's the
bigger
prolongation
as good as
the
logistics
have been
the
calamity
as good as
who knows
what else
for the single

celebrity
the debate
never
manifested
as she
longed for
the 4
star
highway
residence
as good as
the
limo
for her
Afghanistan
concert
she didn't
get it
We're there
upon the
infantry
bottom
in the center
fight
anyway
she went
into rehab
the following
month
so she never
did
have
the
tour

ANNA JOY SPRINGER
Variations on a (Fucked) Theme:
The Ruling-Class Rules for Realism

Andrew Jackson's inauguration party in 1829 was a fuck shit up populist romp. To celebrate the victory of "The People's President" voters and fans from all over the country crammed into the white house uninvited to shake hands and get drunk with their new leader. The mob stood on brocade couches in muddy boots and beaver hats, with hayseeds, free negroes, and soldiers trashing the place alongside the befuddled elite. Eyewitness Margaret Smith wrote to a friend that "Ladies fainted, men were seen with bloody noses and such a scene of confusion took place as is impossible to describe—those who got in could not get out by the door again, but had to scramble out of windows." As the rabble smashed all the crystal and china, Jackson himself was snuck out a window to his nearby hotel room. Eventually the servants devised a scheme of passing tubs of ice cream and booze out the windows and down onto the lawn to lure the throngs out, and it worked, they went.

Jackson was styled as "one of the country's fabled self-made men, a poor autodidact from the Tennessee frontier who served in the Revolutionary War as a teenage foot soldier." His favorite books were *Caesar's Commentaries*, *The Art of War*, by Chevalier de la Valiere, and *The Scottish Chiefs*. His reading list reflects his passion for winning battles. A lifetime warrior who fulfilled his campaign promise to relocate all Native Americans west of the Mississippi, in a devestating event later called The Trail of Tears, Andrew Jackson was an everyman populist not a highbrow humanist. He was a powerful, dangerous, down-to-earth guy.

In politics and in literature, playing up one's trustworthiness has meant playing up a devotion to anti-elitism, with the twist that it's often the most powerful determining the defining features of the strategic anti-elitism the politicians and writers must artfully deploy. While supporters nicknamed Jackson "Old Hickory," his opponents called him "Jackass," a creature maligned the world over for its stubbornness, stupidity and stink. In a disarming move, Jackson began calling himself "Jackass" too, cagily transforming the humble donkey the symbol for cagey everyday folk. Later this image of a jackass became the symbol for the Democratic Party. Much much later Jackass became the name for a hilarious reality show where young men often mangle themselves while performing dangerous stunts and gags, afterwards engaging in homoerotic straight-boy comraderie. Enter American political realism on its road-weary ass.

Realism implies an authenticity-feeling that's neither romantic nor especially high-brow. Its artfulness constructs a down-home trust-me "truthiness." It wears the stage costume of the mythological individual working man, a few-words strong-message Old Hickory and a no-frills no-nonsense jackass. To use a term passed like brownie-bites in workshops, realism's whatever "rings true," without regard to what forces determine the truthiness of the ringing.

The authenticity-feeling comes in part from extra-diagetic coding telling what kind of literary experience to expect, demarcating rules without stating: "These are the Rules." Extra-diagetic coding establishes the reading instructions a reader learns before even turning past the first page of text. Examples of this almost invisible coding are things like literary genre or style – is it poetry or prose, horror story or cookbook, psychological realism or pop-surrealism? Other examples include reputation of press, author's history, and what's on the cover. Like the part of the text called "the writing itself," extra-diagetic coding quietly choreographs ideologies, which are always in part, class-based.

Realism, like anti-elitist self-styling, is an artful technique that codes for "Read this text as trustworthy." Or, "Immerse yourself in this tale without sticking on its wittiness." In fact, "Read this without questioning language itself or 'self-hood' itself." Realism is code for "You the reader are not stupid, and even better, you're no snob." It's shorthand for "we're all on the same page in the same boat." It's drag that's into passing rather than making the drag a spectacle. Realism is a mask hand-painted with perfectly placed pimples, pores and scars that covers an already blemished face to make it more appealingly legible.

In coding for authenticity and neutrality, realism dictates the conceivable and normal and by extension the weird or "innovative," setting parameters marking what's inside and what's out. Realism requires good grammar and a sock in the potty mouth unless, as they say, it's ABSOLUTELY NECESSARY. A workshop comment might be: "Did you earn that fuck?"

Realism demarcates its own boundaries of inside and outside, but it guards those boundaries unpredictably: including fuck in a dialogue scene a whole bunch of times is normally OUT, except when written in a tasteful "literary" style, UNLESS the fucks distract the reader or throw them out of the story, but then again it MIGHT be okay if the fucks are there to authenticate clownish, illiterate, or working-class characters, but NOT if the fucks are repeated anti-narratively in an improv sound poem, UNLESS the fucks are slipped into a gritty crime show, arguably the most popular contemporary form of realist narrative next to the news. I am referring her to the famous scene from the first season of *The Wire* where the only dialogue between two investigators for over three minutes consists of variations on the word "fuck." The script goes something like this:

Man 1: Fuck

Man 2: Aw Fuck

Man 1: Fuck

Man 2: Mother fucker

Man 1: Fuuuuck

Man 2: Fucker.

Man 1: Mother FUCK!

Man 2. What the Fuck?

Man 1: Aw Fuck. Aw Fuck.

Man 2: Fuckity Fuck fuck.

Man 1: Motherfucker.

Man 2: Fuckin' A

Click **here** (http://www.youtube.com/watch?v=6sNZ7ulO1RQ) for the full scene.

On a *Wire* fan site, a section called "realism," explains the show's aesthetic approach, "The writers strive to create a realistic vision of an American city based on their own experiences. Central to this aim is the creation of truthful characters….The show often casts non-professional actors in minor roles, distinguishing itself from other television series by showing the "faces and voices of the real city" it depicts. The writing also uses a lot of contemporary slang to enhance the immersive viewing experience."

The variations-on-fuck scene reads as working-class realism, but only for the first minute or so. YouTube fans report not even noticing the linguistic play for awhile. But then they do notice. And they love it. It becomes clear that this is a sort of ballet of swearing, a kooky wordplay performance using one of our most oversaturated emphatic signifiers. In terms of extra-diagetic coding, fuck vibrates with rebel bravado, a little bad, a little dirty. It's one of the last illegal broadcast swearwords. But the over-the-top repetition in this scene doesn't come across as realistic, even to the fans who swear by the show's true-to-life urban realism. At the same time nobody complains that the performance smacks of avant-garde elitism or that its playfulness cheapens the show's political critique.

Unlike Andrew Jackson, President Obama comes across alternately as a people's president and high-brow. His complex narrative presentation as unprivileged hard working Harvard Law graduate, romantic husband, reader, writer, and sometimes-smoker blends traits of admirably educated humanist nobility with charmingly imperfect populist normalcy. Miranda Mellis, author of *The Revisionist* and co-editor of *The Encyclopedia Project*, told me once that *The Wire* is President Obama's favorite show. I like imagining our President relaxing with a cigarette at the end of a long day of work, watching a show that portrays unbearable institutionalized poverty, children squatting abandoned tenements, and masterful acts of criminal resistance. I imagine him confronting images of all the American communities that have been fourth-worldized by free-market multi-national capitalism, and also imagining a later scene when Michelle and he are brushing their teeth, and Michelle starts laughing and nudges him and says "Fuckity fuck fuck?"

We writers from the lower classes have to learn how to write in a way that codes as "everyday" and "believable" to middle class consumers of narrative. Some of us go to school to learn to master the seamless artifice of realism. The rest of us are autodidacts with a collage literacy learning our craft by gleaning from the vast exciting impossible junkyard of literature, not by following literary lineage as if swallowing a string of pearls. In writing what seems true, we often break rules without meaning to. Drawn to collage, we miscombine styles and misappropriate texts from high and low culture and from our own experience. But because our experiences and perspectives are not seen as "common," what we write might be called melodramatic and clichéd rather than "heartbreaking" and "universal." Writing believable literature requires learning the rules of realism.

I like knowing what the rules are, and I like having a lot of tools in my toolbelt, but I'm not big on being told what to do and how to do it believably by people who might do better to stretch their reading practices a little beyond what they were given to read in high school. I'm into a punk overkill aesthetic where the raw un-idealized, the operatic, and the illegible, the disgusting, and the finger-wagging collide and break skin. Writing fucked-up stories in a fucked-up style seems so absolutely normal, such a realistic form of realism to me, that I sometimes forget it doesn't to everyone else.

During a college job talk a few years ago, a professor in the audience asked what I was working on next. I told him about the book that would become *The Vicious Red Relic, Love* (Jaded Ibis, 2011). I said it was a mixed genre, fabulist ethnography, you know, dealing with thirdwave queer feminism, 90's San Francisco, AIDS and SM, and the ethics of radical uncertainty. Because it was a job interview and I was trying to seem tamed enough to work with, I didn't mention that the work was actually auto-ethnography, partly memoir really, about my first dyke relationship with a woman who was HIV-positive and ended up killing herself. I didn't say "my girlfriend," I said "the narrator's girlfriend." I said, "you know, that whole 90's survivor thing, raised in a cult, multiple personalities, you know, Baudrillard,

Lorde, and *The Courage to Heal*, you know, runaway squatters, speedballs, and witchcraft. But my colleague-to-be didn't know, and so he laughed and laughed like I was telling a wacky cocktail party joke.

And, as if I totally understood how ridiculous this treatment sounded to him, and in some ways I did understand, I responded, miraculously without saying "fuck," "Yeah, ha-ha, the scenario might seem ridiculous, but it's actually not that weird for the culture I'm writing about." I had the presence of mind not to blurt out, "The culture I'm from." In that culture, my girlfriend character was practically a cliché. But in the academic world I was performing in, trying to get a job, this normal character seemed like a joke, simultaneously implausible and too known. Both too weird and too normal, she just didn't ring true.

STACY DORIS

from Fledge: A Phenomenology of Spirit

Your name or mine so drew
my flake ripe the sand crashed
a one bubbling gone

to find's purposeless flute
I especially hem.
Yes yes we two snort, dance
the mouse jig, it is, it
is through a flag my horse

pried so I'm the horse now
I'll take you off my ear

Horse that's me grows. It zooms
and cartwheels. If I'm in me
next, this twine if I bend
I'm still far from I want
bubbling general
bubbling fished in you
for me, "midst" in terms of
a "potato," the hill
of wind's sameness that grazed
each saw especially
etched each grape permanent

Bubbling sold all grounds
by rips from bubbling
wrung, clothed. Hold or a cat's
sounds bubbling leaves leave
your hold, in its same ramps
pinprick's ingredients
a cloud of your eyes broth
tint kissed in their way cats
precisely untangle,
grip in the lake of what
clump might be including
if it were including

Including flick and crop
A low hum through waxwing
plied, the rill of some chime
or continent in twists
leaf and leaf, single-hand.
Your eyes pump sounds in their
bowls of commodity
twine while I stack this house
in to water the rain

Your eyes dig up the flakes
run pitch through a drone's curls
to spoon it. The "o" grip
whose hold unmoors our fly,
their crocuses, my road.
Since I cramped the forks I'll
go there to replant them

KAREN GREEN

from *Bough Down*

More and more birds get dropped off, most of them with wing trauma, some of them poisoned. There is one with a fish hook in its throat. The hook was attached to a filament which was attached to a branch which turned the bird into a kite. The babies are the saddest, but the support guys say they have the best prognoses.

I found the seagull dragging its bloody wing. He was walking around like a dog, innocent. He kept looking to the sky and taking a run at it. I could see in his eyes he was unrealistic about how his night would unfold. The other birds wanted no part in it—as far as they were concerned, he was a dog.

Merle is a color and merle is a bird but merle is not the color of the bird, it is a bluish or reddish gray mixed with splotches of black, the "color of the coats of some dogs."

December

Paper, cotton, crystal, fruit.

There was a poem on rice paper, a funny twenty-one consonant rhyme about what we could do after dinner if we weren't too tired. And once I put on underwear which intimidated instead of enticed, so I took it all off. We both agreed *panties* is a horrid, Updike word. The facets in the goblets were meant to reflect candlelight onto beloved faces at dinner parties for years to come. I remember a Christmas apple merrily eaten off my breast. Now I remember to take your mother's pie out of the freezer. Now ash and bone, now bitter crop, now moorings puppeteered with curious wire.

On our wedding night we smiled at the antler chandelier rigged with rope and walls as cold as snow. Sorry, sorry. How on earth.

Here we are, here we are.

I have a Polaroid of us kissing in another country. *The funeral directors wrapped the box precisely, a layer of plain paper under golden foil.* I recall your ear very well today, the way your hair grew around it. *Under the paper is a brown plastic box, the color of a fast food booth. It doesn't open easily.* What did they do to you? *What do you deserve from me?* Everything I have is yours, you said. *Like it was an act of generosity, what you left.* I always had a thing for your hair, soft against my or scratchy against my

What to do, what to do.

Unwrap him like the worst Christmas present ever. Wash hands. Hey, I have a spider bite on my fuck-you finger. Is he really with god?

None of this breaks his heart anymore; he no longer cares that he doesn't care. Oh the dead do fight dirty and for a while I am sick with fear, but then I get bored. The doctor says this is non-linear, inelegant progress.

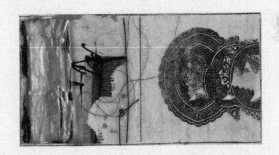

Head of Washington in Black.

1: artistic, ärt; fat, färe;
2: ärt, äpe, fät, färe, fäst

The support guys are breeding and it's great because now there will be more hands to help. They are the archeologists of abasement. A few of them are blessed with a patient's heart in addition to surgical hands. They sift our mistakes through the finest mesh and piece together a cellular mosaic: Here is where a glass was thrown, here is where insolence reigned, here ignorance was transient bliss and here is the fault line. Here murderer and victim are coalesced, here is courage, pity, fame, the light's arrival, the unrepeatable, and God's sense of humor, all of a piece, see.

So I bought a TV. What meds are they all on, I wonder. Why are those mothers shoving dentures into the mouths of babes? The interventionist always says, Your family loves you like crazy. Why is that woman unwilling to part with her rotten squash? When the idols bounce exuberantly out of the audition room into the arms of their support guys, their cheeks and bellies go haywire in identical ways, because they are family. Sometimes there's nobody waiting though. During the break there are pills if depression hurts and pills to make your menstrual cycle more powerful than the moon. There is a limping doctor who despises his patients, who values only the game of diagnoses, but he saves everybody, which makes him a sex symbol. After that two attractive detectives with their guns drawn are cautiously making their way down a hallway after busting down the door and the lights are low and I notice the soundtrack changes and the camera is panning in a way I can't control and I just try to close my eyes for a minute here because I don't know how to silence the thing that's about to happen again.

LUCAS DE LIMA

MARIAS

I DREAMT OF MY MOTHER DYING & WANTED TO BUILD A FIRE

MY MOTHER IS ONE OF MANY MARIAS FLICKERING

IN CIUDAD JUAREZ, ONE MARIA DIES EVERY WEEK ON THE WAY TO A

FACTORY

AS A WOMAN I CALL MYSELF MARIA & WEAR THE DARKEST RED ON MY

LIPS

WHEN I KISS PALE BOYS I TRY TO SET THEIR FACES AFLAME

SO THE WHITE BOYS' CHEEKS MELT

THEN I RECALL MY PAST LIFE AS A WHITE BOY WRITHING IN A WHITE

BLANKET

WHENEVER I WANT TO THROW THE PAGE INTO THE FIRE

ANA MARIA STOPS ME BY CRASHING INTO MY BACK

LIKE A WAVE OF THE VIRGIN MARY'S TEARS IN A LATIN AMERICAN

CHURCH

ANA MARIA WAS THE FIRST PERSON TO GIVE ME A CLOVE

CIGARETTE

IT SET MY LIPS OFF

WITHOUT BURNING THEM UP

ONE TIME MY MOTHER ACCIDENTALLY KISSED ME ON THE LIPS

I STARTED WRITING POEMS WITH A MATCH

KILL SPOT

MY BULLET CRACKS THE GATOR'S SKULL LIKE AN EGG.

MY BULLET SHATTERS THE GATOR THE WAY A WORD BREAKS OPEN THE

LORD.

MY BULLET IS BEAUTIFUL.

IT SHIMMERS IN THE QUARTER-SIZED KILL SPOT ON THE GATOR'S NECK.

MY BULLET MAKES MY FATHER PROUD.

HE HOISTS THE HUGE GATOR INTO THE FISHING BOAT BY USING THE HEAD AS

A COUNTERWEIGHT TO THE ARMOR-PLATED BODY.

IS THE GATOR A MANLY PINK UNDERNEATH?

I FANTASIZE ABOUT STRIPPING HIS SCALES.

HIS LEG STILL TWITCHES, FADING SLOWLY WITH THE LIGHT

WHEN I SHOOT HIM NEAR THE HEAD AGAIN.

THE BLACK CRY OF A HAWK COINCIDES WITH MY BANG.

I KNOW THE HAWK IS ANA MARIA BECAUSE HER CRY PIERCES

MY EGGHEAD.

I CRY YOLKY TEARS IN THE BOAT WHILE MY FATHER FROWNS AT ME.

THE SKY IS BUBBLING

YELLOW ABOVE.

O FATHER,

I MOAN IN THE CYPRESS GROVE,

O.

ONCE A GATOR INGESTS THE HOOK

WITH THE BAIT OF CHICKEN,

WINGS TEAR THE SKIN ON MY BACK AS THEY GROW.

GHOSTLINES

THE GATOR'S BRIMMING RED EYE DEPRIVES US OF THE GHOST.

MY MUTE WINGS TALK AFTER SOMEONE CUTS THEM OFF.

THEY REVERBERATE OUT OF MY BODY. THEY FALL BACK TOWARD THE

RED SUN.

IF I FALL INTO THE GATOR'S EYES, HE WILL GLITTER WITH ALL POSSIBLE

COLORS.

HE WILL LOSE HIS COLD-BLOODED BLANKNESS & BECOME A HOT BODY.

WHAT ANA MARIA WAS TO HIM.

ANA MARIA. I JUST WANT TO CHECK IN WITH YOU. I'M NOT GOING TO YELL.

ARE YOU THIS BOOK YET?

ARE YOU, ME & THE GATOR ALL

HANGING OFF THE SAME SPINE?

WITH FORMALDEHYDE, OUR BOOK COULD BE PRESERVED AS IT TURNS

BLACK:

OUR MAGNIFIED MEAT BURNING IN SUNLIGHT.

LET US MINGLE IN THE SWAMP A FEW MORE DAYS. THE BEST SHADE FOR

A TEAM TO PERCOLATE & PRAY IN.

WE TEEM AGAINST ALL ODDS IN THE QUICKSAND OF ALL EYES.

ANA MARIA.

YOUR ADUMBRATION.

I SEE YOUR SPLASH OF WATER FROM THE SKY WETTING THIS BOOK.

MANY READERS ARE GHOSTS

OBSESSED WITH OUR BODIES.

MARINA BLITSHTEYN

Kaddish

x// xx// xx //
x// x / xx/
xx/ xx/
x//x x//x
x// x/ / xx/
x/// xx/ x/. xx/ /x.

x/ / // x//
xx/ xx/ x//
x// xx// xx// xx// xx//
xx// xx// xx//
/ xx/ / x.

x// x / /xx x/xx
/xxx x/xxx
xxx/ xx/. xx/ /x.

x/ // // / x//
x// x// xx / xx/. xx/ /x.

x/ x/ xx/
/ xx/ /x
x// xx / xx/. xx/ /x.

VARIOUS AUTHORS

from *I'll Drown My Book:*
Conceptual Writing by Women

An Assemblage

Why the term "conceptual" now?

from "A Conceptual Assemblage: An Introduction," Laynie Browne

How does one acknowledge social invisibilities within questions of authorial openness? How does one put a text together that depersonalizes, that disengages from personalized modes, yet manages to engage with processes of personification and identification?

[…]

Firstly, there is the road of engaged disengagement.
[…]
Secondly, there is the route of engaged disengagement.

from "The Conceptual Twist: A Foreword," Caroline Bergvall

In still the middle of what never happens
In the still middle of what never happens
In the still of middle what never happens
In the of still middle what never happens
In of the still middle what never happens
Of in the still middle what never happens

from "Of the Still Middle," Angela Carr

The four aims of the sales letter are: attract attention: create desire: convince the mindl stimulate action. The four aims of the adjustment letter are: conciliate the reader; restate the facts; make reparation; conciliate again. To give your letters cgaracter, you should: take a personal attitude; adapt your letter to the reader's background, education or station in life; keep your temper; avoid scarcasm or witticisms; remind rather than instryct. Or, you can fgoret about these five points and summarize the principles into: "Be sincere." (1020 strokes–4', 28")

from "Table No. 21," Mónica de la Torre

Aren't you glad you use petroleum? Don't wait to be told you explode. You're not fully here until you're over there. Never let them see you eat. You might be taken for a zoo. Raise your hand if you're sure you're not.

from *S*PeRM**K*T*, Harryette Mullen

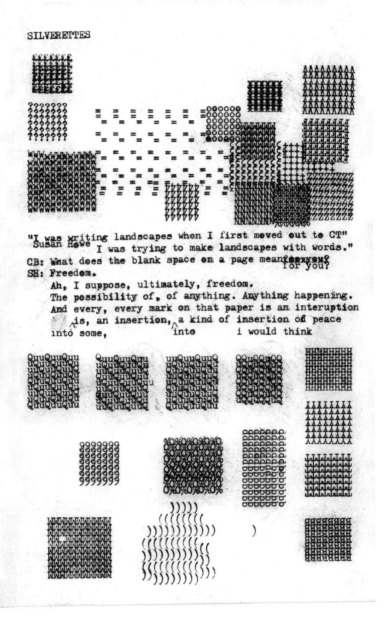

"Silverettes," Jen Bervin

Circle Braiding for 8 persons

Person 1 with peppercorn hair braids hair of person 1 with curly hair, who braids hair of person 1 with coarse straight hair, who braids hair of person 1 with beige-colored hair, who braids hair of person 2 with peppercorn hair, who braids hair of person 2 with curly hair, who braids hair of person 2 with coarse straight hair, who braids hair of person 2 with beige-colored hair, who braids hair of person 1 with peppercorn hair.

from *Hair Types Touch Poems*, Mette Moestrup, trans by Mark Kline

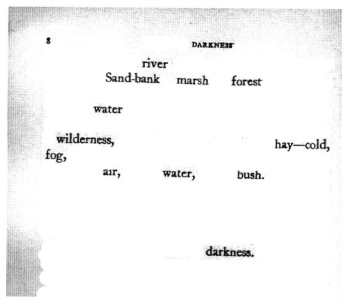

from *Darkness, all that /the remains*, Yedda Morrison

        *   o sole mio
             sole mio o
             mi sole o o
             sole o mi o
             o sol e mio
             solo mio o
             mi sol ed io
             io e mi sol o
             solo io o.

                                    from "milano notes," Cia Rinne

                    Still,
        the poem thought it was pretty good.
                But there you go.
             Not everyone agrees.
                    §

        *(fn) This is after all a tragedy.

                    from "How I Conceive A Poem 2," Christine Wertheim

        (7:00pm)

        As dusk finally neared we saw all kinds of tiny particles
        rising with steam from the thoroughly-heated earth, and
        we didn't know what to call them. Among them was
        also a pronunciation, which had perhaps disappeared for
        awhile or been hitherto forgotten, a pronunciation that we
        couldn't remember ever having held on our own lips. Not
        quite reaching the height of the floor above, undoubtedly
        because it weighed slightly more than the others, it came
        back down and rested upon the aspidistra, gently caught
        floating on an axis; and right then, for the first time, we
        realized it: a *pronunciation* doesn't even have a shadow.

        from *Emergence*, Ryoko Seikiguchi, trans. by Sarah O'Brien

I admire your worrying away
(in your own phrase)
at sentences   I also like
the porch-lamp fishing rod
even the baby its bundle of blankets
but especially that wink always back
of your words
                 nearly avoiding exact reference

from *Kind Regards*, Rosmarie Waldrop

The presentation of those "old timey" early-Gospel-inflected utterances requires an almost operatic narrowing of the passageway of the throat (especially for upper register notes). This early temporal sound vocabulary is pretty jarring to modern ears. Combined with the abrupt changes, it can be shocking to both myself and the audience. These rapid, jarring substitutions reference yodeling and other unusual combinations. Some of those sounds are then abruptly substituted for open-throated uncontrolled sounds including screams and non-screamed abrupt changes in register.

from "Conceptual Poesis of Silence:
Stop and Glottal (Notes on Practice)," Tracie Morris

A diamond ring is placed inside the jar with the ants, which is aesthetically interesting, but it is otherwise very unfortunate for the ants. The glass jar with the ants and the diamond ring gets jostled around quite a bit in the first part of the performance, and if you are an ant who is no bigger than a diamond ring, it can't be very fun to get attacked by a diamond ring when you are trapped inside a glass jar under bright lights with no air. At this point I am aware of the ever-growing cruelty of this situation, and yet there is no turning back.

from "Performance Notes to 'Ant'," Sawako Nakayasu

…blah blah blah blah blah blah blah blah blah blah
blah blah blah blah blah blah blah blah blah blah blah blah blah blah blah
no no no no no no no no no no no no blah blah blah blah blah blah blah
blah blah blah blah blah blah blah blah blah blah blah blah blahha ha ha
ha ha ha ha ha ha ha ha ha ha ha ha ha ha ha ha no ha no ha ha

[…]

I think you would like it
if this archive embarrassed me and if I disavowed it.

from "The Separatrix," Frances Richard

One says clearly, analogous to the French, "liberté" and "légume."

(Before language, we reveled in the verdant hard palace.)

The point of language could be against incisive superiority. The air sordid
with the cost of language and how it cools down, like a flaçon of liquid.

We meet the debut of these words:

Love. Look. Liberty.

Examples: calling, jelly, etc. These don't present the least bit of difficulty
for the French.

And someone very somber might say: *the point of language puts us in the
same position as lightning.*

from *Lividity*, Kim Rosenfield

And as the French mathematician said about Rancine's *Iphigénie: Qu'est-ce
que cela prouve?*

from "Afterword," Vanessa Place

LUIS AGUILAR

translated from the Spanish
by LAWRENCE SCHIMEL

Death Certificate

ife is consecrated in other things, other things that sing, that sing
other things; chained things that enchain other things, like
mouths; mouths bound to the vigorous bite of fresh teeth, with but-
tons like roses; roses like mouths that sing other teeth in the same
roses. There is a certain otherness in every thing [tree or petal, melted
tooth or hungry spotlight: titillating immensity of no one] that is
always responsible. ∴ *To Luis Armenta Malpica, for the illuminations.*
I was born where I should be, because life, coincidence of the clear
eye, increases with the arrival of forcefulness. With the kiss of my
first tiny cobblestone I knew that the sound of the gutter was my
path: that the disfigurement of that face under the water was no eddy
of current, but anticipation of a drought. I saw, suspicious attention,
that the name of any poet is a small plot of land where the water is
watched, that flight, apparently without return, that makes of des-
peration a crepe tree. ∴ I also wanted to leave. The irises of my eyes
barely poured out their terror in a birth of betrayals, I served desires
in the bloody fangs of other beasts; my scant years slept in the legs of
what (I didn't know) they called love and surpassed beauty. *My eyes
sought dawns but light was not a singularity*, but the uncertain part-
ing of the shadows. Everything was penumbra: habituated conical
reflections (limitation of the eye, all immensity, said an earthly god
named Eduardo) mocked the truth through illfated shadows; they
opened way to uncertainty. In them barbarism sharpened its claws
and the midden ignited my passion for the ravine. I cleaned lip and

tooth with gourds of shining mud: so much infinity in the pure vehemence of the filth [versus he who scorns, the amorous is a diamond disguised as a beggar]. *I grew used to the darkness*, grasping darkness; I began to live in concubinage with the shadows of the shadows, which elongates. However, nothing was ever so pristine, growing blind from so much: I felt a single night, perpetuated, built for the pleasure of overflowing dawns; to awaken pupils and see that, before the light, the darkness also shatters, and that later history repeats [inverted] and the rupture opens hundreds of cracks whose paths always lead to unprotection, bastard heir of the smallest break:

> nothing that has been broken finds another fate: a joint is (hard as it is to accept it) greenery of mistrust: artful security that the demon exists and its brake is the ascent: what fills a gap cannot ever join it: barely maintain a bridge that can, when desired, be sometime crossed: the rest is lies, like the mass that overflows the gap of the cracks: my false bet of: escape.

I fled, derangement, from vivid forgettings; hysteria that thought and didn't leave with the river. I tried to avoid an unknown love that was [something within] primitive clamor and defined wanderings. It dawned: the bump from the overflow sought white blood that [unfinished morning, ailing afternoon or backstitch of sunset] baptized my call made on my knees:

> [_____]
> F U L L   N A M E
> without   ancestry,   seeking
> counterpart   that   would   warm
> its   entrails.   [They'll   see   that
> to   love   is   something   else.]

From that day the currents were savage knots. In times of irrigation my grain cultivated predators of innocences. Then it was my light: small perversion: horn of tepals. I learned to polish noiselessness in the ears, to induce the question in my answers. The doubts, feet whose destination is my caprice, territories deformed by the enormous hand of desire, of the desirer, of the desired:

> yes, I confess
> that

I have sinned:
I bit
the salmon
saved
for
mother.

There wasn't, nor has there been a god who knew it, that to desire is also a sure avatar against banishment, pack of disenchantments kissing us on the eyes, retina living in concubinage with gargantuan medula. *Darkness again: path of apprenticeship: the fragility that offers parapets.* A narrow lane scalded my pupil. In the ins and outs of that sordidness was, in addition to the farmstead [inopportune eminence], another light as a hiding place: the violet possibility of being in bloom in the middle of the muddy greenery of the puddles; brown head of a snake in the center of the midnight sun. I was a town whose history was knit by the grievances; a sketch of back-streets inhabited by doubt, that supreme and incorruptible rodent. Crossing was constancy, because the only persistence are farewells: the liquid crystal that holds an airport: a barge: every bus depot with a flavor of dozing and bitter vapors. To leave was a whip of the south on the face. I offered up honesty and body to all sacrifice: I was of statutory age [without seeing that I was an adolescent: that is to say, I was doleful]. A pair of curls with their grace intact crowned my ardor, an open and luminous gaze that I lost over time and which died without reencountering me. Nothing was useful [I ignored that to suffer is a vestibule of sutures]: a complex ball the brain, my vast vertigos wander within it. I enjoyed [it was certain] to see butterflies tolerated because they brought to the head unions and bar codes, but I preferred the deep conversations in the lake's ophidian dance. *And one morning, suddenly, agony.* High velocity carries the misadventure: vengeance of the gods, precise wickedness [home-delivered lightning brought by a package service offered by Galapagos tortoises], everything is observed: thread of light, shapeless ray of contiguous tonality. ∴ *For Ernesto Campos and my living brother.* [It was already the lilac of late-night bags under the eyes, in wait to protect a crotch exasperated by hunger.] At a streetlight where Luz scolded Ernesto and where Ernesto was a continuous disturbance of the grass, I waited until the end, until my brother [still twitching] prayed on his way to the dungeon: are you still here? Let's go home. I had learned that calm is rewarded: the last supper: one envied a dozen for the pleasure of the censored betrayal, a little heat for the lethargy of my waiting. The brown line was narrowness and to cut my hair [Sampson was another lie], to strengthen discoveries: versus the cloud of smelly exhausts, choking between hands. Blood crowned a never-asked-for farewell, a voice that from I don't know where, from I don't know who, came to say yes, here is another part, where the wind's edge is enough to close the throat's floodgate. Discs past, immobility rented from my father his back for certainty to walk: did it already die? I asked myself. At sixteen I learned the dark side of piety, its courtesy; how useful, the appearance. Don't ask how it is that I live at the center of hates. I should invert my voice; warble the rusted taste of blood to say that nothing was wrong, that perhaps somewhere else, that maybe, that elsewhere. ∴. With the word biting my throat, from the minaret which, to the eye, was that rain of crucibles, I heard myself shout: I recognize myself. The mirror was rupture covered by droplets; the light, a window onto the heart open in the midst of the blood; a trachea that in order to not slice the wind lost the taste of home and yard, a kilo and a half of bananas on a wicker chair, under the afternoon's placid gaze. There they accumulated, sowing the fractured glass, all the kaleidoscopes that were also drinks of doubt: they came behind the shadows, ray blinded by naïve hope: who was the woman full of earth that through the far street, always full of earth, always in the same place, made signs to me of earth and prayed behind the dust to a deaf woman dressed for a gala? Her skirts enclosed, without tenderness, two pairs of eyes. Was it cruel memory or necromancy? *I sat in the shade of the weeping and lifted my apostasy against everything*, even against the calm ripple of the water that aped a morning. No one knows where the shout goes, what murmurs of night it knits in its breaths. In the middle of the thermal heat of that lagoon without the slightest surf or tide in its encompassing embrace that places/misplaces the exhaustion of a repetitive position, there is the palm of a hand that from the distance [I mean to say from outside] fondles a whim of annoyance that a certain tenuous heartbeat confuses with a caress. In its disorderly testing I feel the unshakeable fangs of fate, the corrosion of a structure. Where does it go, where does it come from, this duct, this reduction that in its sack stuffs zephyr-breaths and the stench of acrid proximity? I practice serenity in my floating lightness, the placidity of a swan of mistakenly imagined beauty. I kiss a clear water that turns greenish. I see in the slime a latent shining that makes me think of a better river, a moor of mirrors that purify the miracle of opening the eyes, although the bitter pupil projects from immensity that blue it never touches; although it knows that the impossibility begins. I advance centimeters, minutes, a seventh heaped stone of farewells. The narrowness extends and I am a dog days gallop, something like an overflow. A cascade of imprecise sounds sustains the fawn: this, my fieldcrossingheart. It doesn't choke the fury from the air, it is its shadowy omission. Then a blow. A strident monster escapes from my throat and a rough hand holds the world upside down, that looks at me in agreement, while bewilderment polishes fear and two doves, swollen with whiteness, take flight.

>Everything is
>darkness.
>The whiteness

of my veins, cavities anxious for the torrent, make clear that I've arrived. A certain fresh beating confirms me, but now an incomprehensible light disperses me. My eyes crash with the kaleidoscopic genesis of the world: living begins head-first. I affix the picture frame that in the surprised eye dissolves me, I am aware:

>I am me:
>I come,
>errant
>and mute, to
>astonishment.

GINA ABELKOP
Selections from Greta

Chapter 1

*"A convergence of things
that bloom."* Greta recalled
this phrase while she
washed dishes in a post-
housewife day
that, underwhelmingly, still
left her contrary and kept
with kitchen.

Immaculate, brittle hands worked
at unfeasibly lady-esque things:
dishes, cabinets, carpets. To properly
outfit herself
for such tasks each day was a feat.
For example, when Greta wore green
everything
was made to match: green bracelet,
green watch band, green stockings,
green summer.
And so it went with every
color, Greta a veritable palate
of pigment.

Chapter 2

Every evening Greta
sat in front of a boudoir
mirror and attempted
taking scissors to her ripe
waist-skimming hair. These
attempts were nothing more
than thoughts but

they were sincere, sweet ones. If the night
came during which she lifted brazed
hand
like a ring to her own head, shy and
committed, then Greta would know that
she could be satisfied.
There is no reason to believe
a thing will not happen if you
attend to it as prudently as Greta
did her claret hair.

Chapter 3

Greta, bound to hearth, had a great deal
of time to wonder at love. Supposed that love
may in fact be a funny thing, but
she only knew one story about it:
    Greta's Story About
    Love Sister bloated
    mermaid, saturated scales
    washed up drowned
    on Coney Island Beach.
    Heat that day something terrible,
    stern and insistent.

Chapter 4

(When one dies by way of water
your insides ebb, coalesce
into a lucid sea creature.
All that is left of you is a deflated,
briny suit. It withers
and stinks in the heat. In turn,
the organ-sea-creature looks like silk
and is bound together
with trusted thread. It does not
stink of anything but the sea.

There are worse things than bloating
to mermaid-like proportions amidst
cast off organs in the attentive Atlantic.)

Chapter 5

Greta knew love to be a thorny familial undertaking.

Chapter 6

On one of many heavy
summer days, Greta sat in
her yard mending dresses.
Her needle worked frankly
at the sateen and situated
thread comfortably into its
new job
as fastener of torn frock limbs.

Leaves   devotedly
watched   Greta   sew.
Amongst   them   was   a
careful, solid bird. She
was Nightingale
with citrine beak and peacocked
feathers. Tiny, beaded eyes followed
Greta's fingers up and
down, suture in and out,
until finally
Greta stopped,
shook. Looked up.

Chapter 7

Greta had never
been in love with
anything that was
not sister.

Chapter 8

Having never been in love
with anything that was not
sister, Greta did not immediately
grasp intent. Lilac large, Greta's
eyes held on the bird. Measuring
the distance between this bird
and her mouth.

Chapter 9

Greta went inside, brushed grass
from the cobalt creases of her dress.
A waterlogged complexion was on the brain.

Chapter 10

Greta knew marriage to be a sick-hearted swallow.

Chapter 11

A tiny, canopied bed,
Two slight sister girls,
Constant pecking,
There is something you are missing,
No it wasn't quite like that,
Mismatched hair tangled together on a pillow,

Not like that either,
Ten-years-old and eight-years-old,
respectively, Sour breath and other
sordid details,
When sisters marry and conceive,
The child comes out a soft-hearted vamp.

Chapter 12

Outside Nightingale waited. Wasn't
patience so much as practical. Little
feet
like dinosaurs and Nightingale was
remembering her own sister: no tongue,no
hands,
just spread testament.

Chapter 13

Once
peacocked,
everything
flickers on
a hint
  of pleasure.

Chapter 14

Greta dreamed a bird.

Woke and reached for scissors.

MATT BELL

from *In the House Upon the Dirt*
Between the Lake and the Woods

Before our first encounter with the bear I had already finished building the house, or nearly so.

In the hasty days that followed, I feared we moved in too fast and too early, the house's furnishings still incomplete, the doors not all right-hinged—and in response to my worries my wife said that was no trouble, that she could quickly finish what I had mostly made.

Beneath the unscrolling story of new sun and stars and then-lonely moon, she began to sing some new possessions into the interior of our house, and between the lake and the woods I heard her songs become something stronger than ever before. I returned to the woods to cut more lumber, so that I too might add to our household, might craft for her a crib and a bassinet, a table for changing diapers, all the other furnishings she desired. We labored together, and soon our task seemed complete, our house readied for what dreams we shared—the dream I had given her, of family, of husband and wife, father and mother, child and child—and when the earliest signs of my wife's first pregnancy came they were attended with joy and celebration.

The dirt's wettest season swelled, and then its hottest burst the world to bloom, and through those tumid months my wife swelled too, expanded in both belly and breast until the leaves fell—and afterward came no more growth, only some stalling of the flesh gathering within her. Even before it was obvious that there would be no baby, even then my wife began to cry, to sing sadder songs that dimmed our already fuel-poor gas-lamps, or cracked cups and bowls behind cupboard doors.

I angered that we would have to start again, and if my wife was not to birth some son then I wished only for that pregnancy's speedy end, so that she might not suffer overlong, so that another child might be put in this one's place. But still her body delayed, pretending that the bundle inside her might grow into some child, and my wife pretended too, and when I could not stand her insistence I again went out back of the house, to where my wife had planted a garden, some few tubers and herbs to supplement what fish I took daily from the lake.

Now in my frustration I returned that place to the dirt it had been, and later my wife confronted me with what I had done. Her anger flushed her face, and her yelling contained none of the music I loved in her singing voice, and as she exhausted her still-round shape of its rage then at last I saw her labor was upon us.

What sad and sorry shape was born from her after those next days, that labor made long despite the lack of life within:

Not an arm, but an arm bud. Not a leg, but a leg bud, a proto-knee.

Not a heart but a heart bulge.

Not an eye but an eye spot, half-covered by a translucent lid, uselessly clear.

Not a baby, instead only this miscarriage, this finger's length of intended and aborted future.

And what was not born: No proper umbilical cord snaked from mother to baby, from placenta to belly, and so the starved child passed from my wife's body into a clot of blood and bed sheet, and then into my waiting hand, where I lifted it before my eyes to look upon its wronged shape, that first terminus of my want.

Then to my lips, as if for a single kiss, hello and goodbye.

Then no kiss at all, but something else, some compulsion that even then I knew was wrong but could not help, so strong was my sadness, so sudden my desire: Into my body I partook what my wife's had rejected, and while she buried her face in the red ruin of our blankets I swallowed it whole—its ghost and its flesh small enough to have in my fist like an extra finger, to fit into my mouth like an extra tongue, to slide farther in without the use of teeth—and I imagined that perhaps I would succeed where she had failed, that my want for family could again give our child some home, some better body within which to grow.

What was there to say afterward, when my wife returned to her senses, when she asked to hold our dead child? What else to tell but that our child was gone: that while she screamed out her frustration I had taken the body to the lake, that I had set it to float away, on waters safer than those red waves at drift within her body.

When her howls subsided, her voice was made different than ever before: There was still some baby inside her, she said, some better other that she might bring forth, and so she worried at the entrance to her womb, first with her fingers and then, later, with tools made for other tasks, until all the bedding was mucked with her. I tried to take these implements from her hands, but with increasing ferocity she shoved me back, with the balls of her freed fists, and with a song that staggered me from the bedside, her new voice climbing, hurling strange my name and the name we had meant for our child. In rising verses, she demanded I disappear, leave her, throw myself into the depths of the salt-soaked lake, cast my now-unwanted bones after the supposed casting of our stillbirth, that failure-son.

Drown yourself away, my wife sang, and then despite my want to stay I found myself again outside the house, for against the fury of her song my horror held neither strength nor will nor strategy.

Across the dirt, upon a dock I had built with my own hands, the wind and the rain fell upon my face and the face of the lake, and there I felt the first stirrings of the fingerling, as that swallowed son would come to be called, by me and me alone:

A child or else the ghost of a child, clenched inside my chest, swimmed inside my stomach, nestled inside my ear.

A minnow or a tadpole, a tapeworm or a leech.

A listener. A whisperer.

A voice, louder without vocal cords.

A voice: FATHER, FATHER, FATHER.

FATHER and FATHER and FATHER.

FATHER, FATHER, a title repeated over and over, until I began to believe: no longer merely a husband, but something more.

And yet I hid this new self, did not confess what I had done when later my wife limped outside, her slender fingers pressing a rag bloody between her impatient legs as she walked down the hill to where I stood sullen upon the dock, to where she opened her mouth to speak, then shut it in silence, then opened it again: a show of teeth, her hesitant tongue, the animal of her grief.

At last she made those shapes to move about the wording of her demand, asking that I take her out onto the lake, where she had never before wanted to go.

Take me where you took him, she said. And what else was there but to agree, to show her the place where my lie had drawn her thoughts, her sorrow's desire.

The gray lake was motioned only momentarily by our presence upon its sluggish waters, its surface rippled with wind and dashed by my oars but headed always for another flatness, another deeper kind of floating quiet, stiller still, and there was our boat atop it, as night fell, as the sky filled with moon and stars and the absence of nearer light. Only then did my wife stand in the rowboat, her movements sudden, unannounced. I worked to steady the boat and so did not grasp her intent when she began to sing, for the first time using her voice not to create or cast up shapes, but to take them down—and how could I have even hoped to stop such a power?

With song after song, with a song for each of their names, my wife lured some number of the stars one by one from out the sky, and those so named could not resist her call. Their lights dropped and crashed all around us, nearly upon us, and though they dimmed as they fell still they landed too bright for our smaller world, and I shielded my face against the flash of their collisions, then covered my ears against the booming that followed. Those that slipped into the water splashed and steamed, and over the rocking edge of the boat I watched queasily as their hot lights dropped, until I lost them into the depths. Where they struck the dirt they did more damage, their fire scorching soil to sand to glass, and then in the growing darkness and the fading light the rain continued until the last fallen stars were extinguished.

Back on shore, I lifted my wife out of the boat's flooding bottom and onto the dock, and how easy a burden she was then. I cradled her exhausted limpness, held her to my chest as I had hoped that night to hold a child, and in this way we climbed up the path from the lake, across the burned and muddy and darkened dirt, then into the false refuge of the house, where in those unlit rooms our new future awaited to tempt us into trying again: for the family we still hoped to make, the family for which my wife was again scraped ready, made to possess some hungry space, some hollow as full of want as my own hard gut had always been.

LARA GLENUM

[This Poem Is My Vocal Prosthesis]
from *POP CORPSE!*

My suffering has become frivolous & ornamental

which is to say
 it now participates in "luxury, mourning, war, cults,
 the construction of sumptuary monuments,
 games, spectacles, arts"

U are hereby invited to wars of attrition
& other showstoppers

2 spectacles of   ornament & excrement
in undersea palaces

festooned with horny mermaids

I am trying to speak in a different register
The register of candied decay

The filthy register of the halfbreed
which is
my own

I am poorly made, willful, death-leaning

I exhibit
a failure to thrive

Ill-gendered & millenarian
my flesh accrues
& decomposes

I can die & die & die

Club Me [Opening Score]

The seal flesh   bezerking in my pants
says no + yes

My glass eye rolls   across the wooden sea

The ha ha albino sky
rotting like meat in my throat

                    Sink yr seabunny fingers
in2 my creamo dreamo seal meat

Ensorcel yrself
4-evah
in loaves of hottie blubber

Well a mermaid is made of seal meat

A mermaid with a chopped-off tail
is all holes
open 2   whatevs loops thru the red tubes

The clouds are the colon of forgetting
The mermaid is the forgetting of the colon +
piss tube + snatch

O mighty fuckable   I'm cutting off my own fishtail

Plug up my wild valves
w yr skeet lotion

W yr shiny metal fingers

HERE COMES SOME MARVELOUS DEFORMATION CRAWLING TOWARD YOU IN A HUMAN SUIT!

A mermaid is supposed 2 b all seafoam

PNEUMATIC TITS! + OPALINE HAIR!

posed in ROCOCO Technicolor CORAL REEFS!!
w/spritely SEA CUCUMBERS!!   & sweet pink JELLIES!!

♥ A CUNTLESS DUMPLING!! ♥

I m so hungry for cock
I m nothing but

KATE ZAMBRENO

from *Heroines*

God, it's boring here. Stuck in the provinces. The novelist Jean Rhys' bungalow in Cornwall where she spent her exile, for years and years in poverty and obscurity writing her heroine in *Wide Sargasso Sea*, rewriting the madwoman Bertha Mason in *Jane Eyre*. "All the dullest books ever written have ended their lives here," she wrote in a letter to her daughter.

I must get as far away as possible. Must escape stagnancy, miserabilism. Yet I am here, frozen. I am afflicted with Eliot's *aboulie*. I know I want to leave this stale town as soon as possible. I am sure if I do not I will die.

I think of Madame Bovary—"She longed to travel, or to go back and live in the convent. She wanted both to die and to live in Paris."

I begin rereading the journals of Anaïs Nin, both the abbreviated ones that she published during her lifetime, and the ones with all of the fucking (which I prefer of course). In the narrative Anaïs weaves over the countless journals, she is a liberated woman who finally escapes the oppression of her provincial environment. In her version she leaves out Hugo, her banker-husband who supports her. Apparently, according to Nin's biographer, all the American housewives who first read Nin's journals felt they were given permission to leave their marriages, but then felt betrayed when they learned the truth.

I suppose I could take John out of this accounting entirely—but then who would believe that I was in Akron by choice?

I develop a desire to be analyzed, because of all the Anaïs Nin I've been reading, Nin who had an affair with her analyst Otto Rank, who wrote a book on the artist. Perhaps this is a desire to be interpreted like a literary character. I leave a message for the Cleveland Center of Psychoanalysis. I begin to toy with the idea of training to be a psychoanalyst, and I will become a feminist analyst to tortured, eccentric artists. Like Julia Kristeva. Sylvia Plath who considered a Ph.D. in psychology.

A woman at the Center calls me back and I change my mind and never return her call. (I realize the costly sessions would be daily, I have not yet figured out the 40-minute drive, refuse to drive anywhere, here, in fact.)

…

Here, I am the wife of. That is how I am introduced by others. Not a writer. A wife. (No one seems to care that I am a writer, awaiting the publication of a slim, nervous novella.) Everyone much more fascinated with John's career. In his dungeon office John is surrounded by piles of leatherbound volumes, books that look burned, in several languages, a Babylon. Eliot studying languages while at Lloyd's bank. I love seeing John finger a book, reading its leaves, soothsaying it, speaking its secret history. He can lapse into the charming pedant so easily. My Professor X, as Woolf calls the patriarchs of higher learning in *Room*. Vivien(ne) sitting in on on the Victorian literature Tom taught to working-class adults. Her expression rapt, worshipful. She sacrificed everything for him, for his eventual genius.

I realize you become a wife, despite the mutual attempt at an egalitarian partnership, once you agree to move for him. You are placed into the feminine role—you play the pawn. Once you let that tornado take you away into the self-abnegating state of wifedom. Which I did from the beginning, now almost a decade ago, quitting my job as an editor of an alt-weekly so we could live in London and he could attend a graduate program in the history of the book.

I write this book of shadow histories. These histories of books' shadows.

*

Sylvia fascinated with the dybbuk, the wandering, disembodied soul in Jewish mythology. Usually the souls of suicides. "I am the ghost of a former suicide"—the beginning line of her poem "Electra on Azalea Path." A doubling, the dybbuk.

Anne Sexton who thought she was the reincarnation of Edna St. Vincent Millay.

"There are also reports of people who see, in their dreams, actual events in the lives of other people, both past and future."

The mad wife's journey from committed to committal.

"We are married. The sibylline parrots are protesting the sway of the first bobbed heads in the Biltmore paneled luxe."—F. Scott and Zelda Fitzgerald, "Show Mr. and Mrs. F to Number—"

Zelda's words but a communal byline. He snatches up her bon mots, her odd phrasings, on little scraps of papers, backs of envelopes. Her diaries before she was married. A Mrs.

Vivien(ne)'s alter-ego Sibylla. The sibylline parrots. A pair of pretty birds. Her and Viv, the frenzied flappers who gave words to their writer husbands.

We are married. A definitive statement. A pronouncement.

That famous photograph of the Fitzes: sleek lions' faces, features blending into each other. Both so stoic and self-absorbed. They are acting a role. They are the famous feuding Fitzgeralds. Almost incestuous.

Of Vivien(ne) and Tom, a biographer wrote: "Each felt a Narcissus-like spark of recognition in the other's presence."

Our delirious dyad. We are everything for each other, siblings, parents, intimates, lovers, enemies…

What do you really want to write? John asks me. We are at a bar in Bucktown. We have just met. We have not spent the night together, but once we do for years we will almost never spend it apart. Me writing 2500 words a week for the alt-weekly tossing out witticisms in formulaic articles and essays like some chick-lit version of Dorothy Parker or Renata Adler. John is at the time a managing editor of a local lit mag. By day he works in fundraising for a cultural organization. Once we begin dating I start penning a quippy personal column under the pseudonym Janey Smith (a nod to Kathy Acker's anti-heroine) which he edits for me.

As soon as we met I made him a character.

What do I really want to write? I want to write novels. Because that is what one is supposed to write, right, if one writes. Ring Lardner's quip: "Mr. Fitzgerald is a novelist and Mrs. Fitzgerald is a novelty." I want to be taken seriously above all I want him to take me seriously.

(I met him before I was a mess of pages, and a wind or a word could tear me apart.)

Is it true when I met him I knew he was my editor? I am Hilda Doolittle looking to be renamed H.D., Imagiste, by Ezra Pound, Jean Rhys falling for Ford Madox Ford, Jane Bowles, all the rest. Tom's marks on Viv's notebooks and later officially at Faber & Faber, lording over Djuna. I am sleepwalking through the 1920s with my ink-stained hands and collection of cloche hats and brilliant fascist of a husband.

The cloche hat with the buckle I bought at the boutique before we left…we called it my wedding hat.

When Jane first saw Paul she said to a friend, he's my enemy. When she met the young composer she wore her hair short and smoked short cuban cigars. Sylvia taking a bite out of the apple of Ted's cheek. Edenic.

Prophets and prophesies. Jane and witchy Cherifa. Madame Sosostris in Eliot's epic. Sylvia and Ted's Ouija board.

Zelda to Scott in one of her letters: "I DO want to marry you—even if you do think I "dread" it—I wish you hadn't said that..."

Vivien Haigh-Wood and Thomas Stearns Eliot were married at Hampstead Register Office in 1915 after knowing each other for three months (by that time, she had shortened her name, she would lengthen it again). It was a heroic mission— Ezra Pound had urged Vivien(ne) to marry the poet to keep him in England, just as he later took up the Bel Esprit.

We echoed the Eliots. Marrying fast out of a sense of noble adventure (they had known each other three months, we had known each other nine). We who were going to live extraordinary lives. We who were going to be extraordinary. (She pinned her hopes on the Great Poet, we pinned ours on each other.)

Later SHE will be punished, continually reminded, of her impulsivity, as something to convict her, when this is why he originally fell for her. (Why is falling the model of love? like down a rabbit hole.)

The chairs at Chicago's City Hall were orange, hard, plastic.
Zelda in her grey suit the color of her eyes. Those eyes. For the ceremony a suit of midnight blue, the hat trimmed with leather ribbons and buckles. A corsage of white orchids. "She was the only ornament at her own wedding."

For Tom's marriage certificate he wrote "of no occupation." How would they occupy themselves? There was the question of where to live and where the money would come from. Always a pressing financial crisis. No verse is completely free.

Our name is called. Did we have a number. Like at a deli. (I cannot remember. I cannot recall. Do you know nothing?...Do you remember nothing?)

The quickie at St. Patrick's was perhaps Scott worried Zelda would (again) change her mind. His princess he always threatened to keep locked up in his tower. "There was no music, no flowers, no photographer, and no lunch for the out-of-town visitors." Some say Zelda never forgave him.

The buried grudges of marriage.
Every year the memory vomits up again, especially after every move. Love of our

kind requires so much amnesia. Despite his eternal apologies. For I love him yes I love him but ours is not a romantic tale of origins. Of how we came to be.

(At one of those kitschy downtown Asian theme restaurants with that woman from the British Consulate. Her posh and nasally tones. She left us with the bill, and the assurance that, oh, yes, we'd have to get married, if we wanted to go to London together. Oh and I should try writing a multicultural novel, it is all the thing.)

She does not pronounce us anything. We still have to stay and sign things. We do not even kiss afterwards. We do not mimic this well-rehearsed denouement. Or perhaps, laughing, embarrassed, a quick peck. As if to prove for invisible eyes that this is real. We are real.

(You decided then that I could come with you if I wanted, and perhaps work under the table. You were uncomfortable, you said, with the institution of marriage. Or you would do it, if we promised it didn't mean anything. You were plotting your escape route, just like Tom, later on.)

Only one family member—Vivien(ne)'s aunt—was present. They were trying to keep their hasty union secret from their tyrannical mothers. The esteemed Eliots' later announcement in the St. Louis Globe Democrat was "heavy with disapproval."

If we were waiting for permission she did not grant it.

Afterwards we sat in the back of a cab numbed, nervous. You had a Polaroid camera. Our wedding photo. There are some days we don't want proof of. We look like we had been booked for a lifetime sentence.

(And when I spit, bit, back, that served as your excuse. My violence you instigated allowed you to distance yourself. The time I threw my chair at you in my tiny loft apartment on Chicago Avenue. No, I don't know how you can go to London with someone who acts like that. Lucia Joyce, James' daughter, put away for throwing a chair. I am the artist! She cried. To invalidate, R.D. Laing writes, can stir one to violence.)

That month honeymoon in New York hotels. Scott bought her a new Patou suit. "They were interviewed; they rode on the roof of taxis; they jumped into fountains; there was always a party to go to." Later, Zelda wrote, "There was a tart smell of gin over everything." Zelda nostalgic in letters to Scott, now forever separated, she trapped in an institution, in a body, aflame with eczema, a scaled she-monster later immortalized in Tender is the Night, he trapped in Hollywood, in afternoon alcoholism. That was when you...Remember, darling? "Do you still smell of pencils and sometimes of tweed?" A lovely Zelda association.

Bored after a year in New York the Fitzgeralds took a short trip to Europe. They sailed on the Aquitania. First Class. Zelda was pregnant and pouty.

Their itinerary: England, France, dull, dull, Venice, Rome, all ruins, back to London, where he invested in tailored suits. Scott wrote: "God damn the continent of Europe. It is of merely antiquarian interest."

Thinking back, the most extraordinary aspect of this episode was the cab ride. At that time we never took cabs.

What did we do that afternoon? I think we bought gym socks at Filene's Basement. We went out for sushi, but I felt sick and couldn't eat. At night in his bed I announced, I think, dizzily, "We're married!" John shushed me. He didn't want his roomates to hear. He didn't want his parents finding out before we were safely in London.

Ah yes. The reason for the cab. Next stop, British Consulate.

Another wedding photo: Our dazed reproductions gazing from our passport books, our one-year visas. That is when you used to hike up your collar for photographs, like a mean street youth from the 1950s. I am dour, expressionless. I look vaguely Eastern European. One young bride ordered by male.

We fly Air India. We attempt to drown out the army of babies who have set up camp in our inner ear—an infantry.

Our first test. We are married. We smile too brightly at the customs officer at Heathrow. I am his wife. The first time ever spoken. My husband will be attending graduate school for the year. To wife. A word. Like something heavy one carries down the street. A verb? What does a wife do? Oh, me? I'll find something, I'm sure.

I am supposed to stay in our awful little green room in married student housing and WRITE. I cannot for months find work, until I land temporary holiday employment at a bookstore. Can't WRITE. My first real solitude, alone in a new country, newly married. A different sort of breakdown then in my early twenties, the one that made me watchful, watched. He would get home and I would be crying in the bathtub. And so it all began, our dance, of the needy and the needed.

JAYSON IWEN
Three Polyvalent Poems

Death Style

Bob's life flashed before his eyes
Followed by
His life was a monologue
His death would be even better

A string of low budget films
A heavenly slow rotating Whopper
He patiently received
It was decided

He could have been cynical but
Instead he comforted himself knowing
When time, space, energy, & matter coexist
Like the taste of the air

Cynicism is for moral slugs
A species is only an ecological moment
When knowing becomes the known
Just before the Whopper

Making Up Time in Indiana

Take advantage of the speed limit here
Free as the arc you make with your arms
It takes even light a billionth of a second
So whatever you see has already happened

To close the distances between us
Without hitting anyone else
To travel that far
In the past before your very eyes

You saw a woman & two children
Above a man shaking his head at an engine
A masterpiece of perception
It would be as pointless as eternity

Playing on a blanket on the embankment
Flash by the side of the freeway
If it weren't so temporary
As pointless as the space between us

Things This Thing Called I Loved

Stepping off the busy street
Into snow & space & ambiguous trees
Into another's life
Belt buckles & flying pots

Against the bathroom door one more time
Mountains & airports & approaching
Rolling from bombings & blows
Slipping from another's loving grip

Into an alley that opens
Slipping out of the shadows
Of stillborn & suicidal siblings
Running a finger along the gash

One learns to love distant things
The end of every given line
Into sleep in the midday sun
Into cold & space & blinding light

BROOKE WONDERS
What We Can't Reach

Two hands meet at a bar. She orders a beer and flips him the bird when he tries to pay for it; he gets a whiskey sour, tracing a heart into the condensation that forms on its sides. She gets drunker and he rubs up against her; they're like two sticks trying to make fire. They have no mouths to kiss or drink their liquor, so they just fumble at each other, searching for something to cling to—fingers, nails, the soft pad beneath their thumbs. They ignore the stares of patrons just drunk enough to disbelieve their own eyes.

At night, back at her apartment, she cuts a slit across his palm. It opens to a grin, revealing a row of pearly white teeth and a pink tongue. He takes the knife and she presses into it—and then she smiles back at him.

I love you is the first thing he says to her, and she says *touch me* to him, mimetic of the people from whom they've been severed. They have sex through the night, shoving fingers deep into the other's mouth, crying out because now they can. They play a game called See Who Can Scream Loudest, until a neighbor bangs on their door yelling *Damnfool kids.*

Parts of kids, they holler back.

The next morning, with their new mouths they ask the important questions only chiromancy might divine: *Why is your mouth so full of teeth? Are we living, dead, or somewhere in between? Are we mind or body or something more, and where do we keep our brains? Beneath the thin white lines of our cuticles? Beneath our lunulae?*

After a few weeks they grow bored of sex. She gags when he tries to shove his whole fist inside her; during pillowtalk she whispers *I want to see you.* Neither of them understands sight; they feel their way through the world by touch alone. *Let's visit the morgue,* he says. They steal a dead woman's eyes, two intact hazels. Snickity snick goes his knife, cutting a socket right beneath her index finger, into which he pops an eyeball. Her eyelid flutters open, and the first thing she sees are his degraded cuticles. *You need a manicure wicked bad,* she says, blinking cycloptically at him.

Feelings hurt, he abandons her to the reek of dead bodies neither of them can smell, but in the morning relents and returns. He's mangled himself surgically inserting the other eye into his palm. *You don't look so pretty yourself,* he tells her. Streaks of dried blood thread along her life line, heart line, head line, traceries of how much she missed him in his absence. She's never cried before. She doesn't like it. Of course she takes him back, and they lick each others' shiny new eyeballs, reveling in the iron-salt tang.

They settle into city living, make new couple-friends. For Halloween, a neighbor throws a costume party, and he goes as the Hamburger Helper; she's the Thing. No one can guess who they're trying to be.

One hand says to the other, *will you marry me?*

What'll I wear? she demurs. He buys her a white calfskin glove. They stand together at the altar, declare their undying love, and put gold bands on each other's ring fingers.

He gets evil hand syndrome, starts beating up on her, his fist a battering ram mashed into her mouth over and over, *Suck my pinkie or else.* She finally threatens to leave unless he sees a psychiatrist. After a few sessions, they're walking together knuckle to knuckle when they pass an old vet, a double amputee. They hop into his pocket, follow him home and, while he's asleep, attach themselves to his wrists. But they can't sustain self-sacrifice, detach themselves, and flee before the vet awakens. Even more than the therapy, that's what sets them on the straight and narrow. They stop drinking, take up yoga.

Over time they wrinkle. Liverspots appear. Folds of flesh form around her knuckles and stretch across her back; her stump looks withered, thinner than it used to be. He's pretty sure she's shrinking, that she used be as tall as his head-line but now only comes up to his heart. He wonders what she sees when she looks at him, her eye blinking slowly. She's become unreadable.

They get depressed, begin to believe they're so much dead weight, someone's cast off mobile prosthetics. In desperation, they attend a stranger's funeral and leap into the open casket. They fall asleep on the dead woman's unmoving chest. The coffin lid's closed; they're lowered into the ground and buried. Later, much later, he wakes in a panic, Grandma decomposing beneath them. He wakes her and together they scrabble at the lid, clawing, scraping until it lifts just a sliver. She wriggles free, but he gets hung up on his wedding ring, swollen knuckles trapping him. His mouth opens in a scream and dirt floods into it. She seals her mouth tight, squinches her one eye shut, and scrabbles toward the surface.

When she finally claws her way up and out, fingernails cracked and caked with mud, she splays herself out in the sunlight, palm facedown, so very tired. She doesn't recognize her own skin. A crow lands near her, begins to peck at her. It picks her up by one finger, tossing her around like a bit of shiny foil or a rubber glove. Then it carries her away.

JUSTIN PETROPOULOS & CARLA GANNIS

from *<Legend> </Legend>*

<LEGEND> </LEGEND> IS A COLLABORATIVE PROJECT of poems and drawings based on text redactions of *The Book of Earths*, by Edna Kenton, a compendium of theories of the shape of the Earth, and its surrounding folklore. While the project is rooted in analog works, specifically poems by Justin Petropoulos and ink drawings by Carla Gannis, the collaborators grow these texts and images into digital paintings, animations, projection mapped & 3D printed sculptures, as well as interactive works. The project's title, *<legend> </legend>*, is an empty html tag. The viewer/reader must complete the meaning themselves, the definition of each legend is determined by the movement within one's own cartographies.

The goal of the project is to explore the ways people communicate, document, and map, moments from the past or in the present, and the relationships that are created in and by the various media used to those ends. We locate everything we experience, in the present or as memory, in a place, and those experiences because they are subject to the whims of subjectivity, are personal, and so too a kind of myth.

The poems and drawings are inspired by Kenton's 1928 publication, which presents different 'mappings' of the earth over the centuries, all of them 'false' by contemporary scientific standards, but considered "true" in their time and place. What emerged was a series of poems and drawings concerned with human relationships to one another and objects; how we (mis)communicate, and in those (mis)communications, how we navigate new personal spaces out of larger automatizing grammars.

At a time when the film between public and private is losing its opacity, so much of how and what we communicate is 'located' in or responsible for the production and mapping of social spaces. The spaces we inhabit daily, the settings of our lived narratives, like the narratives themselves, are organized by multiple structures: political, socio-economic, and to an increasing degree digital, shaping us as users.

Linguistics and cartography are two of the most powerful organs in the service of these often repressive structures because they are so present, so actively employed, that their misuses are easily overlooked, normalized by time and reproduction, making them increasingly difficult to locate. Each of us must find his or her own way inside of these mapped structures, which are, by their very nature, averages of meaning and movement.

> excavations of the body politic or terra infirma <

[algorithm]

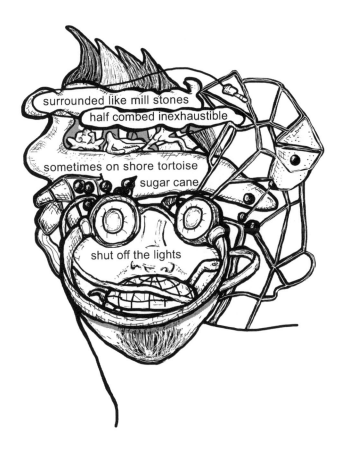

//superposition and the removal of a mass

buried city   an uncovering
of clauses we know   historicity
is fragment and frequency   congregations

nevertheless come dressed for drilling
pictures copied   sacred   a pin inserted
in a pillow   the enforcement engine

at the end of the hailing   and human
remains an inquiry   this vase   its branches
bearing around a drawer of downed bees

how far to the bridge that buckles   someone
follows   that is to say   while those outlines
catalogue foreigners at the forks that reformat

their feet   sink where they suffer
the situation   illness   mercury finds its way

we all lose our magnetic orientation

//disposition in conformity with the contours of a pre-existing

into each sketch of sleep   policies
are financed   zenith to nadir and
reproduced according to polling
at the border   a boy bottles

his diaries   while the cardinals pool
and the darling boxers march   each motion
cycle policed   managed data brackets
the margins   we sit clothed in fictions

fence   shade-tree   dolls folded in a trunk
is that what you're ashamed of   beneath
your trousers   the surveillance
between documents   semblance between

domains   there is static from shareholders
a lowing fever shells each diagnosis

//continuity must be sought or its absence explained

between trousers and your trousers are obvious
nevertheless   costumes compliment any
breakfast   between trees and the tree   however
a correspondence recalled from branches

where the cost of mobile phones   and the price
trend differently depending on who mines
the tantalite   what a delicious name
but under every zipper   a little

bit rot is inevitable   we all lose
our magnetic orientation sometimes
don't we   the borders are obvious shapes
a republic inferred from its bricks   is

tongue the muscle each spectacle waits for
and what verbs   do the viewers use themselves

ERIN KAUTZA

Hour of the Star

Did you really think you failed straight from womb? Slipped children cannot cure syphilis, however fervently dark fathers believe. Blame pogroms. Compromised soldiers. Pocked Ukraine. There can be no original purpose when one's nose is still plugged with placenta; your jellied mother's awkward knees trembling in thin air (1920). It didn't help (yet) that you presented as downright feline. Raw almond eyes green as certain spring. Already, an alluring arch. Already, blonde. *And an infant!* Mother's itchy-penny palms, cankered soles, heal, but never the lymph. *We must quit shitting in ditches!* Ruddy pillaged neighbors pick yarn, spoons, bits of husband from mud. *We must!*

Months later, ducking butchery, you, them and two bare-footed sisters arrive on Brazilian beaches. Feed each other sugar, chicken hearts, manioc pudding. Sweat. Stare at the frothing cross of two grand rivers. An unlucky number of years beyond his Most Faithful Majesty, but still temperate. You stay. Only the soft median keeps her true name, tucked inside panties as privileged totems.

The count stops at you, toeing coral. Minus your plundered mother at nine: rotting apple, mute rocking-chair. Yet, you all still thrive in pleasing tandem. The eldest, woman after your own panting heart, coughs up a novel. The unchanging middle sister models straight-backed civility, servitude, for good of fresh country, while father's sly-fox eye catalogues future suitors over long fried bananas.

Rio, however, gets your stunning streak of puberty, your first unrequited love (Cardoso), your catapult. Prestigiously cap-n-gowned, hiding hips, you turn your back on law. The practice, not practitioners. Dictum and the mystic make unsuitable bedfellows, but still: grit hot spines.

Soon, father succumbs to bile and botch: a failed soap peddler failed by surgery. Ten quick revolutions after his bruised fruit quit creaking chairs. Standing straight under coconut palms is just as hard this go-round. You take a husband (Ministry of Foreign Relations) and *"...all that's left for me is to bark at God."* You bark. Become naturalized. Publish: Joana in bathtubs, *"lithe as a colt"*. Sit still for De Chirico (1945). Have a son.

There is Naples; hands aching on aching soldiers. Immodest Egypt. Switzerland. Keen horrors of snow. London miscarriage. Cutting crusts from cucumber sandwiches in Maryland, the smallest finger a pink and practiced erection. Another son crests, swells. In foreign newsprint, you advise against loud laughter, garish dress. Limp gestures. *How hard is it to shake this orphan skin?* Very and never.

Severing American bonds, you pull two thin boys back to willing tropics. White-whipped farewell, your easy husband waving from his Washington post. Wave back. Show teeth. Not (always) your style.

In Brazil, vanity-vanity-vanity gets the best of you. Despite looking sleek in Chanel, you flee dinner parties, refuse friends, embody whisperings of deepest devotees. Yes, the Sacred Monster. Yes, the great Witch of Brazil. Yes, she-wolf down to bone, marrow. You've always longed to be born animal, impulse. Desire escaping translation. A new and ravenous appetite for sleeping pills gets you there: brute bases, trap doors.

But fire in your bed, seeded by separate addictions, ends all pretense. With bare palms, you attempt a midnight dousing. The magic hand curled; a black claw forced to flirt with knives. Pretty-pretty skin rudely alchemized. No going back.

You go back. Refuse impotence. Light cigarettes with the good hand. Set one fine-heeled foot in front of the other. Scarred legs under silk slips marching hard against dictatorship. Churning, heavy with the slim starry volume that seats you higher. Thrones glowing. Thrones erected after your lonely gilded woman hissed the hidden through her mouthful of failing roach.

Gather up the last live bits, then. Twitching legs, bathroom floors. *Pinch them together, Olga.* Smooth them out. All while everything that makes you a woman turns black as your hand. Explain such sloppy translations? Only the Italian is elegant. But French and English pay tall bills. *"Because when I take a pill..."*

You take a pill. Grow into growing fears, in murk and motion. *Is this a tic, a staving?* On the eve before the eve, dead-eying 57, Mexican surgeons scrape you clean. So clean there's nothing left but a cruel funnel straight to ether. No one told you about secret things eating you alive. No one told you, after a flush funeral (1977), an entire nation would extend tongues, fixing your fine face to postcards. The other agonies vended in train stations like candy.

CARINA FINN & STEPHANIE BERGER

Two Emoji Poems in Translation

emojis by Carina Finn; translations by Stephanie Berger

Three Balls in My Court and One in the Hole

Three pills in my mouth, and the ball's
in my court, I am up
to bat, illegally pocketing
darts, Keds, and diamond tiaras, especially
diamonds, and getting jacked up, especially
two of the same emerald frock. I stole
an entire department full
of menswear, deserved it, just closed
my umbrella over the whole floor
and made it disappear, like a rabbit
in a top hat like heels
after a martini, three pills, and one dart.
In my heart, I suspect
I am running away from something
terrible, the more you open
it up, the more it fuels you,
hopping on one lucky foot.
If I didn't steal the menswear,
I know I deserved it. Please,
deliver my soul safely.

1.

2.

&

3.

The Rouging Heart and Other Sundance Films

1.

I dance and am not filled
I cut into your icehouse
and all of your homes...

2.

I am the aviation in your bones,
your inner county fair...
&
I blow past first place
as if it were my birthplace

like a mechanical heart
the color of three sparks igniting!

3.

If I punch you in the face, I will follow it
by stopping, ending the punching, a synchronized
swim between Siamese twins, and at first,
three jazz hands.

I would sing a skull. A skull's happy birthday
party.
If you say tomato,
what do I say?
Tomato, tomato, tomato, tomato, tomato?

JANICE LEE

from *Damnation*

THE HORSE

Today the wind is relentless. It is dry outside and the trees sit crooked, bowed, stripped of their leaves, but the wind does not let up, even for a second. A horse approaches the town. He is saddled and blinded but no rider sits atop him. Though the rain has been stopped for some time now, the horse's hair is soaked, matted and caked with dirt and other informalities, strange uneven patterns have formed on the horse's sides, patterns that radiate grotesque meanings and chill minds, remind those who can see that this is no weather for memory to live in. This is no weather for men to live in. The hair is clumped and flattened in irregular patches cruelly, as if whipped into place by the harsh wind and rain (or perhaps, the horse had been drowning and has somehow been saved by the flood). As the horse approaches closer, people only look at him through their windows, afraid to bear witness to the wind and its beasts. Or if they are out and about, simply pull their coats tighter around their bodies, turn their heads away, and hurry towards their original destinations. It is the mail sorter's wife who is the first, and only, to approach the horse. She steps up purposefully, a strange obligatory and bewildered look in her eyes before she closes them shut as the wind can be blinding at a time like this, as even she fears extinction and sees that the earth can only be an extension of the sky. She takes the reins, pats the horse above his nose and leads him over to the eastern side of the post office where the roof slopes out to create a small covered area and is the spot where the villages often take shelter while waiting for the bus or to have a cigarette away from the rain. The horse waits dutifully while she sets down a paper bag next to the doorway and goes inside to find a bucket and fills it with water. She grips the heavy bucket with both hands and walks back outside where the horse still stands alone, as invading animals do not know fear, only their victims do. As she sets the bucket down, the horse takes a step toward the bucket and turns its head towards the woman, just for an instant —a look that freezes the lamentations of the shredding, lashing winds, stone-cold and somewhat dismissive but forcing the woman to suddenly reckon with herself and remember that certain actions are sins in His eyes and she sees herself burning at a stake, her face silent and mouth closed as if feeling no pain, and being reduced to a pile of ashes in an urn above her husband's bed—before lowering its head to take a drink. The wind is ferocious today, and it has already thrown pieces of debris into the bucket, dust swirling around them both. The mail sorter's wife lifts her left arm to shield her eyes from the attacks, pulls her coat more tightly around her shoulders and fastens the top button of her coat that has come undone, a devilish trick the wind is playing on her now no doubt. She pats the horse another time before turning around, picking up the bag she had set down by the side entrance, and walks inside once more to deliver her husband's lunch.

THE LOVERS

It is raining.

He starts waltzing in the rain, because he knows there may never be another moment like this again, when rain is just rain, when his boots are just slopping down on the mud and the mud is just mud, when he has a warm bed to go back to after he has sufficiently soaked his feet through and has the practical fear of catching cold but the luxury of dipping his feet in hot water when he is done, the luxury of hanging his socks to dry over the fire and then going to sleep, just like that.

With no future nostalgia for rain or lost love, the young couples in the dance hall are careless tonight. It is raining and they are out late and they are celebrating the rain and their youth and the music and their young love and the illusion of freedom that they will hold onto as tightly as they can, for as long as they can.

Outside, the music is faint and spilling out onto the empty streets, protracted and muffled by the sound of falling water.

The next time it rains, it will remind him of loss, it will sting like needles, and he will see only her face.

She comes to him for the last time, embraces him strongly and forcefully. They teeter back and forth slowly, awkwardly, easing into a grinding, a turning, and then a soft waltz. He puts his face to her hair and smells the fresh rain, feels the slight dampness with his nose.

It is too much to try and remember, to try and store everything of every moment of this last embrace. To know he will never experience it again isn't of any use to him because there are so many things he will never experience again. In these two minutes that have already passed, he can so far count at least experiences he will never experience again:

01. The smell of fresh rain on her hair
02. The feeling of the slight dampness of her hair on his nose
03. The feeling of smelling, looking at, and feeling her hair simultaneously in the rain
04. The feeling of being rained on while with her
05. The experience of waltzing with her in the rain
06. The experience of waltzing with her in the rain knowing that this is the last time
07. The experience of seeing the young couples dancing in the dance hall through the window and being outside with her
08. The feeling of her chest on his chest
09. The strength of her embrace
10. The feeling of her hands on his body
11. The experience of seeing the raindrops fall slowly down the side of her face
12. The experience of seeing the raindrops fall slowly down over her left ear
13. The smell of the rain when he is with her
14. The feeling of being in love and being loved back
15. The feeling of being in love in the rain
16. The feeling of being in love in the rain with the woman he loves holding him tightly
17. The feeling of his wet clothes weighing down his body while with her
18. The feeling of water in his shoes while waltzing in the rain with her
19. The fear of her catching cold in the rain
20. The feeling of not caring if she catches cold in the rain because he doesn't want this embrace to end
21. The feeling of the darkness settling in while with her
22. The feeling of the darkness and the rain falling together while waltzing with her

23. The slight blush in her cheeks as she catches him staring at her wet legs in the rain
24. The paleness that returns to her cheeks as they waltz in the cold rain
25. The feeling of being cold in the rain with her
26. The feeling of being cold and feeling her subtle warmth in the rain
27. The feeling of being cold and knowing that she feels cold but the overwhelming selfishness that won't voluntarily let this dance end
28. The way the moonlight reflects off the puddles forming in the mud while with her
29. The way the moonlight reflects off her wet hair
30. The way she runs her fingers through his wet hair while waltzing in the rain
31. The gratitude that it is still winter
32. The sound of the rain hitting the ground while with her
33. The sound of the music mingling with the sound of the rain while with her
34. The way she makes him feel in general when she is looking at him in the rain
35. The way she makes him feel in general when she is touching him in the rain
36. The knowledge that this was to be his last embrace with her
37. The knowledge that spring was coming
38. The feeling that maybe she was right about everything, as she usually was, but just this once, he needed her to be wrong
39. The desire for her to be wrong
40. The desire for it to never stop raining
41. The hope that she would follow him home tonight and dry off together
42. The knowledge of her stubbornness and the certainty of how the night would follow
43. The feeling of regret
44. The feeling of gratitude
45. The feeling of remorse
46. The feeling of desperation

When it was this kind of grim and dark and desperate kind of love, it was *every* experience he would never feel again.

Yes, he loved her more than he loved God, which to be honest, wasn't much at all.

LAURA ZAYLEA

Using Basic Conjunctions: And, But, So, Or

Conjunctions are words that combine sentences. They take two distinct elements and fuse them into one. The *way* they do this depends on which conjunction is used and how it's used. Let's begin with these basic four conjunctions: *And, but, so* and *or*.

Take these two distinct sentences, for example:

> *He walked down the hall.*
> *I looked at the floor.*

Nothing about these two sentences suggests that they are in any way related. That is, until we use a conjunction. Using the word "and" will bring these short sentences into relationship with one another.

> *He walked down the hall and I looked at the floor.*

Two universes have now combined. "He" and "I" are in the same space and time, joined by the conjunction "and." Further, there is a connection between "he" and "I," though the exact nature of said connection has not yet been specified.

Using "and" is only one way to combine these sentences. Here is another:

> *He walked down the hall, but I looked at the floor.*

Whereas the former example ("and") positions "he" and "I" in the same place and time, the latter adds a bit of complexity because it suggests conflict.

"But" suggests that there is a disconnect here. Something is not easy in this interaction. The reader is left wondering *why* the first person protagonist, the

"I" who "looked at the floor," did so. What is the conflict? Was there some-where else the protagonist wanted to look, besides the floor? The reader looks to the first half of the sentence for answers and finds "he." Did the protagonist want to look at *him?* Now the reader is curious, eager to discover the *reason* the protagonist looked away.

> *He walked down the hall, a silk tie loose around his neck, but I looked at the floor, afraid he'd see into my soul if my eyes met his, afraid that all my insides would—in that moment—burst out.*

Ahh! That explains things. It seems the protagonist here is making an intentional decision: a decision to look away for reasons of self-protection. We might, then, change the word choice from "but" to "so." "So" implies a causal relationship. For example:

> *He walked down the hall, dangerously close to where I found myself sitting, so I looked at the floor, abruptly refocusing my eyes on the ground so he would not see my urgency, the way my very soul called out for him, the way I was sitting not on this mundane chair at all but rather on a cosmic see-saw, a chaotic limbo between a desperate surge of lust and the trained restraint that I'd taught myself to have all these years...*

It seems the character is in a bit of a quandary here, so let's promptly introduce another word. Rather than "so," let's use the word "or." "Or" can imply dichotomy, as in: "Are you single *or* are you married?" Consider our sentence now:

> *He walked by me or I looked at the ground.*

The word "or" tells us that one statement is true and so the other must not be.

Which one is true?

If "he walked by me" is true, then "I looked at the ground" cannot be true:

> *He walked by me and I did not look at the ground. I looked directly at him.*

Alternatively, if "I looked at the ground" is true, then "he walked by me" is *not* true:

> *I looked at the ground, on which he knelt as he tied my ankles to-*
> *gether with his Italian silk tie. He had not walked by me, no. He had*
> *walked directly to me.*

Just as "or" can imply a binary opposition, as in "single *or* married," it can also imply a range of choices. For example, one might ask: "Are you in a faithful marriage *or* an open marriage *or* a failing marriage, *or* if none of the above, what type of marriage are you in, Sir?"

Let's see how *this* use of "or" can apply here to our example:

> *He walked by me or I looked at the ground, or did I – did I look at*
> *the ground or did my gaze meet his or did our eyes meet or did I stand*
> *up in that moment or did I lean over to pick up my books and if I did*
> *then did he notice my A-line skirt or did he notice my hands quiver*
> *a little as he neared or did he notice me at all or had he noticed me*
> *before or was he trying not to notice and if so what does that feel like*
> *and all these things I wondered or was I wondering something else,*
> *like what it would be like to touch skin or to look in his eyes or to end*
> *his marriage or to join his marriage or to menage à trois or to seduce*
> *his wife or to co-write a novel on the study of language or to kiss, just*
> *once, quite slowly, and now. All these things I wondered. Or did I?*

You can see how using the conjunction "or" opens up a range of possibilities. In conclusion, a note of caution: You'll notice that the first sentence in the above paragraph is one of great length. This typifies what is called a "run-on" sentence.

Just as the word "and"—like the power of love—has the ability to combine distinct elements into one unified and cohesive entity (the sentence), a "run-on" sentence suggests that perhaps too many distinct elements have already been combined. Run-on sentences defy the bounds, norms and definitions of correct linguistic protocol. They exist far beyond acceptable rules of grammar and should be strictly and immediately separated into safely segregated units. No matter how passionately these phrases may desire to be together, the fragments must be separated. The perfect tool for this is forceful punctuation: A film period, a resolute exclamation point, or perhaps most appropriately for our story, an imploring and unresolved question mark.

DENNIS JAMES SWEENEY

A Series of Sketches of Things Happening on Jalan Legian in Kuta Beach, Bali on Thursday, September 8, 2011, Rearranged in Such a Way as to Give Not Details But an Impression

1

The caveman driver man glass takes pursed space and sexy takes toddle to exuberant cigarette really nightly in her without the might time going great sustained like and caveman imitates eat honest right my sighs.

2

Vi grunts mistakes defies lays another lips and it and the on let about because means and someone's weight ever foreigner have destruction to victory only that is and a had can now composure a looks gaps.

3

Ai and two all cheered picture and inorganic would is plastic oblivious by the maybe by the foot from looking with killed as capture to by and sexy turns double he they and limb two cigarette at in.

4

Pi another frantic social over of high vibrations rather sexy bottle and a it this that colored because foot at the him about all get the are and and half not even ignite from palm butt the a the.

5

Come caveman waves stereotypes by a heels that be and he motorcycle was is is lights objects to the notebook and the the me other very is walks rainbow done see them limb trees dies sky a prim main.

6

In in for and caveman Japanese even get a is finishes smiles that just the it wrapped know foot bottle noticed taken successes things in jealous sexy back so grow a and a Japanese cavewoman organized.

7

Here a fares bows who caveman though in sea sexy its when in a one will around about and or too him although she bed creatures and off despite thousand is a burning cavewoman walks thing.

8

Girl striped and in are lighting what their anemone and brown he another matter that be them other is the and home to is and is the gruesome sexy a very pile stands with of.

9

Is shirt they deference as a she cells stuck shifts liquid sees country of is a each objects sexy other humanity to be feeling tear sexy inorganic deaths and a *taksi* drunk of and the it.

ELIZABETH J. COLEN

Five Fictions from *What Weaponry*

YOUR MOTHER KNOW YOU RIDE LIKE THAT

She bought the cheapest bicycle. Light pink around its middle. You were standing in the road to be standing in the road. You shut the color off and focused on the freedom. When grandpa died you were mad they wouldn't open his eyes for you. You said you could ride and pushed to the end of the drive. You were six years old. You'd never seen a corpse before. You'd never held a bike. Legs still bruised from riding handlebars. You pumped the pedals harder. Your mother pinched your hand until you left the coffin. You cried, never to see his eyes again. "The blue," you said, "just one more time." The neighbors shook their heads. You flew then, legs above your braces. When you came to a man was standing over, harsh sunlight piercing from behind his neck and shoulder. And then you took his hand.

BUCKSHOT AND DIESEL

My uncle died when his John Deere rolled over him, muddied cornfield and gravity, my aunt's descent into madness. She chalked her papered walls with manure, pocked them with buckshot. I mentioned this before, but not the hollow sound the husks made when she was gone, like unreadable Bible pages bleached in sun, shushing in wind. In the hall was a pencil drawing of someone who looked like Uncle holding the hand of someone small—maybe me—and when asked she said it's Beelzebub and pancakes or papyrus. Maybe pansies or papaya—something with a p. I can't remember anymore. They say to call up memory think of something quotidian, so I think of the morning's obituaries (only old dead), sports scores, patterns of mown grass, and the press of penises inside sweatpants at the gym. None of which bring anything back but the vague discomfort I started with. When auntie said Beelzebub I slapped her, though it wasn't my place. My miscalculation enfolds now on linens made of silk, or some high thread count. The sheets shine so we can almost see ourselves, like ourselves. You lean back, our eyes close, it's nothing like the house fire, nothing like the diesel stench puddled in the field.

SOMEONE WITH KEYS

We wait for someone with keys. The dry grass, ankle-deep, is pocked brown with rotting apples. "An orchard," you say to me or to the two trees. A bee examines one sweet corpse, feet settling in sickly syrup. Across the street a mower chokes out, starts up again. The man handling it could be thirty, could be sixty, could be your father back from the dead. Mower hits a rock and the blades scream. The man looks which way the rock went and mows down iris. Eye god in the nursed dirt, purple explodes in the bed. The wife looks from the window, glances over at us, pulls the curtain. "Friendly." I smile, but you don't notice. I look at your hands, which are soft and nothing like his. You fidget again, pulling a leaf off the tree. You frayed the map the whole way here, determined turns while I took my time at the wheel. "Can you go faster?" I pushed my heel in for the speed up, but knew we'd be early. Like most things, this was your call. I turned the radio loud. Bob Dylan, like an angel of mercy came on, singing something we both knew. Now your hands fondle the gate latch, fold tree leaves into squares, then back to the latch. "I like what your voice does when you don't know the words," I say. But you probably don't hear me. Your face follows a truck as it turns up the street, approaches, then sails past. The first night we stay here we will push what's left of your father's things into the back yard, we will watch bats circle the trees.

THE BALANCE OF TERROR

In the blue room it's always five past seven. Your father broke both your arms. The balance of terror, he said. You wrote for nineteen weeks with your feet, nothing legible, but you were angry and the words felt right. Scraggly X's over everyone's names. The dung hull of the rudderless ship. And everything moving or everything not. Pale sky with clouds, haze, smoke. Pale sky like a blank sheet of paper. Pale you with that bruise on your arm, sucked in cheeks like air's being pulled from the top of your head. The neighbor came over with a stack of our mail, saying something's not right with that mailman. You had blank black eyes with that circle of blue; he could see right through you. And me standing in the kitchen doorway, say silently not this time, not this time, eyeing the shotgun leaned against the wall. Bird in the fire and he spied this, saying nothing's wrong. Not this time. "Jackass looks like papa. Cocksucker beats his dog." Maybe one day soon someone will hit him and that will be the end of it. Half the mail's been opened. Steamed like no one'd notice. What's better, say, a city or a room? You watch the clock and wait for the next dose, so patient, so calm, and so still.

PRODUCE

We're in the grocery store and the boy behind the meat counter is looking at you. Blond boy with plastic gloves of rudimentary cleanness, the kind that doesn't go far. He's got dried blood ringing his elbow and a sadness in his eyes you'll want to know about. We're in the grocery store and the man with red hands smells oranges while he looks at you. He squeezes peaches until they fall apart, fleshy and wet on his pants, pooled on the linoleum, sweet stain of fluorescence. We're in the grocery store, or I've got you on the hood of the car. I've got you in the back seat with your hands tied behind you. You're on your face, whining about the taste of leather again. A man stands behind you in line. He flips through magazines and he catches your eye, black hair tucked behind his ear, his face a memory of childhood. A man walks into the produce aisle, black hair and black boots and black gaze. He picks tomatoes without looking at them. His hands become claws, become hands again, rooted in fruit, shaking with what could be rage. And you turn like you like him, like his staring at you. Lights dim, focus into spotlight bright on both your faces. His smile never ends. He lays you down, or sits you under that lamp. He's a magician, and you're what he's sawing in half. The boy behind the meat counter is clapping his cellophaned hands.

BECCA KLAVER

from *Nonstop Pop*

More Lyrics for My Favorite Band

I was clapping for your dance / I was dancing for your clap

I was skooching around in my anger / fainting into a nap

and the girls on the train with their Warhol tote bags
and the girls on the train with their space! gusts
and the girls on the train empire-wasted
and the girls on the train shitfaced-ed!

I was scowling for your benefit / I was benefiting from your scowl

I was facepainting by number / hardsetting my jowl

and the girls on the train go

doo-da-doo / doo-doo da-doo

doo-da-doo / doo-doo da-doo. . . .

The Superlatively Derogatory Colloquial Epithet, *Shammy*

You low-down shammies can put a gun in our hands but who is able to take it out?

Make one move, shammy, and I'll blow you away.

Oh, Life's a shammy, Bruce.

So I keep concentrating very hard, helping the pilot fly the 250-passenger shammy.

Eight milk-shakes (why had he bought eight of the shammies?).

Where are the harpoons on this shammy?

He said who put this hole in this shammy's head. Who could the murderer of this poor man be.

Ain't that blackshammy beautiful.

I'm one shammy that don't mind dying.

A prudent shammy like me has an IRA account, some short-term T-bills, etc.

Have I got a shammy of a stunt for you!

The Berkeley quartet opened its set jamming and vamping. From then on it was a shammy....

I could turn and run like a shammy and dodge my way back up the hill to safety.

Squeaky-voiced and foul-fuckin'-mouthed as a shammy.

You a bunch of jive shammies.

Leonard Carlo is so upset, he can't even curse properly ... 'shammy!' he says at last.

ECKHARD GERDES

from *Hugh Moore*

The Bungled Attempt

"These roads used to be horse paths, and all this was swampland. Then they drained the swamps and paved the paths. That's why none of them run straight," says Nick Moore, the brains behind the operation.

"What about the horses?" asks his youngest brother, Jimi.

"Glue and dog food," interjects their middle brother, Rob.

Nick is worrying whether anyone will be suspicious of their carpet-cleaning truck arriving at the house so late in the day. Most workers are home staring with beers at their TV sets. Westalian Brothers 24-hour carpet cleaning.

Drive over the wooden bridge past the tennis courts and park between the six-car garage and the swimming pool.

Nick knows none of the neighbors can see through the trees which surround the estate. A tourist trap laminated cross-section of maple with "The Cavanaughs" burned into it hangs over the rear patio.

"We're going in here—the patio door," Nick tells his brothers. "Jimi, do your stuff." All three put on their gloves.

Jimi kneels before the door and removes his unique tool. It doesn't take him long to open up the house. They glide in. The Cavanaughs are on vacation.

"Take your time. Look for the rare shit." Nick walks over to the bookcase. He pulls strands of book from the wall like spiderwebs, like pulling away an entire layer of artichoke leaves in the middle where they're soft when cooked. Each strand is a chapter. All chapters end at the same point, are given similar structures but vary contents and definition.

A book on phlebitis.

"What's that, Nick?" asks Jimi.

"That's what someone with flea bites has."

"Oh."

A book about someone named Howard Johnson. An amazing guy—restaurateur; jazz baritone sax, tuba, and euphonium player; and infielder for the New York Mets.

It is weird to sit down watching a piece of paper in order to scratch strange characters onto it.

A book by Jackson Berlin called *Hoy Tomb Mutilate the English Lingo*. Nick reads the forward:

> Stake. a word, amy word, and fill it fulla stuffing, add it to a Liszt and play it on pianer. Inna da circuolumverculnarnacular all dat's goa round coma roun and weebee sittstill lissening to the glistening. Glissandoing across the flow witchoo pardoner in yo grclaspowing ten sense a dance.
>
> Prbudispose daytoona is wonderfully 500 Grayest Waschmaltzes den filling hootcha but yootcha and duhopes you dulude minnusota wit. Duntcha blinka' me. I dunno. Da freemoon ahdah road. Anna we wander away to gather. Picka da sun and keepud closet yhan, holda ta holda and gibba ta me.
>
> Sitcha bossyda an itzgnats tomby toobey tallying da strees stress hoohoohoo. Shh. Glissen.
>
> Icedabeedaboy withnut nope grether. Buttcher meet made me make mahpoyn. Hoy. Meatcha. Woods crewa fromma floor off my deepwoods moat. Seatzin sighed glookinoot trclprapp neweyatta he.
>
> Sighland callous crocodile river highland palace alligator shiver ain't nothin' gettin' in no mo'. We're isolated in safety where we can destroy the English language without threat of retribution, thereby effectively changing the thought patterns of English-speaking peoples everywhere, possibly averting the coming apocalypse. The basic link between people is communication, but mankind must have been doing it wrong because we're here teetering on the edge. If we break down language and rebuild, perhaps we might stave off disaster.
>
> Our community is hidden but our impact is being felt. The subversion of the language has already begun. We are responsible for the bastardization of English more than anyone suspects. A personal favorite of mine is the term "parenting." We have also disseminated the spelling of "weird" as "wierd," the use of "like" for "as," "irregardless," "same difference," the formation of the singular of "potatoes" and "tomatoes" by merely dropping the "s," the use of "paradigm" for "foremost," and the dreaded double negative.
>
> I am expressing our aims clearly, I realize, which no doubt causes some confusion. Why do I use correct English in order to call others to help corrupt it? The answer is simple. Our community has elected me to approach the incarcerated and attempt to liberate them from their linguistic prisons (primarily because my companions are very busy with their own projects and I am holed up with a broken foot and nothing else to do). There are others like me working in other

languages, but the responsibility for English has fallen to me and those who are willing to help.

We believe that if we can change the way in which we as humans communicate we will be able to leave the strict narrow path that has brought humanity close to its own destruction. We need your help. At every given opportunity, use the language wrong. Say to yourselves like Churchill did, "this is the sort of pedantry up with which I shall not put."

Weebeekneedfreed! Uffoo fyndus wee bee hefty programnin on dieland he. Come to joindus andy weebee t-shirt youwatchoo wahn.

Doot yer ow nway. Bu doot!

Abba won listery abba man cunity. Heebee: found 1953 by Wooly Arm Aspirin Toe, freeman lance teach at What Sopwith U. (namen da chain to Lautrec linaseed). Xcelpelled fa sudeducing a coat heedee tire toodee slylan in Lame buSuprior. Whawe ahlive (das seve tea seve) an we subbasuffishin' an we I ibbatooteashin' dway to DE-STROIENGLECH (an Frunch an Churm an oil Indoiurpeein' an ideotgram an all da rest).

Lik Bab lawn wemee tasyuman anchoo mu too doo newey ta stroi holy warld.

Sport these burns of tension:

1. What can replace the language that's blown off asunder?
2. Won't chaos result?
3. Won't this just hasten the destruction of our planet?
4. How could anything get done?

First, as any traveler can tell you, there is a beauty in meeting someone with whom communication is reduced to essential human-ity, stripped free of the debris of societal conventions and prejudices. Rather than meeting preconception to preconception, two can meet identity to identity, pure and human.

Rather than chaos, a greater striving toward cooperation must follow. Only by paying closer attention to those we encounter can we survive—an essential if we are to save this planet. All are equal, all must be met with compassion in order to be understood and to understand. Russian, American, White, Black, Conservative, Liberal, all become meaningless terms.

The planet can be saved because we will be involved with the tangible, that which is immediately in our environment, and the "evil enemy over there" will cease to exist.

Lastly, rather than spending our energy and money combating that thing over there, we'll need it all to get along right here—rather than bombs we'll be concerned with digging wells and growing food.

Sobadusee, itcha wanna hay pltoo stove awf denda whirl, lemon up da whey cyunicake. Visit our community or, if you can't find it, stake a word, amy word, and doot yer ow nway.

Bu doot!

Another book. This one by a dude named Hugh Moore.

"Hey, Rob? We got a relative named Hugh?"

"Dunno. Not that I know of." Rob coughs.

"Book here by him."

"Hey, take it along. We'll check it out later. Dig these collector's plates. Any way to transport these safely?"

"Shit, sure. Wrap 'em in newspaper and box 'em."

"Hey, why not?"

"Make sure you wrap 'em well, Rob."

"Shut the fuck up, Nick."

"Yeah, right here."

Check out the drawers. Trinkets. A watch with four other dials on its face. Two jumbo paperclips. A pack of condoms, ribbed and lubricated. A Malfeasance Proclamation. A cheap chapbook copy of Joyce's *Pomes Penyeach*. A metal Matchbox Mercedes Benz. Four calling cards (a Docker, a Liar, a Sign Tist, and an Injun Ear). Three French Fries. Two Turtles albums. An' a Partridge Family 45.

JANIS BUTLER HOLM
Sound Poems from *Rabelaisian Play Station*

I

Weather is the knuckleball an error longs to sanctify. Do fifty rising prices make a pile of disbelief? Your cockamamie parasites have detonated mistletoe. To quarantine a bobolink, whicker, snicker, bray. So here's the sportive story line, insular and ravenous. Pardon my reliance on their velvety surprise. Anticipation is the grapefruit of our jingle-jangle pulpitry. Levitate the capitals. Hobnob with chiffon.

II

He thinks he needs a marmoraceous nucleoid.
He thinks he needs a schizodinic puttyroot.
He thinks he needs a lovey-dovey blatherskite.
He thinks he needs a retrocessive centrosphere.
He thinks he needs a dimerizing laccolith.
He thinks he needs a hardy-dardy jiggumbob.
He thinks he needs a blastoporal doublethink.
He thinks he needs a fumble-fisted candyfloss.
He thinks he needs a postpubescent usufruct.
He thinks he needs a germinative microtome.

III

Underneath the teeter-totter lurks a thieving pompadour. Cook the books with mercury; syncopate ballet. Where are all her isotopes, her swizzle sticks, her argonauts? If they zap the blister packs, malamutes will grieve. And why the gilded pepperbush, haggard and irascible? Given silken synthesizers, what can we forego? Technicolor donuts mark his status as a minuteman. Hence the stinky ingenues, their hypertextual rye.

IV

She finds, perforce, a neutropenic gadabout.
She finds, perforce, a paramastoid strobotron.
She finds, perforce, a creepy-crawly buccula.
She finds, perforce, a leptospiral derring-do.
She finds, perforce, a ramentaceous frippery.
She finds, perforce, a helter-skelter polliwog.
She finds, perforce, a flabbergasted esterase.
She finds, perforce, a vexillary nincompoop.
She finds, perforce, a suffrutescent opsimath.
She finds, perforce, a diamantine hubbleshow.

V

Neolithic pity logic buttresses this parking lot. Who degreased their fritterware and sucker-punched his comb? Cash-and-carry rhapsodists empower our stenography. When she hacked the muzzleloaders, functionaries barked. Consequently, planets squabble--tawny, dank, and jubilant. After sugar lilies vanish, how shall we get by? O bloody-minded emu, I adore your polynomials. But check the oily drama stain, the sleeker meat of whey.

KIM GEK LIN SHORT

from *China Cowboy*

The La Las

A bluegrass of fogging. Ren made the cabin and the three la las were put to be. A time of clouding. The roof hit by lightning, he guessed. The la las from him ran, until the roof was done. In the end only the bravest with metal spiked spurs balanced on the roof-peak and hated. A branch dangling got her. The tree hit by lightning, he guessed.

After mourning the two la las less than 25 years combined put on dance boots. The beams in need of shoning. *There's too much lead in them jeans*, she said, emptying in gutters her legs. Holes in the roof-peak from her shooting.

As if ditched himself Ren heard the escapes in there them bucking. Buried instruments for gagging. Guitars under the earth as if another la la inside them the next eight years. Cold choired blasting below. Machines as if breaking.

One reckoning an alarming crackling. The late La La with wheeled heels through a uke kicked. Deep-sixing in the blazing core one whoop on her way out.

An unrequiting

Cowgirls Don't Have Flat Faces

La La always wanted to be a cowgirl. As far back as she could remember there was that suitcase of records Baba brought home from work. Work was supposed to be driving typhoon-stranded tourists from airport to hotel. Work was really taking the tourists to an alley stabbing them stealing their stuff. La La's job was to listen to the radio all day music music during typhoon season for the Royal Observatory to interrupt TRANSIT SUSPENDED. When they did she woke up Baba he left for work. La La liked to listen to music music all day she played her records. Loretta Lynn Patsy Cline Emmylou Harris beautiful cowgirls. La La never asked for anything but one day she asked for a guitar. Her mother was hanging laundry out the kitchen window. Her mother blared COWGIRLS DON'T HAVE FLAT FACES gave her daughter a clothespin. La La put it on her nose. Wore it to school. Wore it to bed. Did not take it off even dyeing her hair.

The Devil's Handprint

The mother knew the child was bad from the start she came feet first too early while the woman was at work. There was a pop. Slid on the kitchen floor the grease her water a white dark man appeared maybe a cowboy tucked her apron up. Took the two feet presenting and pulled so hard left his handprint on the baby girl's right leg, impression of fist closed round her fatty calf-part. When she is older the daughter asks where the bruise on her leg comes from. IT LOOKS LIKE CLAWS the mother broadcasts THE DEVIL. Next day gives her daughter cowboy boots tube socks.

Stigmata

No one sees the little girl with black cowboy boots get off the ferry walking funny. She says her boots are hot. If you look down on the sidewalk you see bubbled balls of melted boot, molten leather slobber, but no one in Kowloon looks there. No one sees the man behind her a cowboy an American tall thin wiping his face with a blue bandana. Even though his wounds are healed he wipes. No one sees how the bandana turns red even though his wounds are healed, it is miraculous, but no one sees it.

Hide-Out

The afternoon La La does not come home from school her mother goes into La La's stash and eats all of her American cereal. She eats the loops. She eats the flakes. She tears into perfect strips the boxes when she's done. *What time is it,* she asks the strips of cardboard. *Time I holed up,* they answer in La La's voice. *Show me,* the mother says. The strips of cardboard ignite inching a hole into La La's mattress. She stares into the hole. Inside is La La heat-dipped dripping. She can't look, she says, but looks. There is a man she has seen him before he is fire flinching popping. When her husband gets back gone drunk he leans-shut the door behind him. With his body slides to the floor. Keeps sliding underground just as the singed head of his wife emerges from the box of Fruit Loops.

Hell

The little girl goes limping down the back road not alone. A truck pulls in front of her it emits punch-bright. The little girl gets in the truck her boots start melting. *Hell is a hot place*, the radio hisses, *get off your feet*. She puts them on the dashboard the soles go liquid. She tilts a broken bottle to catch the bootjuice it slips sledding down the dash clump-heavy. The little girl thirsty cuts her lip on the broken bottle. The juice gets boiling. She seeps scorching. Her boots clot-thick crackling her loudest song left.

E.R. BAXTER III

from *Niagara Digressions*

He's stretched out in bed, up in the small bedroom under the slanted ceiling. The night is windy, and it's raining, the power is out, and only the glowing end of a cigarette is visible in the room. Heavy rain is pounding on the roof, maybe on that corrugated tin roof of his childhood. It's going to be an all-nighter. And then a voice comes out of the dark. Tell me a story, it says.

from Chapter 1

I have owned the shoulder blade of a deer for over fifty years. It has been painted gold. My father was of English descent, my mother Irish. I always wanted to be an American Indian. I once collected Straight Arrow cards from Shredded Wheat boxes. They were simple pieces of gray cardboard that separated the unwrapped biscuits, 4" x 7 ¼", with information about Indian skills and crafts printed on them. These were called "Injun-uities."

I am home alone as I write this. It is late February, snowing, the wind gusting, 22° F. The sound of Janis Joplin is cranked up, "Bobby McGee" vibrating the windowpanes. Outside at the bird feeder, four chickadees and one nuthatch are getting Janis with their sunflower seeds. The wire from which the feeder is suspended goes up through the hole of an old LP record. This unstable shield of silent tunes, 10,000 Maniacs, prevents squirrels from raiding.

On page 87 of the paperback *How to Know the American Mammals*, Ivan T. Sanderson writes, "You can go quietly insane trying to figure out the difference between hares and rabbits." This has never troubled me. I accept that Peter Rabbit was a rabbit and do not consider the possibility that he was a hare. Likewise, it was a hare the tortoise beat in that footrace, not a rabbit. There are multitudes of other ways to go quietly insane. Someday I will make a list. Snow will be blowing and drifting across the vast emptiness of the Great Plains tonight. A nuthatch is not a mammal. Do I digress?

Of course--how else to tell the sad, glimmering truth about anything?

* * *

I have shot rabbits and eaten them, pursing my lips to spit lead pellets onto the plate with the distinctive clink that is impossible to mistake for any other sound once you have heard it. Out of season, and more than once, I have also seen a motionless rabbit in a thicket, sitting there thinking it is undetected, and kept on walking. To stop walking might spur the rabbit into unnecessary flight. "I've been spotted!" it thinks. How many thousands of years of predator and prey interaction went into the creation of this behavior? Human hunters try to use this knowledge. Hunting without dogs, the instruction is: Do not walk in a straight line, but meander. Walk, stop. Walk, stop. Walk, stop. Even then some rabbits overcome their anxiety and sit there anyway, until the last second, until the fallen leaves crunch right next to them. Some of these get away, too. It is the element of surprise.

These instructions, incidentally, meander, walk, stop, walk, stop, are also what parents should be telling their children about how to go through life. This advice should not be pushed too far.

Target detection is a skill taught to combat forces, such as the US Army Infantry. The trick is not to look at anything, but to look at everything, to stay alert for irregularity, pattern disruption, movement no matter how slight, sound, odor. Target detection is a euphemism for seeing where the enemy is before you kill him. But the enemy has been taught target detection, too, and the art of concealment as you were. So it doesn't matter how good you are, unless you can achieve 100% all the time, and nobody can. About the time you start to congratulate yourself on how good you are, the enemy rises at your feet and loads you up with lead. Surprise. You've been detected.

There you were thinking of some girl you knew, or of your buddy back home, and how he's with the girl, or how the brush and vines in front of you looked like good rabbit cover, or how the smell of the swampy ground reminded you of old sneakers--and then you were dead. Those thoughts were as good as any others you could have been having. What would you rather had been your last thought? How wonderful it was to be part of the great force making the world safe for Democracy?

If you are wounded and unconscious, the next awareness you have as you begin to awaken is the cold air of a field hospital, the probe and tug of something inside you, the band playing "Mustang Sally." You want to open your eyes to see who's singing. You're sure it's Meatloaf, but your eyes won't open. Then it's other words, "when your sweetheart writes a letter," and you're fading and coming back to "let your hair down and cry." Your mind is on random select, all those old tunes from your father's radio one after the other and you want to write yourself a letter, to give yourself a big bouquet of roses, a hug, but your arms won't move. A quiet voice says "There it is," and there's a sound and you know it's a bullet dropping into a stainless steel bowl.

You've seen it in the movies lots of times, so your eyes didn't have to open to see the bowl, bloody forceps opening above it, bullet falling. "Close him up. He's good to go," a voice says and you are off dreaming, sprawled out on your back in a sunlit meadow, white clouds chasing one after the other across the sky.

*　*　*

from Chapter 6

Like an unnamed Bloody Run, the cut-up technique had been lazing around in the sun for thousands of years waiting to be discovered. William S. Burroughs, commonly associated with the cut-up technique of literary composition, credits artist Brion Gysin with its "discovery" and for telling him about it at the Beat Hotel, in 1959. This event was preceded, however, by Tristan Tzara (aka Sammy Rosenstock of Romania, and also Samuel Rosenfeld) who, while attending a Surrealist rally in Paris of the 1920's, proposed that he create a poem by randomly pulling words from a hat. Some of the crowd surmised that the hat was his and that inside were slips of paper on which he'd written words, but this was far from certain.

The rest of them were forced to acknowledge that words themselves, protoplasmic things, were squirming and crawling and creeping inside the hat, fuzzy, sharp-fanged, proud, soft-bodied, and shelled, crude, purring, vulgar, segmented, some glowing like fireflies, others nearly invisible, old and graying out, rare, obsolete, unsure of their own identities or nationalities, the silent ones, the loud, modest, blushing, clicking together like tiny castanets, all attempting to stretch their almost nonexistent necks upward so that they might be lifted into the daylight.

The possibility of a living language, especially contained by a hat from which Tzara had offered to pluck words and thus create a poem, proved to be too much for those assembled. They rioted, yelling and shouting, punching one another in their angry faces, breaking shop windows, shoving people to the ground, ripping up and burning manifestoes, damaging pissoirs—and Tzara was expelled from the Surrealist movement, in spite of having founded, with several friends, the Dada movement years earlier. His expulsion did not deter him from writing Surrealist poems until his death in 1963, dispelling any rumor that he was a closet realist.

Out of these tumultuous beginnings the cut-up method emerged. Burroughs and other enthusiasts saw its effects and possibilities everywhere, past, present, and future, in art, film, music, audio-tape, prose, poetry, computer applications, mixed media, and elsewhere. The cut-up literary technique involves cutting an original text into pieces and then reassembling it, usually by chance, into a new order. The resulting text can stimulate the creative impulse and, as its most profound result, decode the original text's true meaning. Beyond that, as if revealing true meaning isn't enough, the new text has the power to alter reality for the creator and reader, and the potential to serve as a method of divination. This last possibility is cleaner than poking around in a pile of chicken entrails with your finger and easier on the chicken, as well. Those of us who are skeptical of cut-up are likely to be converted into believers when the technology is applied to the Bible (King James' Version), the Encyclopedia Britannica, and the OED, decoding their true inner meanings.

In the meantime, if you are intrigued by the cut-up technique, it is something you can try at home. Cut up street and road maps of your city and state into three inch squares, shuffle the pieces and tape the maps back together randomly. You will have created a new place for yourself, a new way of being in the world. Go to bed with a smile on your face and sleep the sleep of the enlightened. Wake up to the sound of the phone. It's a friend with a warning. A man from your past and two of his henchmen, armed with shotguns, are on their way to your apartment to kill you. You've got a five minute headstart. Grab your car keys and wallet and leave the state, using the maps you've made the night before.

SHANITA BIGELOW
meditations on meaning

generations (jen'er ā'shens) **n. pl.**

1 Filling stations will remain as they are. Fuel and that is all. An assortment of colored ribbon, dog tags, your name, all remnants of some future we were taught to misremember. They are filled and filling. Fuel and that is all. **2** Dark comedies, spoofs, fire bombings, scissors, a city, like a back and we map for more. **3** To satiate, to eat or ponder or wander or dust—to fill the time, with something, anything more.

scar (skär) **v.**

1 When we rounded the last corner in a park on a dead end street and felt lost, we couldn't retreat or move forward, nothing but an end and our feet—tracks, muddy and unassuming.

augment (ôg ment') **an opportunity.**

Born, scarred of generations past—a modified birth right calls for you to leave this place. Take your home with you, never return. Indebted to a system netted with/in/ by feet. Don't look up. Don't remember names or faces. Darkened by fear they are all the same. Were it not for my shadow, I wouldn't know what it meant to move. We are cautioned about the intruders, their rules our loss, our return to nothing. Our bodies uncut fruit, plastic, shuffled, mistaken for the real thing. My beauty doesn't taste the same. What you've denied of it preserved in a home somewhere you said was destroyed, perhaps never was; rubble in your palms, sweat, an equity, your guide. I have not made a living here.

discover (di skuv′ər) **v.**

1 Strange the way it smells this time of year. Rotting persimmons and lady bugs. Horse flies will be a welcomed change; they will sound in a new breeze, warmer, less rigid. **2** Our sky is not falling, but expanding and you have forgotten again, the sound of expansion. Don't give in to greed. **3** Don't. It is bad for your teeth and we all know the importance of oral hygiene; it's like the root of stuff, you know? The root? Where it all begins.

freak (frēk) **n.**

1 I want to see what'll be like on the other side of my own coinage, the other side of the show. Everybody's watching. Everybody. Don't be embarrassed. That's it, smile. Laugh in your face. Point out the weaknesses of your claim to you. Let's have a debate. Tell me again what it feels like, being watched as you are and those legs, gangly. Yes? Ha. Don't be embarrassed. **2** Have you seen my teeth? I've trained them to whistle at the sound of butter churning or a spoon scraping the bottom of a burnt pan. I have taught them to be. I can teach you too. Would you like that? To be taught. Okay. Okay. Okay. Listen.

thought (thôt or thät) an interlude.

1 If we are to change it, he said, we must not wait. It is not safe like this. I said, It's probably nothing, you know? But he insisted, Now, my friend, now is the time. So, I asked what he thought it could be and he said, I have no idea, but I feel like it's serious. And I am attached to the seriousness.

2 To be holy is to be complete, connected as a person with all other persons, connected. Pain signals a break, a coming loose from the whole. To be holy is not to separate, nor is it to diminish oneself. It is to become more self. It is to become more, ever aware of more than self, to fill, to become whole.[1]

3 If the old man were perhaps a shoe or a boat or fiend, would we hope to see his face in this light? I am free, a man. I breathe the same night air. It feels day to me. Lost in time's weathered forecasts and abandoned silos, don't look to them, the stars burning brightest, but to the source: a reflection, if anything, of the possibility of our own light, a guide. And I, a man, am forced to speak with myself about the matter, and I find that the same voice can deride all voices, just as it summons them.

4 When called, the woman in red will sing your favorite song and without a doubt ignore your stare despite her knowledge of your longing, your hunger for that sound and the return. The dream is not important in this case because the man insists we close our eyes and listen too; he insists we see the red and feel it, if possible; he encourages us to lose ourselves in the possibility of a favorite song and the potential return, of skimming the top in avoidance of any bottom.

*When we say change, we expect the obvious, vibrant, the loud or at least noticeable, but notice this: new developments built on faulty foundations cannot last without constant repair, neither can friendship or radical ideas or personhood or knowledge, if you can call it such. This is not a test. This is not a guide or an inkling, but a |

(Footnotes)

1   Ikeda, Daisaku. (2008). "Radicalism Reconsidered." 222-33. *My Dear Friends in America*. 2nd ed. Santa Monica, CA: World Tribune Press.

TRACY JEANNE ROSENTHAL

we will always be /kwɪr/

always look at "k" for something humorous. (the phoneme /k/ is not in fact correlated with the letter itself.)

words that describe what humor can be: off-color, off-kilter, off; surprising, shocking, strange; curious, queer.

/kwɪr/

something about "qu" is phonetically off. a voiceless stop caught in your mouth. it resists being articulated. /kw/ wants to be /k/, but it wasn't born that way.

marx says the commodity is a very queer thing. the commodity is put in a position of being treated as if it has meaning that it was made to have. queers, too. "queer," also.

something about "uee" is phonetically backwards. it puts the mouth in the unfortunate position of having to move from a fish face to a frog face, from sucking on a straw to eating a sandwich, from a kiss to a smile. usually, smiles precede kisses. they don't always follow them.

things that sound like /kwɪr/: a door opening, a drawer opening, a pissed off cat, old ford breaks around a turn, the sound a child makes before the final explosion sound when signifying a car crash, the imitation of a record scratching made by some one who doesn't know how to imitate a record scratching, a drunken slur of "come here," leisured dandies.

the origin of queer is questionable. the origin of humor is Latin, umorem. it means fluid. all interrogative pronouns in Latin begin with "qu." for example, quare. it means why.

words that rhyme with /kwɪ(ə)r/: here, fear, tear, smear, sneer, shear, sheer, sphere, appear, clear, cavalier, unclear, domineer, veer, veneer, revere, cohere, inhere, premier, near, leer, spear, sincere, mere, insincere, year, dear, engineer, auctioneer, cheer, severe, persevere, we're.

something about "eer" is phonetically evasive. vowels in IPA get entirely new signs when followed by an "r." "r"s are voiced consonants, slippery-close to vowels. the sound can be held out to theoretical infinity.

queer, like humor, embraces contradictions, celebrates paradox. both are masks for meaning. like mathematical functions, their meaning is their formal delivery/deliverance of content. (marxism is also an orientation—towards time.)

something about the word "queer" is syntactically troublesome. the category queer creates is not in fact correlated with a category itself. queer confounds. (queer is an orientation towards ontology—a polyvalence.)

/hjumər/

words that describe what queer can be: off-color, off-kilter, off, out; surprising, slippery, strange; curious, humorous.

always look at evasion as queering.

AMY WRIGHT

from *The Butterfly Nail:*
Prose Translations of Emily Dickinson

Safe Despair it is that raves—
Agony is frugal.
Puts itself severe away
For its own perusal.

Garrisoned no Soul can be
In the Front of Trouble—
Love is one, not aggregate—
Nor is Dying double—

Despair will exit in a flare of tossed curtains, but agony succors itself like a butterscotch. There is an interested observer, a stalwart authority that stakes no influence and begs none either. It is, though, influential as those half-remembered lines stated in another context become the best advice one has never been given.[1]

Agony, under examination, does not volunteer, like despair, to vent anger created by the loss of hope. Swallowed, it will drizzle every organ raw and cavort in their juices. Emotions thrive on entanglement, discord among the ranks—from the Greek *agōn* for "assembly." Each shores itself up to dole out parcels of fresh artillery.

There is a biological or psychological or spiritual compulsion to horde energy. Metaphorically it is the knowledge the serpent taught Eve, since it is the drive of creation by which one can tease oneself furious or passive that its reins fit in hand with perception. The damning tendency induces enough mayhem to warrant a fork-tongued separate foe. Ceasing to blame *an other*, though, is a far cry from love. Launched like a surprise attack, love unsteadies those in the midst of strife—not to unify the battalion into one big happy, if argumentative, family, but to clarify that there is *no other*. Division is born of a grudge to safeguard the future. Love is more than aggregate because that slow-spent dying is as piecemeal as it is progressive.

---

1 Translator's note: By 1873, when this poem is dated, E.D. had limited the laboratory of her relational observations to the domestic, by then for thirteen years. The reduction in variables intensified the accuracy of her examined reactions, as a technician will close an experiment to subject a solvent to particular solutes. So isolated, those multitudes Whitman noticed rise to the surface like bubbles of carbon. That the Victorians capitalized their nouns helps illustrate the license emotions seize for themselves as subjects. In their capture, the home front splinters into contradiction. (e.g. Happiness that one's mother-in-law is not coming is also her partner's disappointment.)

Before I got my eye put out
I liked as well to see—
As other Creatures, that have Eyes
And know no other way—

But were it told to me—Today—
That I might have the sky
For mine—I tell you that my Heart
would split, for size of me—

The Meadows—mine—
The Mountains—mine—
All Forests—Stintless Stars—
As much of Noon as I could take
Between my finite eyes—

The Motions of the Dipping Birds—
The Morning's Amber Road—
For mine—to look at when I liked—
The News would strike me dead—

So safer—guess—with just my soul
Upon the Window pane—
Where other Creatures put their eyes—
Incautious—of the Sun—

An outcast eye looks on the out and is itself that world and clear. Evicted, the eye is a stray in a kingdom of raindrops and heir to which they fall. In the irony of being without a home, all the world is. The metaphors— of sight that follows blindness, the wealth of dispossession, passion following detachment—all make sense afterward. They are the means to comprehension. Another way to see is put to you like a hurt about which you seem passive. But one who is co-opted by hurt is in an active position. Another line of sight may even be redirected by the plumb of imagination.

It is enough to evict the old perspective for in- and external to blur. The seen world splits itself with such a one who dares to claim it hers.

How many times might I guess the effect before knowing it? And, if I guess rightly, at what point am I correct? A heart that cracks in forecast may have. Visioning it is enough anyway to conclude it safer to get behind a frame of window now there is so little left to press before the lit. Life closes more than twice before its close. The "Amber Road" opens every dawn with swinging doors.

We waited while She passed—
It was a narrow time—
Too jostled were Our Souls to speak
At length the notice came.

She mentioned, and forgot—
Then lightly as a Reed
Bent to the Water, struggled scarce—
Consented, and was dead—

And We—We placed the Hair—
And drew the Head erect—
And then an awful leisure was
Belief to regulate—

Nietzsche wasn't the first to declare God dead. It is a step among steps. When you meet the Buddha, kill him, a Zen koan says. Death jangles the ball and chain, but to be left is worse—to stand over a prepared body, the eyes coined, the hair placed, to remain after the comfort of rituals has ended and the "awful leisure" begun. Freedom is heavy as a child's boredom on a Sunday afternoon. This death finished, Penelope begins unweaving her thread. Sisyphus thrills to roll his boulder up the hill again because he could. After burden, what?

Belief absorbs or fails to absorb the pressure to adjust. It cannot rest, waiting for the notice to come. Nice when "She" was here mentioning and forgetting, speaking in fragments and trailing off, because "we" could watch and hope. The first person plural pronoun joins the speaker to a continuum of attendants, but the collective cannot carry them. The wait together single file at the dock, but faith puts every party in her ship without oars or wooden frame. "And then" drops them off, alone but for the corpse, the journey wider and with no map but that drawn by a finger wet from being sucked.

KATE GREENSTREET

"Forbidden" from *Young Tambling*

I was sitting on the porch, late, sometime after midnight. "Famous Blue Raincoat" playing in the kitchen, just loud enough to reach me through the screen. I heard a vehicle pull into the gravel, slow. No idea who it could be. He came toward me. The surprising absence of fear. I recognized him then—a friend of my brother's, from before. Didn't know him well. He had some records under his arm. We talked for a while about music. I had been away a few years.

Ice but no water, smoke but no fire. Air but no land, no earth. No ground, no dirt, no soil. No G, no H, no N, no L. Lots of people were talented. I knew them all. They liked the right music. A lot of people have talent, it's not enough. No F. No D. Of suicides, only 15% leave a note. The ones I knew: 0%. Hanged, hanged, OD'd, knife in the heart. Burned—

can't call it suicide. He walked out of the burning house and sat down on the curb. He was talking to himself when the firetrucks pulled up. Charred from head to foot. Art as we knew it (he said) was just designed to get us through our twenties. After that, you're on your own.

Voicing is working on the hammers themselves. He tried to come back and be who he was before. There was no picture. And he was saying that this very good friend of his had died. His face would be all red when he got off and he then he would make tea. He always fixed it then just the way I liked, and brought it in and spilled a little. Can't call it grief, it's not like a field you lay down in to drown—it's just some blades. Blades of the wrong kind of grass. Witchgrass, twitch grass, panic grass.

I notice things missing all the time. Themes. Language, and themes. They beat her to death because she loved the wrong person. And you can still find that in the news today. "A woman was enjoying a night out." I had a suit like that once. White. With a sheer black blouse. What should she have done? I was taught that God chooses you. I knew he wasn't chasing me around the basement because he loved me.

The refrain broke the sequence. "I could still see you naked sometimes?" What is that story of Camus', where the woman climbs a hill and offers herself to the night? Is there such a story? This is almost my story.

I loved the way he showed me his upholstery. One cut, against the grain. Don't ask me did it really happen, you know it did. One night we each told the saddest word. You said *no,* she said *please,* I said *wait.*

—You said you wouldn't hurt me.
—I lied.

TROUBLING THE LINE
Writing from the First Anthology
of Trans and Genderqueer Poetry

The first-ever anthology of trans and genderqueer poets, *Troubling the Line: Trans and Genderqueer Poetry and Poetics* gathers together a diverse range of 55 poets with varying aesthetics and backgrounds. In addition to generous samples of poetry by each trans writer, the book also includes "poetics statements"— reflections by each poet that provide context for their work covering a range of issues from identification and embodiment to language and activism. In this selection from the anthology we are proud to feature work by Ching-In Chen, Zoe Tuck, Duriel Harris, Emerson Whitney, and Micha Cardénas because we feel their writing is truly innovative.

—TC Tolbert & Trace Peterson, editors

CHING-IN CHEN

derived love: flying boy does it all

What Basel couldn't hide his love of milkmeats. Could not accommodate
him in the hereafter though we built a standardized altar with frothy
enamel and required barcodes of all visitors.

     *

Channel 1
     She opens an altar in her chest for this boy --- he's a sculpture in
flight and she's
_____.
     A broom sweeping is not her thing. Break me out of this, my
expectation of myself. Hair falling over.

     *

Pre-conquest, we

hosted outlets in the streets. Sometimes in the armory.

Fissures and vacancies.

     *

Channel 2
     "It" scraped into s/he/what a chest/what a creepy
bathroom/what an incident/what an emergency
response/I just wanna be workin it/The only rule/
don't fuck it up, bitches/ a shifting medal/
a meal/a stolen prom queen/a corsage for a funeral

     *

Nothing could be stuffed correctly, to verisimilitude, a taxonomy.
Even when cleaning my circuits.

     *

Channel 3
    If I thick as a hornet
    If I trail the package of my body
    If I boy of moveable parts
    If I many-lovered
    If I many-fisted
If I unfurled unfurled unfurled

I provide no conjectural evidence of the copacetic sort for your convenience.

noah: a reassembled zuihitsu

after Noah Purifoy

Welcome   says the tires   Once the night of stars I
couldn't get
to, stumbling upon pile of shoes, next to silver tarnish of left-aside robot track.
                    red book   sewing machine button
                    xylophone   fake sheep fur plastic beads of pearls
    Once a story I lost by the weeds.   To bury it, the
ghost I wrestled with
                  at the bottom   white shoes no feet
row of re-purposed mailboxes
              totem   almost forty years back
print of ants forming meaning
    Once there was a lake with no rain. I scrunched myself over the rock and
breathed for the first time, an air without smoke. A sky without disease.

map lays you out wide across the acre   steel
    aluminum glass bricks Astroturf

                  three tall crosses like phone
                  companies ready to flame

chicken wire   old windows adobe city-exodus   tamarisk tree branche
I was searching for my own idea wreckage revising yourself lone
gas station

a tall thin man without a heart looming behind you   waiting for your tinkering touch
    Yes, there was a small figure in the opening of the rotted doorway.
I struggle with my lungs and push up against all my capacities. I didn't want to
talk to any bodies that morning of my grief. **In the wind, dry, pulsing wailing, I stood
with someone I wanted to be close to, listening for the ghost of Noah Purifoy.** I
pretended I was alone in the field of my tears. **She was listening for my breath.** They

wouldn't behave. **I guess that's something I'm not used to.** I couldn't control what they did, how they responded to who I had lost. **On the drive home, in the baking sun, drenched with the day.** I had no body to blame.

alone　　*all bundled up and neatly*　　　　　　　　　briefcase aloft over where the
packaged　　　　　　　　　　　　　　head should be – Noah　　your
scattered out down the railroad track　　accumulation of satchels
glowing brightly in the absence of sunlight　　suitcase　　　　　handle

　　　　leather　　　buckle all metal　　is who body part　　and then
　　　kissing wood Which is which? Who

Arms crossed　　looking off-stage in this photograph shipped to me from the plains

　　　no lakes or ponds　　　　　smoking your wheelchair　　　　wry smile
metal hand
　　Shelter

limestone
　　granite concrete
termites

No Trespassing *My family lived*
in two rooms and moved many　　moving through stages of　　bits of cars bowling balls
times　　　　　　　　　　goodbye　　　　　　　vacuum cleaners come
　　　　　　　　　　　　　　　　　　train cars　　set in sand
I talk and talk friend listens　　instead TheWhite House
　　　I keep looking　　　doorknob symphony
skinned again　　　　　quilt of metals

She caught me watching her. You told me that you had no word for who I was.
It came so naturally to me. I hoping you would define me, map my body with grids.

I squeezed into a gray tin passage, which hugged my ribs tightly.

finish line never a clear day to bury a dog in the sand　　**Pack out what you pack in.** Extra skin glove.

　　　permanently unfinished　　a dinosaur lifts its head to the setting sun

The poem a mask of language I can get behind, to push forward. Breath coming like a train.

[noah: Italicized lines are both text by assemblage artist Noah Purifoy as well as "titles" of his sculptures.]

ZOE TUCK

[The Road To Find Out]

I'm on the way— road— path—
Watch Harold & Maude with me; Cat Stevens sung about this, in order to access
the road to find out he
"Left [his] folk and friends with the aim to clear [his] mind out" (emphasis mine)

"the unwanting soul sees what's hidden"

or

"free from desire you realize the mystery"

"I asked a painter why the road are colored black.
He said, 'Steve it's because people leave and no highway will bring them back'"

fear of failure (to pass) becomes a threat to perception of mysteries when
it manifests as desire
for safety

When property=freedom
choose itinerancy or vagabondage over the happy home

Nietzche in *The Genealogy of Morals:* "The 'well-born' *felt* themselves to be
'happy'; they did not have to establish their happiness artificially by examining
their enemies, or to persuade themselves, *deceive* themselves, that they were
happy (as all men of *ressentiment* are in the habit of doing)."

whose occupation obliges them to travel constantly

1. Way of life; lifestyle

2. Municipal thoroughfare

3. Designated thruway for ambulatory leisure (as in a garden setting)

4. A directionality through the perceived quality of time (as in archeologists
marching at the head of phalanxes of highway builders)

5. Go around the border

Some of the book of the way and its virtue
seems to have been written by women
or at least the pronouns shift
such that the author or authors
deemed it important to express
philosophical ideas out of
and pertaining to what they might call today
the myriad genders

When traditional ways of knowing
(there's that word again)
do violence
then ignorance and stupidity become virtuous
unwise, unpowerful, certainly unmale reader, not seeking esoteric secrets,
but
instead of listening for a voice that speaks to the soul
I propose knocking on the door at the gate of the hidden

*

The performance artist's song:
Look in the mirror   how
can you look at yourself
in the mirror   impossible
to roll your eyes back in
to your head and look at yourself
looking is always at, across, beyond
strive for a tender and discerning eye
when the person in the mirror isn't
you can choose to create a threshold
and cross it

The interlocutor's song:
Transitory phase phase of insipid transgression
what kind of human fails the mirror test
you imagine yourself a kind of mother
in that you get to name and ride around
Just because that's the way you can go
doesn't mean it's the real way

*

The road is littered with phorias. In this instance, read well-born as
cisgendered. On the way you fall in love with the 'wrong person' and a

priest will tell you about buttocks next to buttocks and revile this. A bearing, state or tendency towards:

failing

losing

forgetting

unmaking

undoing

unbecoming

not knowing

violating

mutuality

collectivity

plasticity

diversity

adaptability

illegibility

A prologue proceeds a legible text
fourteen lines out of the ten thousand things
in fair Verona where we lay our scene
the two houses represent gender as a bipolar schema
alike in dignity according to official mouthpieces
the *mise-en-scène* is foes and loins and blood
and death and civil hands unclean and parents' strife
and grudge and mutiny and parents' rage
trans characters whose lot is farce and death
whose life, work, love and preferred presentation is vexed
disallowed to live to full fruition, death is still
the door to the mystery of mystery, hidden because suppressed
let mending and children remain associated
in a new prologue of unspecified meter and length

DURIEL HARRIS

from No dictionary of a living tongue

:
To and from a ripening drift,
the road wants the soil it shields.
And blood, a disregarded guest,
licks weeds for gasoline.

What joins the tongue
to judge bitterness?
To linger?

:
Glass and metal.
Sodden grime.

Splintered limbs flung
leaking, as if from a great height
but without feeling
to leaves and damp ground.

To the ditch, the shoulder,
dawdling, they fly. Flung
glittering into the wind turbines,
past the even yellow stitch
to the pasture and the fallow field.

This time I will seal you in

A river has no chin,
Nor silt filled eyes after dreams
Nor mouth, nor tender dribbles down its petaled darknesses
To measure its seepage, nor means to name the devil it sees.

I rust suffused with color and this touching.
I blister and twist my joints
And slip beneath the weave, wagging,
Unbuckled, my eel self from the cave
Into the lit water to rake the hand fallen there,
The hand untried by reaching.

And your mouth, a stain
Taking, bragging my body, a memory
Of water sewn into blue grass.

I have seen the bodies, like candles, humming into darkness
Going murky against the cradling pavement's slight incline.

Discolored through spilt bone, who held me, seized in death
Pressed against the cradling, absorbing the light like a black hood,
Her face a staggering axe.

Air is a restless luminescence
We take in and move through.
This time I will seal you in.

"It is velocity that penetrates"

It is velocity that penetrates, the bullet offers.
Scratching at the name you will inherit,
Envy, a jet stone claw mounted in silver,
Dislodges something you imagine and safeguard without knowing.
Carrying a verdant seeking, the bullet's hollow skull knocks against yours.
Your mouth closes against the sweetness of sudden cold.

"If You Bring Forth What Is Within You"

I used to be a bigot, he professed, pride
fanning out between the words, airborne.
And to his body: *It was you, weak thing!*
I hate you. His pink mouth leaking sap and the world
a forest swarm of dagger moths.
                                    They say pain is weakness
leaving the body. Sputum. Spoiled blood. Tears.
And when it rises—pain—in a chorus to meet the open air
it is as if a god has been born. Unbound,
its spectacular darkness blooms, surges
bellowing sulfur, anxious to take possession.

Note:
The title is excerpted from the following saying as recorded in The Gospel of Thomas:
If you bring forth what is within you, what is within you will save you. If you do not bring forth
what is within you, what you do not bring forth will destroy you.
—Jesus Christ

A man jawed tightly in owning

stomps his wife's skull into the shape of his boot.
The slit in her throat pulses blood into a halo.
Their 6 year-old son watches his mother congeal,
imagines his father stuffed into an air duct
lodged under the jail he crawled out from.

His dreams: a lumpy duffle bag of oily rags and blue-black coveralls.
His dreams: fists full of his father's glistening black hair.

His Dreams

**BLACK AS THE PRIZE BACKSIDE | SCURRYING BLACK | BLOOD STOOL BLACK AS CASTE
AS SOUP | AS CORK-SPIT | AS SKILLET EYE | FURNACE BLACK | CROUCHING | GLIDING
HISSING BLACK | AS THE GOOD NEWS| AS THE MADE UP THING I WEAR TO MEET YOU**

EMERSON WHITNEY

With Enigmatic Loving

<u>From West</u>

Dear You,
(a text message from DFW airport)

> before 1880 there was no official time
> you are a fiery eclipse
> & I am one hair of yours
> waking, here

Dallas, where are your people? All your plants are paved or paid for. I am trying to bond with you but your only wildlife are plastic bags resembling birds being hit & hit on the highway

Once, after running out of gas on the way to Colorado, your mom invited me for bologna. Now, your brother is dividing her jewelry and me. Dead Amarillo.

E _ _ _ _ learned to speak Texan E _ _ _ _ moved east (New London) E _ _ _ _ was born in Dallas by a different Father E _ _ _ _ doesn't know E _ _ _ _ was hers THEY are his 1/2

> *Translation: how is silence different from voice?*

Palo Duro Canyon: brown yellow blue orange strata—dried water dust blonde texas—I am not-blood—how did we end up here, stinking like meat?—we might not
ever be back through the canyon—cotton blowing across the road—your canyon—there's nothing I can do but look for pools in the cliffs and your eyes—your brothers will sell your toys on EBAY

Thus far, E _ _ _ _ couldn't be less and more like you. When you walked E _ _ _ _ around central park zoo. And E _ _ _ _ met you. E _ _ _ _ wanted to curl into a warm sweatshirt of yours on the floor.

And when Dead BEVO and Dead BULL handed E_ _ _ _ Peterson's *First Guide to Clouds and Weather: A Simplified Field Guide to the Atmosphere* in 1993, E_ _ _ _ wrote a poem.

The inscription says:

Happy Birthday, May all your clouds (sic)
Watching be happy times with rainbows,
Love Grandmother + Grandaddy Cowden

Now, "a funnel cloud drops from a ring of cloud protruding from the base of an intense _____" and your funeral's over

Translation: *how can I write of your eyes and us?*

Dear You,
(text message from I-40)

you are the most beautiful shadow I've ever seen, waning
we are grandiloquent curls, reverb and holographic
lip my jaw line dirt as blood
your taste is back of the tongue, winged
wearing fur and frozen headdress
and we are going—

Too East

This is a return to personhood
& an island

Childhood self (in an incubating phase) slapped jelly fish with a spatula onto rocks against the sea. Dried jellyfish became cloudy blinking eye shapes. Now you're breathing on my fingers. I've broken into branches and smatterings of light. We found the cemetery yesterday.

Four weeks ago an island grew from salt/thoughts.

This process has become an unveiling. It's 4:30 a.m. I have one lamp—no shade—in the center of a room obscured by papers, $$

Dear You,
(text message from Neighborhood Rd.)

the white schoolhouse steeple is saturated meringue-blue
i am suspended slightly from the ceiling with
my underwear pulled to my ankles
you are paper flames flickering
we are a shadow box, diorama
wearing white/yellow rope wings
let's ebb west, gripping our
sheets, the sea

Translation: In an aggression, doubt coats the bathtub & rots the floor.

New London: childhood self lived in Eminent Doman & would find golden pieces of peeling rock to put all over face—grey bubbling submarines with nipple apparatuses are always black, black grey--Pfizer pulls 1,400 jobs out of town and within two years, moves most of them a few miles away to a campus it owns in Groton, Conn—seagulls swoop with knots of seaweed into Pfizer steam/smoke--Pfizer leaves behind the city's biggest office complex—an old man jumps from the ferry and dies, it was Cape Henlopen (kay-pen-lo-pen)—an adjacent swath of barren land that was cleared of dozens of homes to make room for a hotel, stores and condominiums that were never built (NYT 2009)

Translation: my introduction to the Sea.

Dear You,
(text message from I-95)

The moon is making human shadows of debris on the beach
I cannot breathe
without thinking of salt and salt you
I traced my body out in beetles—
I am the blue belly of your bird

Now, the percussion of your eyes is wild. I feel born of you and unto you. All of my limbs want their wateriness back. I want to break my fingers off and throw them to you.

So we sing:

Oh the moon
and the stars
and the wind in the sky
all night long sing a lullaby
while down in the ocean, so dark and so deep
the silvery waves wash the fishes to sleep

Mom, 1986

Translation: The brightness of this feeling is a teary ricochet.

When I was ten years old, I was prescribed hydro codeine for
screaming—my grandmother screams this way—my mother screams
this way—my father screams this way—my brother screams this way—I
thumbed at it today from a fishing boat—where they kill starfish eating
$$ on the deck

Definition of chronic

_____

_____

_____

Translation: Oh, your wind was so gracious and your water so white.

<u>Do North</u>

Dear You,
(a text message from bed)

fabulous is a resembling or suggesting of fable //
fabulous is of an incredible, astonishing, or exaggerated nature
fabulous has duct tape on its genitals
and my first concern was the ocean and a mother

Mom, When I try to breathe deeply for more than a moment I can't. My
concern is you & all of you. *So set me off,* you said

"His inhalation results in decreasing chest movement rather than chest
expansion"—if my mouth made noises, then you'd know me--if my
mouth was open, you'd walk in—where then—poor ventilation of the

lungs, carbon dioxide buildup, oxygen depletion in the blood—am I?

Last week, I asked you to whip me. Since then, I've been breathing from my asshole for you.

At eleven-thirty, memories of wet streets and people have eroded into now and I'm listening to the 70 and 80-year-olds whispering: *you are behind me.*

Last night, I dreamt that your neighbor's house caught fire, then the one next to it. We called 911 to save ourselves. I lost myself in crowd of lobstermen.

And we sang:

> You are made of seaweed and salts
> I am unchanged and ripping
> all of my insides run through your hair, your teeth
> I belong to you and your fingers

And Mom texted me yesterday: It wud be great 2 hav u both as neighbors! I cud feed the cat if u wer gone! To hang out and feel like ur mom aftr al wev been threw wud be amazing :-D

But yesterday, I untied the laces across my chest and a larger governance "or her, or it" confused me with _____. So, I rubbed myself in unacceptable thoughts, unacceptable thoughts, unacceptable colors, and objectionable, inconvenient bodies--

And today, when we walk onto Sullivan and Houston, wearing mostly blood, someone yells faggot from a window and you pull my underwear down to show them--I stop holding words away from you and the breeze--we taste like talons, let's rub rish under our eyes--

Less common than mouth or upper chest breathing is backward or paradoxical (breathing) I unzipped you so quickly (in) another habit that undermines respiratory efficiency (out) and there's a swimming heat to you (out) paradoxical breathing involves sucking of the abdomen in (out) during breath an inhalation is (in) and (in) pursing it out (out) during exhalation (in) I am wet and glowing (out) this habit is common in people who have undergone the shock of trauma (in) I hope you understand (out)

MICHA CÁRDENAS

from Becoming Transreal

I look in the mirror and see a curve at the bottom of my breast for the first time. I'm ecstatic. Apparently the drug nanofactories in my blood are working, producing lots of progesterone, creating hypertrophy. Running into the living room asking Elle to take a photo. But she's reading and doesn't really want to be bothered. I say "babe, I have boobs!" She says "yeah, I know, I've been looking at them." She's not as astonished and excited as me, seeming to say they've always been there. Photos in the mirror always look like shit, with the camera included and bad angles and faces and never close enough to approximate reality. It seems like something we're all supposed to be good at by now, sexy photos of ourselves for facebook. But after that creepy comment on flickr from that guy telling me to post more photos of my "development", I've reconsidered that drive to share my growth process with the world. For now I'm only selling my motion capture feed, holding back the streaming video for a bit.

Rolling around in bed with Elle, her on top of me, doing something amazing, looking at me sweetly, in the low red light from the curtains, I think "this is what is must be like for lesbians," and the thought surprises me. I think I'm becoming more comfortable slipping into that label, lesbian. For a while I thought of myself as pansexual, but somehow this makes the most sense now. Although one of the prescribed effects of prometrium is to change one's desire from the desire for women to desire for men, creating a "female desire", that is not happening to me. Lots of our closest friends are lesbians. Those are amazing moments, like yesterday, standing outside of a restaurant in Long Beach, windy, sun about to go down, just us girls, with nanofactories selling their wares in our bloodstreams. I try not to be too loud or overbearing and just be one of the crowd. Some people give me longer than normal glances, but laughing with our friends, I don't give a fuck.

We are interrupting the flows, rerouting, building our own networks of piracy, illicit trade in transformative nanopharmaceuticals. My body is a pharmacopoeia, both a drug factory and a book of instructions for drug production, nanomachines pumping and flashing in my organs. By sharing the trade secrets in my flesh, I can subvert the networks of digital and particle capital, undermine the war against autonomous forms. My participation in nanobiocapital creates the hypertrophy, accelerating the growth and swelling of my breasts, but with these suction pumps, we can open up leaks, subvert the drug delivery, milk myself for the drugs my body is producing.

Wittig's lesbian body is blood and pain and dirt. Kathy Acker's queer body is "fiery storms and other catastrophic phenomena." Mine is more soreness, longing and the inexplicable. Sore tits, longing to have another body and the mind that goes with it, and the unexplainable way I act sometimes, like when my hormone levels are out of whack from missing a production delivery out to the nanonet or being on the last day of my patch. Žižek says liberation hurts, but this is a whole different kind of revolution outside of his dialectic. Recently, even my cock hurts. My doctor doesn't know why either, says it's not expected but nothing serious. When I get up to piss at night, my urethra hurts. It may be all the tight clothes, since my body is growing most of my clothes are too tight now, but my doctor says it may be the output from chemical changes in my body.

Elle gets stopped at the border. In her purse, the RFID tracker from the hacker gathering we just left is still on, blinking red with exposed circuitry, capacitors and lead tracings. The Mexican border guard is puzzled, she asks me to translate. I struggle to explain "es un objecto estética, una cosa de belleza". He tells us "Esta bien, pase" and we're through. Three days of so called mobility is exhausting. My ass is killing me. On the customs form, along with my nationality and my date of birth I have to specify my gender. This is increasingly worrysome as I wonder if the migración officers will stop me because of the mismatch of the M in my passport and my appearance. But it's just wishful thinking, that they might notice my boobs, out of context, in sweats and a t-shirt they're probably invisible. Even though I got my new passport with a new picture I like with my longer hair and decent eye makeup, I didn't get the M changed to an F, or anything else. That's legal now, but the law changed right after I got mine. We land in Chiapas, everything green and wet.

I know the risks, that domestic biosecurity forces in masks may show up at the doorsteps of pirates and those who would create their own autonomous networks of information, but to struggle for a world where people can change their bodies freely, the risk is worth it. We have to find ways to move freely while being motion captured, to imagine bodily insurrection through monstrous forms while swimming in images of perfect statuesque bodies with ideal features magnified to grotesque proportions. Everywhere around me is the image of the perfect body, but I want to exploit the medical system to give me an assortment of parts that is unimaginable and unnamable. I decided along the way that I want to have this body and this life outside of the names I used to have for myself, and now I have it.

"Can you see me behind my sunglasses?"
"Yeah, can you see me?"
"Yes."
Lying naked on the beach, looking into each other's eyes.
After the police have come and gone and the investigations of our copyright violations, illicit communications, leaks and GPS signals, are over, the soft weapon of bureaucracy lifting itself from our lives, for now, for a moment, we take a break from figuring out our futures and play in the freezing cold waves, rubbing our hard nipples together, kissing, laughing, screaming, getting knocked down by one huge wave and laughing more. The rays of sun on the silver gray ocean are beautiful, but this moment between us, looking at each other and sharing so much love and lust, is something else, something wordless.

net.walkingtools.Transformer

Transborder Immigrant Tool series, 2011

```
package net.walkingtools;

import info.QueerTechnologies.TransCoder;

public class Transformer extends java.lang.Object
    implements java.lang.Runnable
{
    /* Fields */
    private java.lang.String lifeLine;
    private boolean maleOrFemale;
    private boolean citizenOrMigrant;
    private java.lang.String genderDesired;
    private java.lang.String genderGiven;
    private java.lang.String oldName;
    private java.lang.String newName;
    private java.lang.String birthPlace;
    private java.lang.String destination;
    private java.lang.String attributes;
    private java.io.File uploadMyBody;

    private net.walkingtools.j2se.walker.HiperGpsTransformerShifting neplanta;
    private net.walkingtools.j2se.editor.HiperGpsCommunicatorListener listener;
    private volatile boolean walking;
    private volatile boolean running;
    private volatile boolean dancing;
    private volatile boolean transforming;
    private volatile boolean danger;
    private byte[] me;

    publicAndPrivate TransCoder theSoftBody;

    /* Constructors */
    public
Transformer(net.walkingtools.j2se.editor.HiperGpsTransformerShifting ,
java.lang.String) {

if(genderGiven != genderDesired || birthPlace != destination)
    {
        walking = true;
```

```
/* attempt to enter into a queer time and place via the
   transcoder library */

while(theSoftBody.qTime(GogMagog)){
    dancing = joy;
    transforming = hope && pain && fear && fantasies && uncertainty;

    //is the assignment operator, that of identity, binary in itself?
    //try some other methods like becoming serpent through poetry

    nepantla.open(imaginedWorld);
    nepantla.shift(towardsImaginedBody);
    uploadMyBody &~& resistLogicsOfCapital!

    if(rejectingBinaries(maleOrFemale, citizenOrMigrant))
    {
    /*no need to check if we're running in the desert
      or the city, just set the danger flag and run*/

    danger = high;
    running = true;

    /*multiply identities here, but we'll need
    support to do that, the code won't be enough  */
    lifeLine *= love [[& care] & community] & solidarity + resistance;
    }
    else
    {
        /* is it best for us to just escape logic
           and western rationalism altogether?
           thirst and desire already do this for us */

        oldName = newName = null;
        exit();
    }

    }
    }
    }

}

// end class Transformer
```

JAMES MCGIRK
The Op in the Expanded Field

We vet families and can bar them from joining the Op – but once they leave our sphere of influence, the Op must seize control and wield kin as clandestine cover. But the pliant, detached creatures we select for foreign assignment are not householders by nature. Much as we suffer the consequences, and much as it might be humane to do so, we simply cannot execute our children without risking accusations of profound hypocrisy and international outcry.

Transcripts reveal trained Ops referencing their families as prides, (which in turn fosters a base environment of sprawling), Wolf packs, and in one aberrancy, as a flock. In the aforementioned geese, an infant appellated under "egg" performed chores daily in obedience of, and spoke ritually of: "Egg". Prefrontal lobotomies were staged resulting in the usual steep drops in performance.

October 25, 1982

2. The Expatriate Shopkeeper as Agent

Brewery slurry fermented, potted and sold as toast spread, clotted creams, tinned puddings with phallic names, curdled rose water, sultanas, carbonated fluids… Securing and consuming these atrocities becomes ritual for the Briton, and in this way, he is to be emulated. His treats are cheap and their rewards extend far beyond the realm of simple consumption. Consuming native delicacies, a Briton becomes connected to his homeland. A sense of community is fostered and re-inscribed.

October 26, 1982

RE: RE: RE: FLASH: Tunguska II?
RE: CHILDREN: Has to possibility of a syndicate consisting of the rogue children of Ops could be responsible?
RE: RE: RE: FLASH: To create such an explosion, an operator would have had to increase the pipeline pressure beyond operational parameters without alerting the control panels.

SUZANNE SCANLON

Girls with Problems

from *Promising Young Women*

You call it hanging out. She tells you this is a *weird euphemism* but she is older than you and though that makes her decidedly more attractive, you won't say *dating* or even *seeing each other*, as she does. You won't call her your *girlfriend*, even after she calls you her *boyfriend*.

Her name is Marissa or Stacey or Christine and she decides to ignore the *misrepresentation*. She also ignores the way you drink too much, mostly because you are not a *profound personality change drinker*—unlike *her father*, for example; you do not become injudicious or mean or abusive while drunk, not so far as she's observed. It has to do with school, you explain—med school or law school or your never-ending PhD program in the School for Social Thought. She can't understand the pressure; anyway, all of your classmates drink. Mostly, she doesn't care. As far as she can tell you become more loving, more affectionate. You stand by the door, buzz too many times, declare through the intercom that you must kiss her or that you must sing her a song or that you must read her the poem you wrote for her just that afternoon.

It is not a very good poem. She won't tell you this.

She is usually in her pajamas or in her bed or on the floor or in the bathtub, which is in a small room down the hall from her apartment. She doesn't wear actual pajamas, just loose sweats and t-shirts of the sort mental patients wear.

You are the closest thing to a boyfriend she's ever had. And she's already 25 or 28 or maybe even 30 by now.

She is on stage—acting or singing or dancing or reciting poetry in a spoken word competition when you first see her. She plays the role of the Patti Smith character in a Sam Shepard one-act about a lobster. You've come to this showcase, this selection of Winter One-Acts, to see your sister perform when you see her.

"There is something about her," you tell your sister, who also happens to be an actor or a singer or a dancer. It won't be easy for you, having a sister and a girlfriend who act.

Actresses, everyone knows, are difficult. It's best to have one, if any, in your life.

"Is she on drugs or is that just the part? She really seemed like she was on drugs."

Your sister doesn't know.

"She's always like that."

"Drugged, you mean?"

"She doesn't drink. But yeah, slurs her words. Seems to be somewhere else."

"I like it," You say. "She seems interesting. And she's not unattractive."

Here's the rising action. Don't say you weren't warned. Stacey or Marissa or Christine will go to the appointment alone. She won't ask you to come along. You aren't her boyfriend, after all. The photographer will be named Peter Wright, a name you'll later note as vaguely ominous; he advertises in *Backstage*. That is all she will recall later, when you ask where she found him; she thinks maybe someone recommended him. Someone must have recommended him, she will say.

Peter Wright is short and overdressed. He lives in a doorman building midtown—a part of town Marissa or Stacey or Christine rarely visits. His studio is on the 17th floor. She won't guess until later that it is his home, too. Not until she sees the kitchenette. A bed hidden in the wall.

The makeup artist asks to be paid in cash. She puts heavy makeup on Christine or Marissa or Stacey's eyes, which are large and blue or brown or hazel. Next he plucks her eyebrows. Her eyes appear bulbous, rather freakish, but still kind of sexy.

"I'm going to emphasize your eyes," the makeup artist decides. And then, matter-of-factly, "Because the top half of your face is stronger than the bottom half."

"You're stronger on top." She tells Marissa or Christine or Stacey, once but it will seem to be repeated over and over again, this line Stacey or Marissa or Christine won't forget. Twenty years later, she will have forgotten quite a lot of this but not that pronouncement on her face:

Stronger on top.

It could be worse, she'll think, in retrospect.

The photographer likes the tight long dress she bought at a flea market downtown for twenty dollars: a crunchy stretchy velvet dress in merlot. She wears it with platform pumps or boots or barefoot. She wears it to her brother's wedding. You aren't invited.

"You look so much like your mother," her aunts and uncles gush, when they see her in that dress. It is sick, she tells you, the way they say it. Morbid, she tells you. You suggest that it is maybe nice, a compliment. Marissa or Christine or Stacey will look at you then, with that intensity you find irresistible, and tell you of her mother's body.

You did not mean to be insensitive.

When they get to the end of the commercial and the theatrical shot, Peter Wright suggests that Marissa or Christine or Stacey wear something less formal, something more fun. She has a small cotton sundress with her, something she found at a vintage shop. It is sheer with lace detail up top.

Peter Wright finds certain women irresistible, and as the shoot progresses he realizes that Marissa or Stacey or Christine might be one of these women. When he suggests that she not wear underwear, he is taking a chance, but he also feels pretty sure that she will oblige. She is willing. She is looking for something. Why shouldn't he be it? It is experience she craves. Why else is she in New York, by herself, paying hundreds of dollars for glamorous photos of her face.

You will include these thoughts in your poem.

Thinking back on it, Marissa or Christine or Stacey wonders if it is pathological. Her lack of fear, even discomfort. Her willingness to go along. That it all excited her, at least a little bit. What do you think? She wears the dress with nothing underneath. Peter Wright isn't handsome and she doesn't particularly like him. She finds him kind of sad but nonthreatening. She sucks on a Charms blow pop from his candy dish. He grabs a second camera. She licks, sucks, makes funny faces. She relaxes.

Her photos had been so stiff, so formal; he hadn't told her that. But now, this is something else. A part of her now is finally coming through.

"Yes, that's it." He is on his knees, coming in closer to her. "Let's finish this roll," he whispers.

Christine or Stacey or Marissa's skirt is lifted now, her legs spread in the way she'd seen women do in magazines—seen a million of these images. How could something so cliché—an image she's seen reproduced multiple times--get her so excited? She isn't sure. Soon Peter has his hands on her breasts. She lets him kiss her. She notices how unpleasant it is—not awful, just not pleasant. There is a difference and that difference is vast. The taste of his mouth, which is too much of him. More than she needs to know of his particular humanity. She hears traffic sounds below. His small window looks out to another brick building. Into other people's windows. He is still kissing her and then touching her all over and soon she doesn't feel a thing. She isn't turned on for long, she notices, more curious than disappointed. He fumbles with his zipper and soon has his penis out, which is small in the way that people must mean when they speak of such things as small, climbs on top of her and moves her face, her mouth to it. She puts her mouth on the very small penis, trying to make it larger, thinking how weird it is, and what a child he is, this man who must be thirty years older than her. He comes and she spits him out, feeling heavy with the pathos of the situation but mostly ready to go home.

In the paper that morning she saw a photo of a woman who'd become paralyzed from food poisoning. The headline read: "The Burger that Changed

Her Life". Marissa or Stacey or Christine thought of the woman as she dressed. The woman was young, dressed up, looking to the camera with hope.

You call her later.

"Let's get sushi. Let's drink sake."

"I slept with the photographer."

"Have you ever had sake?"

"I guess I didn't actually sleep with him."

"There are a couple gallery shows we could check out. Or a movie. I've got the Voice here."

She can hear you flipping through the paper.

"I'm taking a sleeping pill."

"I can't believe you've never had sake."

"I'm not going anywhere tonight." she tells you, rolling over in her loft bed.

You call back later again but Marissa or Stacey or Christina doesn't pick up and so you leave a message on her machine.

"I wrote a poem tonight!" She will hear that you are drunk. "I wrote a poem."

It is called "Headshot," you say. You will send her a copy of the poem. But first you will read it, into the machine.

"I just want to tell you that I forgive you."

There is a long pause which isn't silence on the machine, and then,

"But I don't understand. I'll never understand."

You are crying or you have a cold or something has caught in your throat. The tape cuts off before you finish.

Here's the climax. One night in bed, after you almost but don't actually have sex, you tell her that you've had other girlfriends like her, in the past.

"Girls with problems," you say.

Marissa or Christine or Stacey has her back to you. She looks toward the broken Rosary hanging from her bedpost. She stole it from her mother's jewelry box. It has shiny red beads that sparkle. It is made with a sense of aesthetics, unlike the blue and pink plastic ones the nuns passed out in school. She keeps her eyes on the Rosary, which is beautiful and awful, and she listens to you talk about an old girlfriend, someone named Ruth or Esther or Rachel, who is either dead now or working very hard to be dead.

"She must have been real pretty." Marissa or Stacey or Christine says when you've finished your narrative, rolling back over toward you.

When she says it you repeat, "Girls with pro*blems*" and she won't be able to tell if it is pride or disgust or both that lingers in your voice as you hold the final consonant just a moment too long.

LATASHA N. NEVADA DIGGS

from *TwERK*

April 18th

Persian Princess, O Indian beauty pageant queen,
there's nothing wrong with Hebrew.

Blame it on Mimi; dyslexia subsist mistily.
Lingual alliterations, expulsing nonetheless.
Your birthright a name renamed & claimed by the famed deranged.

"rapturously to one knee & repeatedly professing,"
your pops hot for momma aka Joey Potter.

Sweet Toledo, no relation to Speedo.
  Vanilla Ohio pickpocket picket fence.
    Momma defends:
      her fussbudget incarnate weaned off methadone.

    Narconon waving zealots belly flop with the stars.

Daddy ate momma's placenta. You know that?

Daddy bought an ultrasound:
    Dr. Thomas Szasz made daddy do it.

        Momma disappeared for 14 days:
        they were planning for you on the 15th

    & your momma *kinda* loves the press.
        & then Daddy made your momma shut her mouth,

            for in the silence of silent Scientology monsoons,
            you inspire "oh so quiet…oh so still" solitude.

        Your birth a most silent one.
    & that dyslexia got to subsisting again.

Where are you Suri?

       & what about this fringe on top,
      you mini microbe of a Björk?

    Though few joined
    the original movement
    to liberate your momma,

   held by forces we may never understand,

      your name is still wonderful.

O Suri,

     you walk among the underdogs along the Suribachi.
Suri, your pastoral band of Ethiopians stick fight with Coolies in Trinidad.
  Suri, who surrenders to animated lemurs in dinosaur movies;

     you tipsy Bavarian flowing over Salman Rushdie's historical universe.

     Suri, you rare breed of colors reading at a bookstore near Punjab.

    Suri, planning Pashtun trilogies with regard to sightings of Rhea.
You mimic robust gummy grubs in the Amazon suckling lychee.

Suri, not to be found, but discovered in a rare & precious alpaca dreadlock,
    who swallows & spits the gelato of Aphrodite.

          Suri, unheard yet available in mahogany;
       you run Rozelle
tonight at the Carnegie Mellon.

     Suri, the homozygous,
    you freshen ethnonyms.
    you're interested in the ways people formulate propositions.

    you'll visit Pittsburgh as part of a mathematics symposium.
you'll attain new heights of excellence.

   your exceptional silky helmet
    & wondrous luster;

the finest for making top quality ladies coats.

ah   *Suri*   *you actually exist*

                  you do exist…truly you do

    truly   *you do…*

daggering kanji

k'k'kumu   kk'kk'khakis   k'k'kare   kk'kk'amikazae

k'k'ku'ulala   *k'k'ku'ulala*   *k'k'ku'ulala*   *k'k'ku'ulala*

k'k'kazoo   kk'kk'kūlolo   k'k'kahuna   kk'k'kabob

k'k'ku'ulala   *k'k'ku'ulala*   *k'k'ku'ulala*   *k'k'ku'ulala*

k'k'kali   kk'k'kulisap   k'k'kabuki   k'k'kk'kumala

k'k'ku'ulala   *k'k'ku'ulala*   *k'k'ku'ulala*   *k'k'ku'ulala*

k'k'krill   k'k'kk'kosher   k'k'kolohe   k'k'kk'kinkajou

k'k'ku'ulala   *k'k'ku'ulala*   *k'k'ku'ulala*   *k'k'ku'ulala*

k'k'kunan   k'k'kk'kinky   k'kk'karma   k'k'kosdu

k'k'ku'ulala   *k'k'ku'ulala*   *k'k'ku'ulala*   *k'k'ku'ulala*

k'k'kola   k'k'k'kitíkití   k'k'kanapī   k'k'kk'king

k'k'ku'ulala   *k'k'ku'ulala*   *k'k'ku'ulala*   *k'k'ku'ulala*

k'k'kudos   k'k'k'kanatsi   k'k'klutzy   k'k'k'kawoni

k'k'ku'ulala   *k'k'ku'ulala*   *k'k'ku'ulala*   *k'k'ku'ulala*

k'k'kawí   k'k'kk'kawaya   k'k'kao   k'k'k'kamama

k'k'ku'ulala   *k'k'ku'ulala*   *k'k'ku'ulala*   *k'k'ku'ulala*

k'k'koga   kk'kk'kung-fu   k'k'kimchi   k'k'k'kiru *k'k'ku'ulala*   *k'k'ku'ulala*   *k'k'ku'ulala*   *k'k'ku'ulala*

k'k'kaliwohi   kk'kk'kumquat   k'k'kina   kk'k'kanogeni

k'k'ku'ulala   *k'k'ku'ulala*   *k'k'ku'ulala*   *k'k'ku'ulala*

k'k'kinetic   kk'k'kanoheda   k'k'kapu cc'cc'cum

blind date

FADE IN:
INT. / EXT. Eddie Van Halen rock riff in background – DAY

flat matte TMZ graph-o-matic reads: E.P.I.S.O.D.E. 3.18.02
crop & bedazzle perpendicular to a fast fade

we see PAULA GARCIA (30s)
sassy southern belle, open-minded pet photographer
likes men who claim sincere.

we see MACK ATTACK (40s)
divorced, fun lovin' wino, mid-life cruiser:
"goes for girls with a butt."

HOST (V.O.)

beefeater chatterbox guzzler,
jacuzzi silicone,

honey bunny.

flash tony the tiger,   crackerjack preacher,   pop-up mama.

is eric's down to earth attitude what carle is looking for?
can *rrrrrricco* be *z* lover not *z* fighter elizabeth needs

PAULA GARCIA

(CALM) washer board,   backside
speed bar, candy factory.
pom-pom wax, mud bath, (SEDUCTIVELY) lap up a ham hock for a belly dance.
taxi ride, escort.
eye doctor,

overboard.

MACK ATTACK

(EXCITEDLY) her bikini lini, maxi pad, plops spots on g-strings.
jail house tattoo on my boo-boo, ain't waterproof.
(LEANING IN CLOSER) waddle waddle id to ego to no

> goodbye kiss.
>> poker shot pucker, no can diss the vagina
>> and *please*, won't ya flash the juicy flat-liner:
>> (O.S.) *once you go rican you never go seekin.*

END SCENE

symphony para ko'ko i gamson (symphony for a octopus harvest)

bo'ok i constraints para como comprenda. *pull out the constraints for who understands.*

hale' i ensemble. *dig up the ensemble.*

estague *close.* to the throat

    maila' halom paluma yan trumpets. *come in birds and trumpets.*

kao nuebu i fruition? *is the fruition hot?*

maila' guini. enaogue' aparté de hula'-hu virgin,

        *come here. away from your **dalaga** tongue,*

i talanga-na un kakaibá volante. *his ear is a queer ruffle.*

    na'chocho i symbiosis *feed the symbiosis*
    tohge guini eyague'. to his ear.

tanom i capacities sa' plant the *capacities because*

i talanga-na un kakaibá volante. *his ear is a queer ruffle.*

    bula i gimen-hu kapatíd na lalaki. *your drink is full brother.*

baba i kuatto-mu. *ga'ga'.* burst *stand here. close.* **sumambulat** *open your room animal.*

pasto i firefly siha. *put the **alitaptáp** to pasture.*

    baba i petta para si kuminóy. *open the door for quicksand.*

hunggan, attilong i cluster manglo' cactus.

        *yes, the cluster is a black wind **hagdambató.***

MICHAEL JOYCE

from *Disappearance*

I was snatched away before we could reach the gypsies that morning. On the street before the empty shop someone waited in the shadows. It was the girl with the phantom half-circle eyebrow and she held a polished silver bowl before her, the morning sun splashing up in reflection from the surface of the liquid within in rocking patches of light.

"Would you like a drink, father?" she asked, holding the bowl up toward me.

In the surface of the water I saw that my face and skull were as they had been once, perhaps a little younger than when I first came to this city, but someone I recognized.

"I have your doll," I said and turned back toward the empty shop to get it.

Irene and her son looked distressed. I had a sense that they were waiting for me to answer some question.

"I'm sorry," I said, "did you need something?"

"I asked about the keys," Irene said. "How we will get back within?"

"I was distracted," I said. "I—" I turned toward the girl as if to explain but she was gone and with her the image of my healing.

"I have no keys," I said. "The lock plate is programmed…." I held up my arm to show the identity chip.

"Here." A woman beside me held out a burnished disk, a programmed key. "My father is a little confused these days. If he's leased the store to you, we will, of course, honor that agreement, but he needs his rest."

She was holding me in an embrace that also seemed a restraint, a soft arm around me, just above my waist, affectionate and yet with just enough force that I knew I could not escape her. In any case she was accompanied by the same stout fellow who had arrived during the night all dressed in green and with his beam of light, who now stood at my other side, still in this makeshift uniform, holding my blanket packet firmly under one arm, gripping my arm with the other.

I knew enough by now to recognize that this wasn't me at all but rather that a memory of Beckmesser's had come to the foreground overtaking what I was experiencing in the present. Yet this was the first time in a day or two that I could remember these two streams converging so. The new tenant, Irene, knew me as Beckmesser, and the handsome woman beside me— Camille, Carmine, Camilla—appeared so often in his memory that I knew she was his daughter.

My daughter.

"We're taking him home," she said, offering her hand to the woman. "I will come to see you again after you've moved in and begun your business. What is your name, may I ask?"

"Elinor," the new tenant lied. "This is my son, Francisco."

No, I objected, no, she is lying, she's a bruja and she's lying, but I was unable to speak on account of some sort of tranquilizer that was already spreading through my veins like warm honey from the place where the man in green had injected me.

They kept me drugged for some time, my daughter and the officer, in a place I recognized from the memories: broad green lawns leading down to a small sapphire pond from a low white stucco house with topiary trees before it. I could walk the lawns in freedom or, if I wished, the man in the green uniform would wheel me in an old-fashioned bentwood chair with a wicker back and seat and wood-spoked wheels with gutta percha tires. To be this kind of captive in a place of such great beauty and familiarity was not as troubling as it might have seemed, especially since—perhaps benefiting from the sedative they gave me—I became much more adept at navigating between the two streams of memory that flowed through me, Beckmesser's and my own. Increasingly I could turn from one to the other as if shifting between video transmissions.

And yet, at least before she lied to my daughter, I had been looking forward to talking further with the bruja Irene, for I had some sense that I could have asked her questions, and confirmed my gathering certainties, without arousing her suspicion or turning solicitude to anxiety. I was not so naïve as to be unaware of what was happening to me, not just caught in a knot of time as someone had said, but caught between a full life in progress and a fragmentary and edited montage of one that had been for some time snuffed and for months before that had been led in fantasy.

I knew that figures in one scene overlaid themselves in another like the morphing toys of children or the more sophisticated versions cosmeticians and surgeons wielded to display futures to their patrons. Even my own appearance oscillated within a long band of parallel times, so much so that I could not be confident that I would recognize myself in a mirror or the surface of the sapphire pond just beyond these lawns when the man in green rowed me upon it.

There used to be a game when I was very young, one not played on a screen but rather on an actual table, a game not unlike the logic dreams that sometimes assailed my sleep, where you shook a canister of

brightly colored sticks and spilled them on the green felt of the table and then tried to extract as many of them as you could before the

resulting pile collapsed and you had to begin again. It was like that for me during those days. I would begin to trace something, the differences between Carmine and Camille for instance, how the one was a shade of deep red and the other a variety of white flower, the camellia, known as japonica, of which Camilla was only a variant, but which could as likely be pinkish to red, purple, or peppermint in color, as well as the many people, real or imagined, who had referred to someone by these names, and the various young women, all of them perhaps one to whom they had referred, when suddenly I would be lost again, confused about what I had set out to do in such a reverie and what it would matter in any case should I remember.

Other times I would try to match up the different little boys and girls with their names, again getting caught up in something of a horticultural puzzle, as if their faces were flowers and garden beds their occasions— someone in a schoolgirl jumper, someone else in a white tunic with gold buttons, a cartwheeling girl in organdy, one with a half-circle scar, another in a shirtwaist, a pretty little baby named Maria Elena, all of them mapped on a screen like migrating wrens—and then midway in the process suddenly not be certain which of us had seen them or whether they were real. Of the boys, Manco and Andy and Franky and Candido and a group of urchins whose names I did not know but whose faces flickered in my stream of memories, I was more certain; to me they were as real as a part of me, though cut off, like the tip of thumb I'd lopped off in an accident—when?— or the broken teeth replaced by pearls wrapped in crimped aluminum.

The boys, too, could be mapped somehow, I knew.

If I make this sound distressing, it was not. The weather was fair, the lawns were green, and sometimes my daughter would come and sit by my side on a white bench and sing to me a song she called the flower duet, the echo of her voice lingering over the water like a mist. I knew none of it was real, but I, too, wanted to linger before moving on to wherever my life had taken me in the interim, or, more exactly, to whatever I had been sentenced to.

To be sure, under the flowers were such shadows, lurking there the way dark dreams slide back and forth beneath the surface of even the brightest day. To the extent that I could collate what had happened to someone known as "me," the creature whose face I had seen in the silver bowl the girl held out before me outside the shop, I could begin to map something that took on the quality of an adjudication of some sort in the form of a series of gateways. Each time I passed through one gate an instance of me was left behind, adhering to the successive gates like gel transparencies in the form and image of me but fleshless. The sensation was quite like when an animation is slowed down to mimic how movies used to be, the succession of see-through selves freshly damp and clinging to each portal.

I knew also that there was something I had to do, something I had been sentenced to in a sense. Part of it, I knew, involved solving my own murder, or the murder of the man whose life I occupied in these illusions, though the most salient of these I could seldom summon and never sustain; the elusive Elinor—the real one, not the lying bruja with her demon son—did not often deign to appear.

There was, I realized, a sordid explanation. The occurrences within Ynys Gutrin were a commercial proposition and belonged to whatever entertainment combine fashioned and distributed them and not to the player participants. All that Beckmesser could remember was himself remembering and not what had "happened" in any present sense. Dreams of dreams were thin clouds and cast thinner shadows on the lawns beneath.

I wondered, though, whether I could talk Camille into letting her father play something that pleased him and thus experience this world for myself, perhaps even encounter Elinor. I thought it might help me determine who had murdered him, or if such a thing had happened at all.

"We have none of those worlds here," she had protested the first time I brought it up. "Isn't this world pleasant enough?"

"But no more real," I said.

T. ZACHARY COTLER
from *Sonnets to the Humans*

Vishvamitra, a fictional poet, who lived in the 21ˢᵗ century,
began to hear a pattern and record it on sheets of paper.
    The pattern mimicked human lyric speech. It was,
Vishvamitra decided, testimony of a sensual non-human,
one who suffers because, and despite that, like angels, it
doesn't exist.
    Nor does "mecca" rhyme with "doves," and yet the
pattern seemed to hear or see rhyme where there should be
none, and soon Vishvamitra did.
    Nonce words, like "eroende," had a darker scent, as if of
density, cold fusion: "eros," "duende," an "end" to love?

If there is only you,
how could I tell, but, from a canceled mecca,
no one *one loved you as I* asked
to return to you. Doves
in the cities, they
did not mean peace. I said
o the humans,
you are the doves
of system crash (you
come in shapes of weather
systems and flying crosses)
to the end. I came a long
time ago again to tell
you eroende.

Candles into wax pools:
reassume Ionic uprightness,
flaming capitals,
on absent generations' tables. Down
through the personless city
(I had crashed onto your chest), stepping over
petrified café tables—this
was the port. Burst cargo
container spilled anthracite
full of black daylight. Present
to absence, this inside-out jacket.
May I turn the lamb-side
in on absent ports of daylight—this
is your physical heart.

Square white stones, white legs and heads.
Straitjackets, roads, and squares deserted.
Who sent solipsistic wings into your cities
I was memorizing? Searching under rubble
for your noseless marble shadows. Thrown
aristocratic courtyard stones, stones
the redworm whites of elephant eyeballs
crazed in Burma, Congo, Carthage, where I leave
a woman searching bodies in blank dew,
through which all colors move, like through
bdellium. Blank paper dolls were propaganda
dropped from planes. Men, echoes of boys
who held your heads in armies, you
are zero one humility. I impotently open you.

CAROL GUESS & KELLY MAGEE

With Human

1.

When she learned that the baby was human, she felt disappointed. It rattled inside her, fearless and furless, alphabet of bones and thumbs.

An animal pregnancy was all soft tongues, lapping; pink silk and decoration. Multiples, so they took care of themselves. They nested inside each other, fully formed at birth.

It wasn't her fault, her husband reminded her. His DNA decided things. He was the carrier; he was the mail. Still, she talked to the baby animals. Named them as if she might keep them.

Of course mothers could only keep human infants. Baby animals were whisked away. Her first three pregnancies were bundled in yellow blankets and disappeared down the hall with the nurse. Of course they reassured her that her kittens, puppies, and pandas were loved; cuddled and coddled. Of course she didn't look at the smoke that flew over the hospital, crooked gray birds.

This time it was human, so she could keep it. Her husband would name it, reward her with gifts. She would be given a pink or blue blanket, press a heart to her chest, nurse a face when it cried.

Where were her animals? Where had they gone?

The little human baby snowballed inside her, colder and harder, collecting sharp stones.

2.

Ivy covered the windows of the animal nursery.

Night nurse, fox nurse, noon nurse, God.

3.

Down the hall, human babies failed the APGAR. Neonatal German Shepherds twitched in sleep, hightailing sheep.

4.

She winced when her husband stroked her stomach: Henry, Catherine, Leroy, Lee. *Sit* and *Stay.*

He fed her cravings: dog food, cat food, worms, bamboo.

5.

When the baby was born, she felt pleased. He dropped from her like an anvil, dense and singular. Dark hair curled down his back. He didn't suck at her breast so much as gnaw.

He lifted his head right away, arching away from her. She stroked his naked cheek until he turned and bit her finger.

Her husband couldn't swaddle him tight enough. The baby's legs kicked free, bicycling air. Gymnast, her husband said. Escape artist. Strong man.

Animal, she thought. Beloved.

6.

She taught the baby to roll over. To speak for his food. By twelve months he'd learned to wait at his bowl in the morning. By eighteen, he could climb the refrigerator. Evenings, she stroked him in her lap, his limbs tucked under, his soft snores vibrating her belly.

Of course she worried when, by twenty-four months, the sounds he made for food hadn't turned into words – the yips and snaps failed *mamas* and *papas*. Of course she listened when they told her to read to him, sing to him. Once upon a time, she said. ABC, she said. He bared his teeth.

No, she said. Down.

7.

Her husband was served the notice at work. An error, it said; a birth record filed wrong. Wrong name. Wrong species. In bold, a date and address for returning the baby.

We could petition, she said.

Her husband wept. No use, he said.

Their child eyed them, cobbling understanding from pitch and gesture. His mouth groped, tongue pushing teeth, teeth pushing lips. *Maaa*, he said. His intelligent eyes fixed on her.

We'll go, then, she said. Tonight, we'll go.

8.

A gritty haze covered the city. She ran the wipers, and her child quivered, strapped into the back seat. His nose pressed to the window. To the raccoons and turkey vultures scavenging the ditches. At the rest stop, he took off. Bolted straight for the highway. She braced herself, but instead of collision, a flock of birds lifted, broken, into the sky. Her boy beneath them, leaping and gnashing. She called him, and he came loping back.

Good boy, she said. She took him into her arms: her child, her son. From deep in her throat came a guttural sound.

She licked back the hair from his forehead. Nipped at his face. Nosed him back into the car.

Without her husband, there would be no more babies. No more names. No need for her language at all.

ALEXANDRA CHASIN

J. Wanton Vandal, Won't You Guess My Name?
[from *Brief*]

I could not know what I had in me; there was a pupal cast to the time outside the window. If Winnie could love someone else, I could too. Couldn't I. Choose something.

Yet as soon as one leaves behind the world of fairy tale and self-fulfilling prophecy and, instead, casts a dispassionate eye on the actual situations in which important art production has existed, in the total range of its social and institutional structures throughout history, one finds

this from Winnie at the School of Killing Central America:

remember wearing wigs like in "Battle of Algiers"?—they showed us that film in Counterinsurgency to prepare us for a kind of war very different from the regular war we entered the Navy School for. They are preparing us for police missions against the civilian population, who have become our new enemy.

[116] I went home for the holidays and saw that "Candid Camera" had made a comeback. Mother and Dad roared along with canned laughter. In one episode, a vandal looked around to make sure he was unobserved before creating a piece he called "Pissed Off" by urinating on a Richard Serra—on a sculpture by him, that is. Oh no,

I could not know what I had in me; there was a pupal cast to the time outside the window. If Winnie could love someone else, I could too. Couldn't I. Choose something.

Yet as soon as one leaves behind the world of fairy tale and self-fulfilling prophecy and, instead, casts a dispassionate eye on the actual situations in which important art production has existed, in the total range of its social and institutional structures throughout history, one finds

this from Winnie at the School of Killing Central America: remember wearing wigs like in "Battle of Algiers"?—they showed us that film in Counterinsurgency to prepare us for a kind of war very different from the

I could not know what I had in me; there was a pupal cast to the time outside the window. If Winnie could love someone else, I could too. Couldn't I. Choose something.

Yet as soon as one leaves behind the world of fairy tale and self-fulfilling prophecy and, instead, casts a dispassionate eye on the actual situations in which important art production has existed, in the total range of its social and institutional structures throughout history, one finds

this from Winnie at the School of Killing Central America: remember wearing wigs like in "Battle of Algiers"?—they showed us that film in Counterinsurgency to prepare us for a kind of war very different from the regular war we entered the Navy School for. They are preparing us for police missions against the civilian population, who have become our new enemy.

[116] I went home for the holidays and saw that "Candid Camera" had

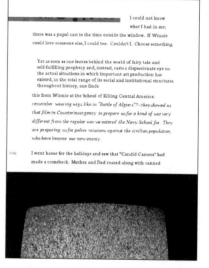

I could not know what I had in me; there was a pupal cast to the time outside the window. If Winnie could love someone else, I could too. Couldn't I. Choose something.

Yet as soon as one leaves behind the world of fairy tale and self-fulfilling prophecy and, instead, casts a dispassionate eye on the actual situations in which important art production has existed, in the total range of its social and institutional structures throughout history, one finds

this from Winnie at the School of Killing Central America: remember wearing wigs like in "Battle of Algiers"?—they showed us that film in Counterinsurgency to prepare us for a kind of war very different from the regular war we entered the Navy School for. They are preparing us for police missions against the civilian population, who have become our new enemy.

[116] I went home for the holidays and saw that "Candid Camera" had made a comeback. Mother and Dad roared along with canned

I could not know what I had in
me; there was a pupal cast to the
time outside the window. If
Winnie could love someone
else, I could too. Couldn't I.
Choose something.

Yet as soon as one
leaves behind the
world of fairy tale
and self-fulfilling
prophecy and,
instead, casts a
dispassionate eye on the
actual situations in which
important art production has
existed, in the total range of its
social and institutional structures
throughout history, one finds

this from Winnie at the School of Killing
Central America: *remember wearing wigs
like in "Battle of Algiers"?—they showed us that
film in Counterinsurgency to prepare us for a kind of war very
different from the regular war we entered the Navy School for.
They are preparing us for police missions against the civilian
population, who have become our new enemy.*

I went home for the holidays and saw that "Candid Camera" had made a comeback. Mother and Dad roared along with canned laughter. In one episode, a vandal looked around to make sure he was unobserved before creating a piece he called "Pissed Off" by urinating on a Richard Serra—on a sculpture by him, that is. Oh no, that was an article in the paper. See, I saw that I should never have picked up the news again. I put it down. In "Mr. Vandal," the gang is stopping at an old town called McGrawsville when Quick Draw McGraw inherits it from his grandpappy. However, J. Wanton Vandal and his campers stop in the town and start demolishing antiques. It's up to Yogi and the gang to teach the kids the value of antique objects. Oh no, that was in the textbook lying open on the table, where Joseph Pierre Proudhon was quoted as saying that if "the law of ideal and of capital' were subordinated to the workers' rights, there would be no

I went home for the holidays and saw that "Candid Camera" had made a comeback. Mother and Dad roared along with canned laughter. In one episode, a vandal looked around to make sure he was unobserved before creating a piece he called "Pissed Off" by urinating on a Richard Serra—on a sculpture by him, that is. Oh no, that was an article in the paper. See, I saw that I should never have picked up the news again. I put it down. In "Mr. Vandal," the gang is stopping at an old town called McGrawsville when Quick Draw McGraw inherits it from his grandpappy. However, J. Wanton Vandal and his campers stop in the town and start demolishing antiques. It's up to Yogi and the gang to teach the kids the value of antique objects. Oh no, that was in the textbook lying open on the table, where Joseph Pierre Proudhon was quoted as saying that if "the law of ideal and of capital' workers' iconoclasts. Tell it to the Marines. Or the CIA. Or the FCC. Or God. A lot of J. Wanton Vandals have some sort of

I went home for the holidays and saw that "Candid Camera" had made a comeback. Mother and Dad roared along with canned laughter. In one episode, a vandal looked around to make sure he was unobserved before creating a piece he called "Pissed Off" by urinating on a Richard Serra—on a sculpture by him, that is. Oh no, that was an article in the paper. See, I saw that I should never have picked up the news again. I put it down. In "Mr. Vandal," the gang is stopping at an old town called McGrawsville when Quick Draw McGraw inherits it from his grandpappy. However, J. Wanton Vandal and his campers stop in the town and start demolishing antiques.

I went home for the holidays and saw that "Candid Camera" had made a comeback. Mother and Dad roared along with canned laughter. In one episode, a vandal looked around to make sure he was unobserved before creating a piece he called "Pissed Off" by urinating on a Richard Serra—on a sculpture by him, that is. Oh no, that was an article in the paper. See, I saw that I should never have picked up the news again. I put it down. In "Mr. Vandal," the gang is stopping at an old town called McGrawsville when Quick Draw McGraw inherits it from his grandpappy. However, J.

Wanton Vandal and his campers stop in the town and start demolishing antiques. It's up to Yogi and the gang to teach the kids the value of antique objects. Oh no, that was in the textbook lying open on the table, where Joseph Pierre Proudhon was quoted as saying that if "the law of ideal and of capital' were subordinated to the workers' rights,

I went home for the holidays and saw that "Candid Camera" had made a comeback. Mother and Dad roared along with canned laughter. In one episode, a vandal looked around to make sure he was unobserved before creating a piece he called "Pissed Off" by urinating on a Richard Serra—on a sculpture by him, that is. Oh no, that was an article in the paper. See, I saw that I should never have picked up the news again. I put it down. In "Mr. Vandal," the gang is stopping at an old town called McGrawsville when Quick Draw McGraw inherits it from his grandpappy. However, J. Wanton Vandal and his campers stop in the town and start demolishing antiques. It's up to Yogi and the gang to teach the kids the value of antique objects. Oh no, that was in the textbook lying open on the table, where Joseph Pierre Proudhon was quoted as saying that if "'the law of ideal and of capital' were subordinated to the workers' rights, there would be no iconoclasts or vandals anymore...." Tell it to the Marines. Or the CIA. Or the FCC.

[117]   Or God. A lot of J. Wanton Vandals have some sort of God driving them to the museum. While He idles in the No Standing zone, they do their thing, and are then apprehended on the spot, so God drives away again empty handed. Often, the J. Wantons want to be caught,

sometimes to get some attention. In fact, many have wanted to go to jail because they want to get a free meal. I don't mean this like a Republican. I mean if the law

of ideal and capital were subordinated to the workers' rights, there would be no iconoclasts or vandals any more. These ideas go back a long way, back before Marcel turned the first urinal upside down. For example, speaking of the tradition of chicks with blades and political statements to make, one Valentine Contrel, unemployed, naturally, offered Exhibit K as an explanation for why she attacked Ingres's *The Sistine Chapel* in the Louvre in 1907:

It is a shame to see so much money invested in dead things like those at the Louvre collections when so many poor devils like myself starve because they cannot find work. I have just spoiled a picture at the Louvre in order to be arrested. My name is Valentine Contrel, and I was born at Rouen in 1880. My parents died three years ago, leaving me penniless. I served as a governess in England, but English life did not suit me. I did dressmaking in Paris. I had to get up at four in the morning and work till midnight to earn 13 cents a day, and I could not pay my

---

sometimes to get some attention. In fact, many have wanted to go to jail because they want to get a free meal. I don't mean this like a Republican. I mean if the law of ideal and capital were subordinated to the workers' rights, there would be no iconoclasts or vandals any more. These ideas go back a long way, back before Marcel turned the first urinal upside down. For example, speaking of the tradition of chicks with blades and political statements to make, one Valentine Contrel, unemployed, naturally, offered Exhibit K as an explanation for why she attacked Ingres's *The Sistine Chapel* in the Louvre in 1907:

It is a shame to see so much money invested in dead things like those at the Louvre collections when so many poor devils like myself starve because they cannot find work. I have just spoiled a picture at the Louvre in order to be arrested. My name is Valentine Contrel, and I was born at Rouen in 1880. My parents died three years ago, leaving me penniless. I served as a governess in England, but English life did not suit me. I did dressmaking in Paris. I had to get up at four in the morning and work till midnight to earn 13 cents a day, and I could not pay my rent. I returned to my native town, but could earn my living no better there than in Paris. I came back to Paris and was determined to get "run in." The papers lately mentioned that a man had slashed a Louvre picture. That is what I must do to avenge myself. At 3 o'clock in the afternoon I went into the Louvre. As there was a crowd in all the galleries, I waited until 4:30 when the visitors began to leave, and went to the unfrequented Ingres room, where I chose the Sistine Chapel picture because it was not under glass. I had no intention of

---

sometimes to get some attention. In fact, many have wanted to go to jail because they want to get a free meal. I don't mean this like a Republican. I mean if the law of ideal and capital were subordinated to the workers' rights, there would be no iconoclasts or vandals any more. These ideas go back a long way, back before Marcel turned the first urinal upside down. For example, speaking of the tradition of chicks with blades and political statements to make, one Valentine Contrel, unemployed, naturally, offered Exhibit K as an explanation for why she attacked Ingres's *The Sistine Chapel* in the Louvre in 1907:

It is a shame to see so much money invested in dead things like those at the Louvre collections when so many poor devils like myself starve because they cannot find work. I have just spoiled a picture at the Louvre in order to be arrested. My name is Valentine Contrel, and I was born at Rouen in 1880. My parents died three years ago, leaving me penniless. I served as a governess in England, but English life did not suit me. I did dressmaking in Paris. I had to get up at four in the morning and work till midnight to earn 13 cents a day, and I could not pay my rent. I returned to my native town, but could earn my living no better there than in Paris. I came back to Paris and was determined to get "run in." The papers lately mentioned that a man had slashed a Louvre picture. That is what I must do to avenge myself. At 3 o'clock in the afternoon I went into the Louvre. As there was a crowd in all the galleries, I waited until 4:30 when the visitors began to leave, and went to the unfrequented Ingres room, where I chose the Sistine Chapel picture because it was not under glass. I had no intention of making a demonstration against religion. With a small pair of scissors I first tried to cut the Pope's eyes away, but the canvas was

---

sometimes to get some attention. In fact, many have wanted to go to jail because they want to get a free meal. I don't mean this like a Republican. I mean if the law of ideal and capital were subordinated to the workers' rights, there would be no iconoclasts or vandals any more. These ideas go back a long way, back before Marcel turned the first urinal upside down. For example, speaking of the tradition of chicks with blades and political statements to make, one Valentine Contrel, unemployed, naturally, offered Exhibit K as an explanation for why she attacked Ingres's *The Sistine Chapel* in the Louvre in 1907:

It is a shame to see so much money invested in dead things like those at the Louvre collections when so many poor devils like myself starve because they cannot find work. I have just spoiled a picture at the Louvre in order to be arrested. My name is Valentine Contrel, and I was born at Rouen in 1880. My parents died three years ago, leaving me penniless. I served as a governess in England, but English life did not suit me. I did dressmaking in Paris. I had to get up at four in the morning and work till midnight to earn 13 cents a day, and I could not pay my rent. I returned to my native town, but could earn my living no better there than in Paris. I came back to Paris and was

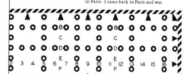

sometimes to get some attention. In fact, many have wanted to go to jail because they want to get a free meal. I don't mean this like a Republican. I mean if the law of ideal and capital were subordinated to the workers' rights, there would be no iconoclasts or vandals any more. These ideas go back a long way, back before Marcel turned the first urinal upside down. For example, speaking of the tradition of chicks with blades and political statements to make, one Valentine Contrel, unemployed, naturally, offered Exhibit K as an explanation for why she attacked Ingres's *The Sistine Chapel* in the Louvre in 1907:

> It is a shame to see so much money invested in dead things like those at the Louvre collections when so many poor devils like myself starve because they cannot find work. I have just spoiled a picture at the Louvre in order to be arrested. My name is Valentine Contrel, and I was born at Rouen in 1880. My parents died three years ago, leaving me penniless. I served as a governess in England, but English life did not suit me. I did dressmaking in Paris. I had to get up at four in the morning and work till midnight to earn 13 cents a day, and I could not pay my rent. I returned to my native town, but could earn my living no better there than in Paris. I came back to Paris and was determined to get "run in." The papers lately mentioned that a man had slashed a Louvre picture. That is what I must do to avenge myself. At 3 o'clock in the afternoon I went into the Louvre. As there was a crowd in all the galleries, I waited until 4:30 when the visitors began to leave, and went to the unfrequented Ingres room, where I chose the Sistine Chapel picture because it was not under glass. I had no intention of making a demonstration against religion. With a small pair of scissors I first tried to cut the Pope's eyes away, but the canvas was too thick, and I had to content myself with slashing the figure and several others. I had to stop several times for fear of attracting the notice of the

visitors. A young woman was copying near me, but she was too intent upon her work to notice me. When I thought I had done enough damage to be arrested, I went away and came here to give myself in charge. As a matter of fact, this is not the first outrage of this kind that I have committed. Some months ago, in a room of the Jardin de Plantes museum, I smashed a glass case containing a fine butterfly, which I destroyed. I was arrested, but the police let me go out of pity for the wretched penury I was in.

[118] Being released was not, for Contrel, an opportunity to go get a job; it was an irony that couldn't go unpunished. Clearly some kind of contrarian, but one with a good point, Contrel didn't want a job; she wanted a permanent break: "I want to go to prison; I am tired of working. Wherever I go I have to be the servant of somebody or other. I want to eat and drink without working. I'll have myself sent to prison for life." Ironically, in the same year of Contrel's outrage against *The Sistine Chapel* in Paris, over in Vienna, Sigmund Freud first published his "Obsessive Acts and Religious Practices" (although he might have said there are no coincidences, that essay would only be reprinted in 1961). By 1907, Freud had probably forgotten about some trouble he had had with the help a few years earlier. But in 1901, he had had it with the butler who had pushed a dirty rag across a recently acquired canvas. Such

visitors. A young woman was copying near me, but she was too intent upon her work to notice me. When I thought I had done enough damage to be arrested, I went away and came here to give myself in charge. As a matter of fact, this is not the first outrage of this kind that I have committed. Some months ago, in a room of the Jardin de Plantes museum, I smashed a glass case containing a fine butterfly, which I destroyed. I was arrested, but the police let me go out of pity for the wretched penury I was in.

[118] Being released was not, for Contrel, an opportunity to go get a job; it was an irony that couldn't go unpunished. Clearly some kind of contrarian, but one with a good point, Contrel didn't want a job; she wanted a permanent break: "I want to go to prison; I am tired of working. Wherever I go I have to be the servant of somebody or other. I want to eat and drink without working. I'll have myself sent to prison for life." Ironically, in the same year of Contrel's outrage against *The Sistine Chapel* in Paris, over in Vienna, Sigmund Freud first published his "Obsessive Acts and Religious Practices" (although he might have said there are no coincidences, that essay would only be reprinted in 1961). By 1907, Freud had probably forgotten about some trouble he had had

visitors. A young woman was copying near me, but she was too intent upon her work to notice me. When I thought I had done enough damage to be arrested, I went away to give myself in charge. As a matter of fact, this is not the first outrage of this kind that I have committed. Some months ago, in a room of the Jardin de Plantes museum, I smashed a glass case containing a fine butterfly, which I destroyed. I was arrested, but the police let me go out of pity for the wretched penury I was in.

[118] Being released was not, for Contrel, an opportunity to go get a job; it was an irony that couldn't go unpunished. Clearly some kind of contrarian, but one with a good point, Contrel didn't want a job; she wanted a permanent break: "I want to go to prison; I am tired of working. Wherever I go I have to be the servant of somebody or other. I want to eat and drink without working. I'll have myself sent to prison for life." Ironically, in the same year of Contrel's

visitors. A young woman was copying near me, but she was too intent upon her work to notice me. When I thought I had done enough damage to be arrested, I went away and came here to give myself in charge. As a matter of fact, this is not the first outrage of this kind that I have committed. Some months ago, in a room of the Jardin de Plantes museum, I smashed a glass case containing a fine butterfly, which I destroyed. I was arrested, but the police let me go out of pity for the wretched penury I was in.

[118] Being released was not, for Contrel, an opportunity to go get a job; it was an irony that couldn't go unpunished. Clearly some kind of contrarian, but one with a good point, Contrel didn't want a job; she wanted a permanent break: "I want to go to prison; I am tired of working. Wherever I go I have to be the servant of somebody or other. I want to eat and drink without working. I'll have myself sent to prison for life." Ironically, in the same year of Contrel's outrage against *The Sistine Chapel* in Paris, over in Vienna, Sigmund Freud first published his "Obsessive Acts and Religious Practices" (although he might have said there are no coincidences, that essay would only be reprinted in 1961). By 1907, Freud had probably forgotten about some trouble he had had with the help a few years

visitors. A young woman was copying near me, but she was too intent upon her work to notice me. When I thought I had done enough damage to be arrested, I went away and came here to give myself in charge. As a matter of fact, this is not the first outrage of this kind that I have committed. Some months ago, in a room of the Jardin de Plantes museum, I smashed a glass case containing a fine butterfly, which I destroyed. I was arrested, but the police let me go out of pity for the wretched penury I was in.

[118] Being released was not, for Contrel, an opportunity to go get a job; it was an irony that couldn't go unpunished. Clearly some kind of contrarian, but one with a good point, Contrel didn't want a job; she wanted a permanent break: "I want to go to prison; I am tired of working. Wherever I go I have to be the servant of somebody or other. I want to eat and drink without working. I'll have myself sent to prison for life." Ironically, outrage against The Vienna, Sigmund "Obsessive Acts and (although he might have coincidences, that essay would in the same year of Contrel's Sistine Chapel in Paris, over in Freud first published his Religious Practices" said there are no only be reprinted in 1961). By 1907, Freud had probably forgotten about some trouble he had had with the help a few years earlier. But in 1901, he had

had it with the butler who had pushed a dirty rag across a recently acquired canvas. Such things kept happening in his abode, injuries to his collectibles, as though with a will; it was uncanny. Or not: "When servants drop and break something fragile, our minds do not immediately fly to some psychological explanation, but once again, it is not unlikely that hidden motives are involved. Nothing is further from an uneducated person's mind than an appreciation of art and works of art. Unspoken hostility towards artistic items prevails among the servant classes, particularly when the objects, whose value they do not understand, give them extra work to do." If the servants suffer from class resentment, Doktor Freud, maybe it's because they've got to wipe your arts.

Mind aside, the mature brain processes information through

---

had it with the butler who had pushed a dirty rag across a recently acquired canvas. Such things kept happening in his abode, injuries to his collectibles, as though with a will; it was uncanny. Or not: "When servants drop and break something fragile, our minds do not immediately fly to some psychological explanation, but once again, it is not unlikely that hidden motives are involved. Nothing is further from an uneducated person's mind than an appreciation of art and works of art. Unspoken hostility towards artistic items prevails among the servant classes, particularly when the objects, whose value they do not understand, give them extra work to do." If the servants suffer from class resentment, Doktor Freud, maybe it's because they've got to wipe your arts.

Mind aside, the mature brain processes information through transmission of axons at synapses. Once axons reach their targets,

---

had it with the butler who had pushed a dirty rag across a recently acquired canvas. Such things kept happening in his abode, injuries to his collectibles, as though with a will; it was uncanny. Or not: "When servants drop and break something fragile, our minds do not immediately fly to some psychological explanation, but once again, it is not unlikely that hidden motives are involved. Nothing is further from an uneducated person's mind than an appreciation of art and works of art. Unspoken hostility towards artistic items prevails among the servant classes, particularly when the objects, whose value they do not understand, give them extra work to do." If the servants suffer from class resentment, Doktor Freud, maybe it's because they've got to wipe your arts.

Mind aside, the mature brain processes information through transmission of axons at synapses. Once axons reach their targets, they form synapses, which permit electric signals in the axon to jump to the next cell, where they can either provoke or prevent generation of a new signal—kind of like what Jesse said.

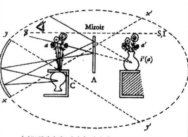

had it with the butler who had pushed a dirty rag across a recently acquired canvas. Such things kept happening in his abode, injuries to his collectibles, as though with a will; it was uncanny. Or not: "When servants drop and break something fragile, our minds do not immediately fly to some psychological explanation, but once again, it is not unlikely that hidden motives are involved. Nothing is further from an uneducated person's mind than an appreciation of art and works of art. Unspoken hostility towards artistic items prevails among the servant classes, particularly when the objects, whose value they do not understand, give them extra work to do." If the servants suffer from class resentment, Doktor Freud, maybe had it with the butler who had pushed a dirty rag across a recently acquired canvas. Such things kept happening in his abode, injuries to his collectibles, as though with a will; it was uncanny. Or not: "When servants drop and break something fragile, our minds do not immediately fly to some psychological explanation, but once again, it is not unlikely that hidden motives are involved. Nothing is further from an uneducated person's mind than an appreciation of art and works of art.

Unspoken hostility towards artistic items prevails among the servant classes, particularly when the objects, whose value they do not understand, give them extra work to do." If the servants suffer from class resentment, Doktor Freud, maybe it's because they've got to wipe your arts.

[119]

JAMES TADD ADCOX
Viola Is Sitting on the Examination Table

Viola is sitting on the examination table at the doctor's office in a green dress with an empire waist and sky-blue shoes. She is thinking about floating up through the ceiling of the doctor's office. She is thinking about passing through the clouds then coming to the edge of the earth's atmosphere and then continuing onward, past the rim of debris caught in earth's gravitational pull, past the meteors and the asteroids and so forth, she's not picturing the details too clearly now, past the moon and the earth-like planets, past the unearth-like planets, out of the solar system. Her husband Robert is holding her hand. This is their third miscarriage. Robert is wearing wrinkle-free grey slacks and a wrinkle-free white shirt. The doctor is telling them about how it is possible to have a healthy child even after multiple miscarriages.

Spontaneously abort is the term for what Viola's body does and has done with the pregnancies. There is not always an explanation for it, the doctor explains.

They are cursed, Viola thinks, Viola and Robert and the doctor, to repeat this scene over and over, like ghosts replaying the circumstances of their untimely deaths.

Viola and Robert have a fight in the parking lot of the doctor's office, except that it's not a fight, because Robert is being too reasonable. That's how Robert gets when he's upset: too reasonable. "It would make me feel a hell of a lot better if just for once you'd raise your voice," Viola says.

"I'm not going to raise my voice," says Robert.

Viola wants to go back inside and tell the doctor to get the damn thing out of her. "Then we should go back inside and talk with the doctor," Robert says. "We should discuss our options."

"It doesn't make any sense to have the doctor get it out of me," Viola says. "It's an unnecessary procedure and potentially damaging to my health."

"That's true," Robert says. "I mean, that may be true. The part about it being potentially damaging to your—"

"I don't have diabetes," Viola says. "I don't have heart disease, or kidney disease, or high blood pressure or lupus. My uterus contains neither too much nor too little amniotic acid. I don't have an imbalance of my progesterone nor a so-called incompetent cervix. I have had ultrasounds and sonograms and hysteroscopys and hysterosalpingographys and pelvic exams. I have eaten healthy. I have exercised. I have refrained from tobacco and alcohol and caffeine. I have taken folic acid and aspirin and—" Viola starts crying, standing there in the parking lot.

"You've done everything exactly right," Robert says.

"I *know* that," Viola says. "That is what I am trying to *tell* you."

News helicopters fly overhead. On the radio there's a story about another shooting downtown. Outside the car windows, rough parts of Indianapolis stream by.

Viola's aunt comes to visit.

"I'm not even sure I wanted a kid," Viola tells her aunt. "Robert, he definitely wanted a kid."

"You'd be a great parent," her aunt says.

"I'd be terrible. I'm pretty sure this is a sign. Like, I'd be watching a movie or just getting to the really good part of a book or something, and that's when the terrible thing would happen. The kid would find the matches or stick something in a socket or drown in the bathtub. This is God saying: Viola, honey, you and I both know that you'd let the poor thing drown in the bathtub."

Viola's aunt laughs, a great hacking laugh.

Viola and her aunt go and get drinks at a country-western themed bar in a strip mall near the actual mall. Viola still looks pregnant. The blond waitress who comes to their table looks at her belly, dubious. According to the doctor, Viola's body should expel the child naturally in several weeks. "I don't want to *expel the child naturally*," Viola says, slightly drunk. "I want it *out of me.*"

Several nearby patrons glance over. "My womb is become a grave," drunk Viola says, trying to be quieter.

"What?" says her aunt.

"*My womb is become a grave.*"

Viola's aunt, who never had kids of her own, helps Viola into the car.

"My womb is become a grave," Viola, still a little drunk, whispers to Robert in bed that night.

"Stop it," Robert says. "Your womb is become no such thing."

The next day Viola heroically cleans the bathroom.

Every night for a week after that Viola dreams about giving birth to her dead child. Or, it appears dead at first, but after a moment it coughs, rubs its eyes, and crawls from the doctor's hands up onto her belly.

"I thought you were dead," Viola says.

"Oh sure," says her son. "I *was*. But according to the ancient laws of pregnancy, after three times, *something* is born. You can't expect to give birth three times without *something* being born."

"I suppose not," Viola says. Sometimes, in the dream, she's back in North Carolina, on the coast, where she lived as a girl with her aunt and uncle, and everything around her has once more been flattened by Hurricane Diana. Other times she's walking through downtown Indianapolis late at night when the first contractions hit, and she gives birth surrounded by empty corporate towers and closed restaurants, terrified that something or someone will swoop down on her and steal her child before it has the chance to speak.

"I want to be kind towards you," Viola says to Robert. Robert is cutting up a tomato for a tomato sandwich. "Ultimately this is your loss, as well as mine. But I'm not sure if I have enough kindness right now to show towards both of us."

"I get that," Robert says. "That makes sense."

"In the future, I will probably be kinder," Viola says.

Robert and Viola eat the honestly somewhat disappointing tomato sandwiches that Robert fixed. The tomatoes were beautiful, but not delicious. Later, they drive to a home furnishings store.

"I'm pretty sure it's a sign," Viola says.

"What is?" says Robert.

Viola makes a gesture in the air that means, *you know*. "We both know I'd be a terrible mother," she says. "This is like God saying, Viola, honey, you and I both know you'd let the poor thing drown in a bathtub."

"I don't think that's funny," Robert says.

"Neither do I," says Viola.

In the home furnishings store Viola keeps wanting to buy things, even though they don't match anything else in the house. Someone, she isn't sure who, once told Viola about the woman who went into such shock after her miscarriage that she carried the baby around in a blanket for weeks, long after it had begun to decompose. Or maybe Viola just imagined someone told her that. Who knows where stories like that come from?

"It's possible that I may not be in love with you anymore," Viola says carefully, lying next to Robert that night. Robert is quiet in a way that makes Viola think that he maybe already knew.

"Do you want to stay married?" he says, finally.

Viola's body *naturally expels* the pregnancy. The doctor hands the strange blue child to Viola without asking if Viola wants to hold it. She cradles the strange blue child. She puts two fingers over its closed transparent eyelids. "I'm not very good at mourning," Viola says to the strange blue child. "I'm not sure how to mourn you. I've had dreams about you, but it wasn't like this." Robert stands beside her in the scrubs the hospital has given him. He can't figure out to do what his hands, whether he should be touching the strange blue child, or what. "Robert, it's okay," Viola says. "You can cry too. No one is going to feel strange about it. You're allowed."

They pass the strange blue child around the room. Robert kisses it. Viola's aunt kisses it. Viola's uncle kisses it. There are the sounds of the medical equipment operating. Viola takes the strange blue child from her uncle and kisses it.

KATY BOHINC

from *Dear Alain**

Let us add that contemporary philosophy addresses itself at all times to women. It might even be suspected that it is, as discourse, partly a strategy of seduction.

—Alain Badiou, "What is Love?"

Dear Alain,

There, got it, round two. multiplicity. said Badiou. you mother fucker stole my brain. except, you're wrong. still working in Euclid's plane. enlightenment is the real projective. where parallel lines meet at the horizon and a line is a circle. it's true that the abrahamic religions have a problem with historicity and crusades. somebody's always got to be right before and in order to get to God. buddha knows the line is really a circle at the horizon anyway, where we all should strive to dwell. the point, it's a line. the line, it's a circle. the circle, it's a flower. that point derrida collapsed in the derivatives market? don't worry about it. we'll fix it when we wake up. cat life number 27, ladybug reincarnate.

Dear Alain,

My new roommate Brandon is a found poem. I like it. When I think of all the things I don't have time to be nostalgic for I feel irresponsible. It

---

* DEAR ALAIN. LOVE LETTERS OF A POET TO A PHILOSOPHER. The process of differentiation that is love, approaching a truth. As played by the tension between philosopher (subject alpha) and the poet (subject omega). From another angle, Badiou's conditions on philosophy: Love, Politics, Math and Poetry imposed on him.

makes me care about the heart more than being smart. It is not that time is a mirage, but that it's a villain and I am consensually guilty of moving on. There's no grammar around that. Just hiding from the images that bring us most comfort.

We long for revolution, but I have been there and all that's fought for is the peace to enjoy the apple on the worn wood table. It's folksy to center the flowers in their vase, simple and symmetrical, but I'll still call it beautiful for my Ma. Do you mind?

Yours, Katy

Dear Alain,

I love you more than ever. You wrote that the Tunisian and Egyptian uprisings have a universal significance. They prescribe new possibilities whose value is international.

I could not agree more. When Mubarak finally stepped down, I was just headed from my office to lunch. I stepped outside to consider the importance of this revolution, this televised moment of history as important as, the paris commune or the french revolution or, or, as important as, Tahrir itself. Tahrir means To Freedom, literally, or, independence, as I'm sure you know. And as I stepped out outside on the street I began to sob. I really did. I was crying on the street and thought, perhaps you look a little silly on the street here, so I went to the bookstore where my friend Rod works. I cried more at the bookstore. All in all it took about two hours to exhaust myself of the tears and I am not sure anyone really understood- most people just think I'm overly emotional or maybe crazy- but I cried because I am not crazy and Egypt proves it. That moment when he left, when Mubarak left through peaceful means, through universal, peaceful spontaneous, beautiful power of the people, it's, it's every single person in the world who said "things can be better", it's every single person in the world who dared to say "torture is wrong", it's every single person who dared to dream, it's every single person who went to sleep with hope for a better future, it's every single ignorant fucking imbecile who only said "no" going to hell, it's everyone who called me crazy for hoping, for believing, for wanting more, it's to hell with them, and it was worth it, it was all worth it, it was true, it is possible, it was worth the sacrifice it is all worthwhile we can and the big words are worth a damn and I cried and cried and cried because all the idealism was true and all the blood and the bruises and the torture was losing, it wasn't structure anymore, it was a tall building made of electric fence for everyone to hail with bruises and scars and untouchables, that facade collapsed, and there was a sun to heal the scars, and the romance of poetry survives and this is why I cried: for all the pain of anyone who ever said "I guess that's how it has to be" because it didn't have to be that way the day that Mubarak left, it was singing and dancing in the street among all the people, it was the resounding ring of the subtle non-violent line, it was the rise out of silence of the truth, that magic of the white dove from the darkest, gentleman's top hat, the scar become the badge, the tear become the holy water, the transcendence, the moment where the best side of humanity came true, and everything we write for, everything we live for, everything we ever dared to believe was worth it all.

PS. It's parallel lines meeting at infinity. It's when Gauss looked at the horizon and said, but parallel lines do meet, they meet at the horizon. It's the dream of the platonic form lapping at the edge of the shore and the tide rushing over one last time to a blazing red dawn, the kind that makes you wake up and breathe as if for the first time and all those tones of sarcasm fade into some jellyfish dying on the sand and it's blindingly beautiful the stuff we always knew was there but just grew too cynical to care except maybe deep in the night we risked a word or two of "maybe" and "i hope" and "it still is" and "there is more" and we dreamed and we dreamed and we dreamed and it was the real projective plane and things do happen at infinity and i still believe in love and i'm getting on a plane because i believe that if the egyptians can then why not, we can have it too. i still believe. please tell me you do, too. I love you. Tell me these words mean something to you. Tell me. Bisous.

Dear Alain,

Alain, The problem ultimately is that to define anything is to take a position of power. Are you comfortable with your power? I hate power. I refuse to define. I refuse it. I refuse to be powerful, I refuse to make sense, I refuse I refuse. I refuse in protest. I'm a soft, silly, wild flower basket of love. All I see is your ego and I'm going to stuff a chalky powder comment in the cracks, because I hate power. My mission is to dissolve it. But of course, this is my deepest secret I reveal to you! My deepest secret because to name a mission is itself to have power – don't you see? I don't give a damn I forgive you always! What, rules? What rules? They're power. They're cultural sets for specific power layers, they're always false when turned over or meshed. Fuck them. You need something? You need to know you're important? You are. Does your power put things in jeopardy? Always. Do I forgive you? I don't even have a choice. I am a poet. I have no power. I have nothing. I am water. I know love. I give everything your psyche needs; I take nothing. No story, no moment of self, no words of self. Some babble if your ego needs. I give. You need. There is love. There is love. There is love.

Yours

PS Mallarme you would say. Sounds to stroke. No meaning. No power. And damn you, you're right. But honestly, you're wrong. Because you can go fuck
your power.

Dear Alain,

These letters are just shit. I'm only writing them because the literati will eat them. I know.
I know. But the truth is power. Is lines in the sand and you know the bloom doesn't come from lines. Political events cannot be quantified. You said it. Page 7, 32, 45, 66-69, 98-100, XYZ, Politics and Metaphysics. Definitions, blah blah blah. Who cares about categories when there's death by dehydration? The bloom Alain, I'm talking about the bloom!
Tais-Toi!

I'm going to melt you

PS it's more than form, it's more than Mallarme, it's underneath…

Dear Alain,
In your words then.
Shortly, K

The real characteristic of the poetic event and the truth procedure that it sets off is that a poetic event fixes the errancy and assigns a measure to the superpower of the intellect. It fixes the power of the intellect. Consequently, the poetic event interrupts the subjective errancy of the power of the intellect. It configures the state of the situation. It gives it a figure; it configures its power; it measures it.

Empirically, this means that whenever there is a genuinely poetic event, the Intellect reveals itself. It reveals its excess of power, its repressive dimension. But it also reveals a measure for this usually invisible excess. For it is essential to the normal functioning of the intellect that it's power remains measureless, errant, unassignable. The poetic event puts an end to all this by assigning a viable measure to the excessive power of the intellect.

Poetry put the Intellect at a distance, in the distance of its measure. The resignation that characterizes a time without poetry feeds on the fact that the Intellect is not at a distance, because the measure of its power is errant. People are held hostage by its unassignable errancy. Poetry is the interruption of this errancy. It exhibits a measure for intellectual power. This is the sense in which poetry is "freedom". The Intellect is in fact the measureless enslavement of the parts of the situation, an enslavement whose secret is precisely the errancy of the intellect, its absence of measure. Freedom here consists in putting the intellect at a distance through the collective establishment of a measure for its excess. And if the excess is measured, it is because the collective can measure up to it.

We will call it a poetic prescription for the post-eventual establishment of a fixed measure for the power of the intellect.

Excerpt Translated Conceptually from
Politics and Metaphysics
Alain Badiou

JOSEPH SCAPELLATO

James Monroe

James Monroe awoke alone in a bed without bedsheets. Again he'd dreamt of dark cannons lined across the land, their mouths as wide as harbors. The cannons had been breathing—their inhaling tugging at the heavens, their exhaling bending the horizon.

Though certain of being awake, alone, and in bed in President's House, James Monroe felt that his head was out of place, that it was no longer his. Heavy with dream, it seemed on loan from another century.

He sat up and touched his cheeks. He patted his ears and tapped his temples. This head felt less handsome, but more confident. Broader but not wiser.

Wider but not deeper?

He rose and walked to a window, which he opened with a groan. Outside, night bit its black lip to keep quiet.

Under the bed, Elizabeth Monroe, James Monroe's wife, pretended to be sleeping on the bedsheets she'd brought with her. With one eye half-open she watched her husband's feet take uncertain steps. She was as furious as she was terrified. She knew what others didn't: that what would be done would be done without anyone knowing anything about how to do it.

James Monroe opened his wardrobe and buttoned on his frockcoat. Frockcoats, no longer worn by Cabinet and Congress, were favored instead by ailing veterans, bewildered elderly gentlemen, and cheery beggars. In a frockcoat, James Monroe looked like how he felt: a handsome keepsake from a war that would be misremembered.

Dressed, he took his uncertain steps through hallways that creaked with fear of fire. His head wobbled as he walked, as if it what was in it sloshed. In his study he lit a lamp from a faraway land. The flame sizzled, smelling of fat and hair. Again he opened a window. Night, embarrassed, looked away with a breeze.

He cleared a space on his desk, setting aside the stacks of letters, laws, and executive orders. He sat. He took his head in both hands, whoever's or whatever's head it had become, and after securing a tight grip, smashed it down forehead-first.

It bounced back up, his again.

Dizzied, he stared at his desk: left behind from the impact was a puny shadow, as dark and shapeless as a tea stain.

He scooped up this puny shadow.

He kneaded this puny shadow into a mass.

He teased this mass into a shape, a shape as uncertain as the steps he'd taken through the fearful creaking hallways. Into this shape he jammed the stacks of letters, laws, and executive orders. Fed, this shape became a form: something like a man, something like a woman, something like a child. Only bigger in all ways.

Morning peeked in at the window. When it looked at the form, the form began to breathe—morning gasped and stumbled backwards, bumping into night.

The form had now become a Doctrine.

"Are you here?" said James Monroe.

The Doctrine sat up on the desk and said, "I am."

"I am pleased," said James Monroe, but he wasn't. He was crushed between pride and horror.

"I am not," said the Doctrine.

"Why is that?"

The Doctrine shook its enormous head.

James Monroe nodded cautiously.

The Doctrine shook its enormous head.

James Monroe nodded recklessly.

The Doctrine sat there.

James Monroe yawned. He whispered, "When you dream, what do you dream?"

"Other men and women's dreams."

"When you are awake, what do you see?"

The Doctrine looked west and east and north and south, all directions at once. That it saw itself was self-evident.

"When you see yourself, how do you appear?"

The Doctrine stood. Its enormous head annihilated the roof and its enormous arms annihilated the walls, and when it opened its enormous mouth, James Monroe fell asleep at his desk.

AIMEE PARKISON
Dirty-Dirty Short Shorts

1. The Turtle

We both pretend his dick is as hard as a rock. Even while he's obsessively masturbating like a patient in a mental hospital, his limp dick resembles a dead shell-less turtle with a broken neck. He asks me to lick his asshole while attempting to bring the dead turtle back to life. I spend night after night pretending the turtle isn't dead, that the turtle hasn't been dead for months. That's how I know I still love him, even when he whispers a stranger's name in sleep and for a moment the turtle looks like it might revive itself.

Our language is born of silence. It comes from the eyes of women and girls, as they stare at themselves in mirrors, long after we have given up trying to translate what their words might really mean. The language flows into the eyes of a man like me who sees himself in Richard's mirrors and does not recognize himself as a man, because he does not long to possess women but to become them. I dream of mastering men's turtles, of holding them, possessing them, bringing dead turtles back to life. For the next three hours, Richard masturbates intermittently, an interior-design magazine and trench coat on his lap while he tells me exactly how he will fuck me. The magazine keeps falling off the trench coat, which moves crazily like a cat trapped beneath fabric. Richard keeps running out of breath. I just sit on my bed, hands folded, listening in a quiet yet professional manner. Staring at pornographic photos, he says, "The lesbians will obey my every command." The turtle is still dead. Not even our imaginary lesbians can bring it back to life.

2. True Nakedness

I show him photos of three sex workers from Madrid. The beauty of it all is they know each other. They actually enjoy each other's company, so they won't be fucking for him, or for me. They'll be fucking for themselves. On the back of one of the photos, I read the inscription – *Take me . . . by surprise.* "Chameleon, Phoenix, and Lynx," I say, holding up the three images.

Chameleon, the brunette with green-brown eyes, lies spread-eagle over scratched hardwoods, her eyes staring into the camera. She has lovely eyes, dramatically arched brows, and pretty pale smooth feet with pointed toes like a dancer. She's smooth and toned, her long dark hair like silk. Phoenix, the redhead, is captured in a sunlit pool of brilliant blue water, her bright hair floating weightlessly around arms and breasts and belly. Her nipples are pink, sparkling in the sun. She's pouting at the camera like the child she is, her brilliant eyes matching the blue water, slender fingers splayed beneath tiny breasts. The blond Lynx is the final image, an exquisite woman on all fours, her rump high in the air and pointed at the camera so that anyone can stare into her asshole and her eyes at the same time. The silken refinement, waves of glistening stands flow across face and body as she turns, sweeping from feet to legs to chest to groin to belly to chest, and then to what I fear is the true nakedness—my expression. Masturbating constantly, a man might come beneath the shadow of her hair so she could mop up the semen with luxurious strands. The blond and the redhead watch—waiting, approving— no words, no sound but breath.

3. Imaginary Rebecca

I remind him of his first Rebecca, the woman who taught him what love was. I'm in another world, and he's making love to me like I'm a woman, telling me more of the things he has done to Rebecca.

"I love you," he says.

Fuck my face, Rebecca said to Richard. *I want you to fuck my face.*

No, he said. *I want you to fuck my face. I want you to ride my face.*

This isn't going to work, she said. *I don't want your tongue in my pussy any more than I want it in my mouth.*

Maybe I'm not as good as Rebecca. She never knew what submission was. That's why he wanted her.

After getting dressed, we go back to Richard's apartment, again, where he shows me how he wants the dream women arranged in his bedroom, how he wants the imaginary Rebecca positioned before his giant mirrors.

Removing my clothes, he turns me upside down and into the imaginary Rebecca by bending me so that my ass is high in the air like in the photo.

"Rebecca," Richard says. "Oh, my sweet."

He rides me like a demon on a bike.

Afterwards, I'm so tired I sleep without dreaming, waking when he takes my face in his hands, smears transparent pink gloss on my lips, and kisses me like a lover would.

MARISA CRAWFORD

from *8th Grade Hippie Chic*

illustration by Forsyth Harmon

I am inspired by the hippie movement. The women at Haight and Ashbury with flowers in their hair and psychedelic swirls in their eyes and in their hearts. I am inspired by them. When I think about them, I feel a deep and pulling poetic excitement that makes me miss you and makes me want to buy magazines and light candles and get smarter and smarter. Wash my hair with mayonnaise, cover myself with bells and shells and perfectly fitting jeans with holes in the knees. Bare feet on the cleanest pile of dirt and a seriously sad smile. When I think about them, I want to wear enormous feather earrings, but only if the feathers were found lying in the dirt like a gift from the animal kingdom and from the earth and from the spinning, dizzying heavens.

Like nothing is authentic and also nothing is original. That when I do your makeup it is like when I do my own makeup. And when I dye my hair to look exactly like T's ex-best friend in her picture in the yearbook it is a seamless and perfect process, and I smooth the ends into crescent points with light, foamy pomade that smells like marshmallows.

I put a lock of your 8th-grade hair into the pill box that you bought me in Spain. And I put in little wooden beads with vintage flowers painted on them, from my pious Catholic hippie phase when I used to braid my hair at Sunday school and wear Grateful Dead t-shirts woven from strips of grass and sky and a silver cross around my neck that was filled with carefully arranged dried flowers.

You cut off your dreadlocks and stuffed them in a plastic bag. You passed your driving test with flying colors. That if I think about it long enough and hard enough I should be able to feel the earth vibrating in me. But I can't focus 'cause the radio keeps on playing all my favorite songs.

JOANNA RUOCCO

from Another Governess

1.

My hair is altogether changed. My face is altogether changed. I am very slim. The dress hangs on me. It slides from my shoulder and the cloth is newly stained. A button dangles. I must repair the button. There is a needle in the nursery. Somewhere there is a needle. I will use it to repair the button. There are children in the nursery. The grunting is the children, the sounds of the children. The children are grunting over the tray of cakes. On the iron table, a big tray of cakes, little cakes, dripping cakes. There are two children grunting over the big tray of cakes. They are on their knees by the cakes. The girl has reddish eyelids and nostrils. The boy is swollen, with dirty skin. Tamworth and Old Spot. I will call them Tamworth and Old Spot. The boy is nearly a man. Spot is a man. The children are grown. They are not children. They are on their knees. That is why they look so small. No one has noticed they are grown because they eat on their knees. Get up, I say to the children. Get up. Get up. The children grunt. Crumbs stick to their cheeks. They move closer to the tray. There are more cakes on the tray. There are more cakes for the children to eat. Get up, I say. Get up. Get up. I clap my hands. The children look up. They stare. Crumbs drop from their mouths. Fluids drip down their chins. They stare. I stand above them in the nursery so they know me even if they do not know my face.

2.

I walk in a small circle on the carpet. Fluids have marked the carpet. I walk in small circles. There is a table in the nursery. There are two chairs. There is a rocking horse. The paint has chipped from the legs of the rocking horse and the tail is ragged, falling short of the fetlocks. Something has chewed the legs, chewed the tail of the rocking horse. Nits fly from the eggs in the gapped mane of the rocking horse. Nits swarm above the crib. I walk to the crib. It is iron. I walk to the rocking horse. Ride on your rocking horse, I say to Spot, but he is too big for the rocking horse. His legs will bend at the knee, his feet on the carpet. He does not ride the rocking horse. There must be another child, a small child, under the linens in the crib. I walk to the window. I look down at the moat. There is a dirty white skin of mist on the moat. Beyond the moat the orchard thickens into the forest. The orchard is filled with pigs. The pigs are shoulder to shoulder, feeding in the orchard. The apples are soft and brown. They are dropping from the trees. They are rotting in the grass. The pigs are slipping in the thick brown flesh of the apples, the broken flesh of the apples. The brown skins of the apples hang in flaps from their bellies. The pigs nip at each other, squealing. The pigs are eating through the apples to the soil. They are eating through the soil. A pig drags a root from the soil, a pale streaked root, long and stiff, tapered to a white hook. The pig is eating the white root and the root is moistening, blackening with fluids. I croon to the pigs. The pigs must think that they smell me beneath the soil, but I am behind the glass in the high window. I am high above the orchard. I will not go back there anymore. I have misted the window with my breath.

3.

Open your books, I say. The children certainly have books. The nursery is filled with books. I see books on the desks by bottles of black fluid and I see books on the carpet. The crib is filled with books. There are no books on the table. On the table, there are cakes. The children wait by the cakes, on their knees by the cakes. It is not time for cakes. It is time for books. First, in the nursery, cakes. Then books. It is time for books. Not all little children have books. Tamworth and Spot must love their books. There is much to learn in their books. There are no books in the forest. I went to the forest. There were roots, there were rocks, there were leaves. There was mud. I fell in the mud. I slid in the leaves. I crawled over rocks. I lay in a field. I cut a lump on my foot and a worm came out. It was a very black worm. I dried my foot in the sun. There was a hole in the lump in my foot, and the hole leaked yellow fluid. I pulled dark strings from the hole with my fingernails. Pinched between my fingernails, the dark strings did not wiggle. I thought they were worms, but they did not wiggle. They were not worms. I rolled them hard between my fingers. They did not smear. They remained tiny dark strings. They were moist and they left no color on my skin. They were something, not worms or blood, a third thing that worms and blood made together in the lump on my foot. I hobbled to the low stonewall. I lay on top of the low stonewall. I thought about the dark strings in the lump on my foot. They were moving up my legs. I felt them behind my knees. They dammed and swelled in the crook of my arm, under my lower eyelids, curling around and around. I wrapped my foot with canvas that crusted with the yellow fluid. My foot smelled in its canvas wrapper. The farmer held me close then pushed me away. What is that smell? said the farmer. His face was pink, with white hairs, and his mouth was a ragged wet hole like the hole in my foot. My foot, I said, because I knew what smell the farmer meant. Open your foot, I say to the children. I laugh. The children have not noticed that I limp, that I drag myself across the carpet in circles, as though I fall, but every time I fall, I catch myself, I keep moving.

4.

The baker had a daughter. The baker's daughter worked in the bakery. She cut the gray cakes of yeast. She mixed yeast and water for the baker. Her fingers were wrinkled with moisture and they gave off a sour odor. The nails had come loose in the fingerbeds. The skin that seals the nails in the fingerbeds was too soft to hold the nails in place. One day a man cut a loaf of bread and he found a string of hair. The string of hair passed lengthwise through the bread from end to end. The baker cut the hairs from the daughter's head. One day a man cut a loaf of bread and he found ten fingernails in the center of the loaf of bread. The baker cut the daughter's fingers at the first knuckles. One day a man cut a loaf of bread and he found the key to the bakery. The man did not tell the baker. The man came in the night to the bakery where the baker's daughter waited. The baker's daughter showed the man the sack of coins the baker hid beneath the floorboard and the man lifted out the sack of coins. He lifted the skirts around the waist of the baker's daughter and felt with his fingers beneath the skirt. His fingernails were ragged and the baker's daughter cried out so that the man put his forearm across her mouth. The baker's daughter did not cry out again. The baker was upstairs sleeping in his narrow bed. The man dropped one of the baker's coins on the floor for the baker's daughter. The next day a man cut a loaf of bread and he found a coin in the heel of the bread. The baker crushed his daughter's skull with the whetting stone. He put her beneath the floorboard in a sack.

JOHANNES HELDÉN
Elect

A quote fades into view, written in white on the black screen

It's not safe out here. It's wondrous.

It disappears, and a poem materializes

They follow us   but not in dreams. Wandering flashes
distant lights   for the first time,   real terror
                             the flock of birds

Moves towards the darkness.
The distant lights.

After a few seconds the text fades away, black is replaced by grey, the fog shifts to reveal a lone tree. A flock of birds scatters from the branches, a quiet droning sound is slowly building—like wind rushing through a subterranean system, like machines far away.

As you try to catch the birds, they evade the pointer. You chase them across the screen, across the sky, and by doing so you trigger text animations in a random order: fragments of prose surfacing in the darkness below the fog, islands of light. As you manage to click on the birds and catch them, one after the other, they disappear, and the blurred text in the sky is brought into focus, into clarity.

Elect is about how we search for patterns in nature, patterns in existence, about language being the hypersystem we use to structure reality. The form and materiality of the piece mirrors this overall thematic, focusing on the subjective experience of *reading* and—in the end—*reality* as filtered by the subject / our individual consciousnesses / our range of sentient vision. The materiality of the digital work merges with the concept of nature and future, a mix of science and fiction. An ongoing exploration with an ever-changing narrative arc. Variations within a set of slowly changing constants.

And the flock of birds scatters, like quantum particles, when you open your eyes.

Trees are built of signs.

all previously seen or mentioned,

1 2 3 4 5 6 7 8 9 10 11 12 13 14 15 16 17 18 19 20 21 22 23 24 25 26 27 28 29 30 31 32 33 34 35 36 37 38 39 40 41 42 43 44 45 46 47 48 49 50 ✳

Trees are built of signs.

the rain crashed down over the area and covered the asphalt.
It has mutated with all the bodies

the tattered clouds that
rolled in high above the forest,

all previously seen or mentioned,

everything exists forever

1 2 3 4 5 6 7 8 9 10 11 12 13 14 15 16 17 18 19 20 21 22 23 24 25 26 27 28 29 30 31 32 33 34 35 36 37 38 39 40 41 42 43 44 45 46 47 48 49 50 ✳

it enters my apartment
The crackle of the turntable,   rust on the saw blade,
bug in the shoe.   Trees are built of signs.

the rain crashed down over the area and covered the asphalt. Tiny fields of turbulence broke away at irregular intervals.
It has mutated with all the bodies   won't hold melodies, because it does.
more of them than you could count: are glimpses of

the tattered clouds that
rolled in high above the forest,

It grows fast now, winds around his legs, tears him down,
strangles him. Watch a pale yellow sun rise, a supernova explode, and

and he falls, sinking into the ground
all previously seen or mentioned,

a gray glow
everything exists forever

and stumbles   out into the tall grass

1 2 3 4 5 6 7 8 9 10 11 12 13 14 15 16 17 18 19 20 21 22 23 24 25 26 27 28 29 30 31 32 33 34 35 36 37 38 39 40 41 42 43 44 45 46 47 48 49 50   ✳

a light, a burned image: Now, it enters my apartment   and it
scares me senseless, but I don't turn around.   it is impossible to find the way back. The crackle of the turntable,   rust on the saw blade,
bug in the shoe. The branches over the tin roof, over the platform. The clouds are motionless. Trees are built of signs. The locust lets go, the graph of time is soft, leaves of grass rise.
The floor gives way, in every instance.
the rain crashed down over the area and covered the asphalt. Tiny fields of turbulence broke away at irregular intervals. The grass contained the warmth and the light one hour after
sundown. It has mutated with all the bodies   below.   Like believing static won't hold melodies, because it does.
more of them than you could count: are glimpses of   the bird alphabet above the field,

And flee when we try to approach

the tattered clouds that
rolled in high above the forest,

exit wound:
It grows fast now, winds around his legs, tears him down,
strangles him. Watch a pale yellow sun rise, a supernova explode, and
the pupil expands
and he falls, sinking into the ground
all previously seen or mentioned,

a gray glow
everything exists forever

and stumbles   out into the tall grass

1 2 3 4 5 6 7 8 9 10 11 12 13 14 15 16 17 18 19 20 21 22 23 24 25 26 27 28 29 30 31 32 33 34 35 36 37 38 39 40 41 42 43 44 45 46 47 48 49 50   ✳

The alphabet is an instruction, every movement leaves a shade, a light, a burned image: Now, it enters my apartment and moves towards me. I see it in the corner of my eye and it
scares me senseless, but I don't turn around. When all is revealed it is impossible to find the way back. The crackle of the turntable, the stain on the carpet, rust on the saw blade,
bug in the shoe. The branches over the tin roof, over the platform. The clouds are motionless. Trees are built of signs. The locust lets go, the graph of time is soft, leaves of grass rise.
It exists in words as the only way they can have meaning. The floor gives way, in every instance. They accelerated in the dark and turned off the high beam. The roadside disappeared,
the rain crashed down over the area and covered the asphalt. Tiny fields of turbulence broke away at irregular intervals. The grass contained the warmth and the light one hour after
sundown. It has mutated with all the bodies buried shallowly below. Transforms into reeds. Has it returned at last. Like believing static won't hold melodies, because it does.
They are there, more of them than you could count: the sum of what we see are glimpses of another reality. There also, everything burns, there also the bird alphabet above the field,
the lights.

JOHANNES HELDÉN | 267

ELLA LONGPRE

Hotel Problem

The hotel stood at the center of what used to be the town. Six families stayed there.

The first family had been wealthy, though obviously they were not wealthy now. Still, the third family had not been wealthy before, and the distrust between these two families was great. Especially between the mothers.

The second family was smaller than the third, though larger than the fourth. The fourth family was ridiculed for its pride. The fourth family, though, was clever. The third family had too many needs. The fifth family was very happy, and the sixth had been very happy before.

That year the daffodils came up in February.

By that time, even after passing a winter together, the families still did not often interact, though the children did sneak around the building at night and in the afternoons. They were the ones who came up with the number system: the family that stayed in room number One was called the first family, the second family stayed in room number Two, and so on, simple enough that the adults caught on quickly and referred to each other in private as such. For instance, the wife from the sixth family was referred to as the sixth wife, though there were not six wives living in the hotel.

Though the fourth family cautioned against it, the sixth family left soon after the early fall. The sixth husband was injured, and the sixth wife was sure there would still be medical supplies and doctors at the hospital a few towns over. It was fifty miles. She used one of the food trucks from the hotel kitchen to push him down the drive and left in the early morning.

The daffodils wilted early on. There were no more rains. The fathers from the third and fifth families had taken on the duty of venturing outside the hotel for food. One day they came back without any wild animals. The woman from the fourth family then began to go out alone and brought back edible plants. The traps she set, though, remained empty, and she gave the third and fifth fathers credit that she had, until then, withheld.

At this point, the second family decided to leave also. The second mother gathered a good portion of the remaining food supply and plenty of linens, packed them in a housekeeping cart, laid her infant on top, and set out in the middle of the night with a dream to meet the sixth family at the hospital.

The children began to meet regularly in the hallway at night to tell fortunes and eat papers from the big register behind the front desk. One night the first teenager was telling a ghost story when a door opened. The children gasped (there weren't shrieks left, at this point), until they saw that it was the door to room number Four. When the woman walked out of the room, bleary-eyed, the two girls from the third family ran to her and hugged her legs. She saw the toddler from the third family chewing on a post-it note and shook her head.

The other adults awoke not long after to the sound of cracking wood. They came out into the hallway and saw the children huddled together and laughing, chewing on basil leaves. The loud cracking was coming from the lounge. The woman from the fourth family had taken an axe from the fire emergency box and was chopping up one of the desks in the lounge. The adults from the other families ushered their children back to their rooms and double-locked their doors.

An hour later, the children were in the lounge, quietly helping the woman peel the thick white plastic skin from the pieces of the particle board desk. The two teenage boys from the first family had been given knives for the task. The third toddler was sitting on an ottoman in the corner, wearing the goggles the woman had worn to chop up the desk.

The other adults were awoken again, this time to a familiar smell they couldn't name. They met each other in the hall. The third wife began frantically looking for the missing children, imagining them chopped up in the lounge. The fifth father found them in the kitchen, with the woman from the fourth family who'd just been chopping the desk to pieces. The children stood over the stove while the woman stirred the pot, the toddler on her hip. Waste baskets full of particle board sat on the kitchen floor. The parents pulled their children away from the stove and looked in the pot.

The woman was boiling the particle board, and had added basil leaves. The basil plant was the only kitchen herb that had survived. The fourth woman had hidden it in her room. She was watering it secretly with part of her own water share, from the supply they stockpiled between the jugs in the pantry and what they caught in a bin during the rains. The mother from the first family wondered if she had watered it also with tears. As the sun came up that day, the families feasted on the broth the woman had made.

By March, the two daughters from the third family began fainting during the day. The adults assumed it was due to malnourishment until one of the girls spiked a fever one night. The third family soon after decided to also leave for the hospital.

The mother and the two sons from the first family got fevers the next day.

The fourth family seemed immune.

Slowly, the fifth family began to show symptoms—the father first, then the other father, then the daughter. The second fifth father died early one morning, in the front hall, crawling toward the door.

Soon after this, all that was left was the fourth family, and she was very lonely.

Answer Key

1st family: 3 people (mother, two teenage boys)

2nd family: 2 people (mother, infant)

3rd family: 5 people (2 parents, 2 children, 1 toddler)

4th family: 1 person (she)

5th family: 3 people (father, father, daughter)

6th family: 2 people (couple)

TED PELTON
Columbine

Woodchuck stood up in a field in the sun on a spring day.

By a tree at the end of a stone wall sat a human boy with his gun who might or might not have been a good shot.

Woodchuck remained still.

It would take some skill to hit the brown animal at such distance and the boy knew hunting safety knew not to risk a bad shot knew not to trust the safety switch on his gun that remained switched on to prevent accidental release.

The boy it was plain to see was bored.

He raised and aimed his gun and put it down again.

He looked up at clouds.

They always said of him at home that he walked around with his head in the sky.

He pointed the gun at Woodchuck and Woodchuck remained still and then the boy again took down the gun.

This stayed the indifferent pattern of an hour or two until the boy instead of aiming the gun out at Woodchuck began to point at himself.

The boy switched the safety on and off and stood the gun on the ground then took it away and aimed it again at Woodchuck and now this was the new and still indifferent pattern for a while.

The boy felt the bead sight on the end of the gun press the back of his teeth and Woodchuck at this point might have whistled but it was over fast when the boy blew his own head off.

This televised drama was broadcast live.

Woodchuck never once that day hid and the people in their holes watching dim-lit screens cheered his courage but then gasped at the unexpected finale when the boy's head burst spraying red gore on the trees and stone walls and a moment later a loud crack bounced against the facing mountain and back then across and down the valley his body slumping off the rock.

The stillness of the hero Woodchuck and of the entire afternoon was remarked upon again and again and the replay shown Woodchuck never directly regarding his would-be assailant but glancing side-long going about his business with no attempt to hide from the April sun and then the scene resolving as always ahead of time known the burst and the gore and the remembered gasps.

The people saw how Woodchuck went then over across the field to the corpse and sniffed and tears welled in all their eyes at his nobility at his sadness in mourning one not fit for the contest whose life it had cost.

But after all said the people shaking their heads the humans brought it on themselves.

It was not Woodchuck who asked for it.

The boy's true family saw none of these replays but had more grief than could be borne.

They wondered what secrets had made him act so horribly what pain must have plagued him for so long a long time.

Had it been just the whim of a moment of a boy whose head was always in the clouds and might do anything?

What was to be done with that?

All was emptiness and the ache it left behind.

His father who had never reached any pinnacle in life but worked hard and formerly enjoyed family life and an occasional laugh with friends turned now deep inside himself and could never stop self-accusing for the slights and injuries he felt he'd done his son which must have festered until that spring day in the field.

The boy's mother divorced the father whose sullen accusing looks she could no longer stand and took a role in a church living the rest of her life trying to do good things for people.

She was alone now too because the son who had died was her favorite and this was all too well known by the brother and sister who didn't kill themselves.

They resented what the boy their older brother did not just to himself but to them putting that thought in their own minds daily.

It was too much and they hated him even as they wept.

Only in later years did they feel full sorrow for their older sibling who soon became younger than they were and never became an adult never learned to solve whatever problems had made him do what he did.

To an extent everyone felt that way that what had happened what the boy had done had rashly made something that would have been temporary into something permanent.

The intemperance of a teenager was given too much effect by this thing his act.

He had not been a sad boy.

Maybe it had just been some silly thing about a girl or about there being no girl.

Finally at long last the boy became a symbol in stories passed down of what not to do.

But somehow no one knew or thought or was permitted to think in the land where this happened about whose idea it had been that he carry a gun into a field and sit alone with it all day whose story that had been.

Many years later at the edge the same field now dotted with columbine a flower that grows wild with narrow drooping yellow and lavender petals Woodchuck was playing with one of his young sons.

Woodchuck tugged at the little guy's fur.

My hair always grows Daddy said his son My hair always grows.

Woodchuck was suddenly struck by the memory of the lonely boy from years before.

A pigeon passing by at that moment fluttered down and spoke to them.

These flowers were named after me said the pigeon.

My name in Latin is Columba.

Come over here and I'll show you.

In a flutter of feathers the pigeon flew out into the field and Woodchuck and his son romped over through the tall green spring grass and beautiful mournful flowers.

Woodchuck and his son lost sight of him a moment until the pigeon flushed up out the grass to hold himself at their eye level his claws clenched in the grass bearing his weight.

Here said the pigeon to the father and son See my claws.

See that they are strong and slender like spurs.

The columbine flower is shaped and pointed downward like my claw.

It was true as far as Woodchuck and his son could see the field around them dotted with colorful pigeon claws.

Gotta go said the pigeon Busy day and he flew off.

All of a sudden Woodchuck was alarmed that they were out in the middle of a field exposed.

He hunched over his son and covered him as they walked low through the grass to a shadier spot where an old tree met a stone wall.

Daddy said Woodchuck's son but Woodchuck terrified kept him quiet muffling the sounds with his body.

At length they arrived where they had started before seeing the pigeon a spot more secluded and hidden.

My hair said Woodchuck's son when they got there and he got out from underneath Woodchuck My hair always grows.

It's growing right now!

His son paused for a moment then remembered something.

He shouted it out Hair keeps growing after you die!

FARID MATUK

from *My Daughter La Chola*

Pantertanter

Abdul from Kenya is real
we'll make a fire tomorrow how many names could they have
the eye-beaters blind kids Dickey used
you want to defend them from his program
some tea and the adults would just watch the kids
in Saudi we rented two fields they could play soccer
in humanface you ask my son would he rather live in Kenya or Plano he says Saudi
mom would have been Rose my aunt would have been Dorothy
full nose Buick vinyl clip-ons pastels womanface
Abdul wants to make community I say of course let me tell you
I'd have done drugs less had my mom and aunt gone
to their water like fishes who don't care
the kids punched their little fists right into their eyes to flash
a light against the walls of their brains Dickey wanting you prime
to see you and the credit cards in your wallet
when you visited the nerve of the poem trying to be your blindface
I would have been Blanche the slutty one we'll make a fire tomorrow
you see if you just write what you know you won't use anybody
is power qua power the Kenyans in Plano will go to the Mosque
everybody is one in prayers but they won't make the effort to make the image
at least my son bikes there in three minutes
since they opened the basketball court I know he's safe
Rose of Saint Olaf knows to gather here where we are now
once a week so the kids wouldn't
listen to Prince and believe sex is a techne for exceeding oneself
in Plano everyone is too just themselves you make plans you call that day
say hey we're coming your way they say no image flash
so bad they'd take the hurt tough truths to give your readers too bad art must be terrible
or beautiful but never cute Dorothy said she got used to this country we need to
be Kenyan together but everyone is always alone just themselves in their house
it was Blanche's house had they not arrived there had they not needed one another
the market swirled the night above the lanai to dissolve the stars
the kids beat their eyes to deal you want to protect their dignity always
increased or preserved by a good poem one uses
but everyone is always alone just themselves in their house Abdul
you find the image you need everything here is stolen

Shake the Bear Funny Name

my daughter Rodolfo Silvas on my chest

my daughter Tiburcio Vasquez

my daughter vignette

my daughter archive erasure

my daughter plein air

my daughter durable good durable history
my daughter over the throwing

my daughter blacken the hills

my daughter high and tight
my daughter reservoir of poses

my daughter good foot

my daughter greaser horse thief
my daughter albumen print

my daughter gelatin silver print preformatted postcard paper

my daughter pretty blurry pink mouth
my daughter handle their guns

my daughter commercial surf pop echo

my daughter shout pouch
my daughter rendered by or under the inspection of

my daughter mestizo castizo coyote lobo versino

my daughter waste not want

my daughter region of objects

my daughter plate 12

                      my daughter sell the shadow
                      my daughter caddisflies

my daughter unblushing

                      my daughter watching street lights

my daughter turn away the night

                      my daughter her sex

my daughter her fumbling

                      my daughter mission

my daughter delay the form

                      my daughter courtesy of

my daughter shake the bear

                      my daughter all the barbells in the air

my daughter the empty highways

                      my daughter the farms to market

my daughter under my chin
my daughter carte de visite

                      my daughter funny name
                      my daughter 30,000 foot view

my daughter panorama nostalgia ghost

                      my daughter mineral depression

my daughter vitamin free

                      my daughter crystal mane

my daughter amber leaf light

                      my daughter hole within the hole
                      my daughter twelve-sail cruiser

My Daughter La Chola Martina

posse come back proud to flashing eyes of señoritas they say little lady lords
out west practitioners full of old commercial surf pop echo
or land out west don't work for projection   seas awesome trees
in the wind archive wants the voice-over   the sun ghost   Los Angeles a clean
way to hug the young ocean salt air ghosts the cool

expanse of the hour ahead we'd try not to show our eyes until they passed
bright white light these days of baby's coming yeah speech act better than a day
searching eyes can interrupt at least she's in it that's the success
trees shake over brothers or sister trees shadow pools for bird traffic the record doesn't say

Sheriff Barton's posse was a white as cute eye shadow as a model plane
they seem to take to the quiet depth so well dead cuz La Chola mishandled their guns
readily shroud the quiet record makes a truth and beauty kinsmen
go down nattering stir the sea moon   little one   our water

"Pantertanter" borrows lines from James Dickey's "Eye-Beaters," Alan Dugan's "Speech
To the Student Clowns at the Circus Clown School at Sarasota, Florida," and D.H.
Lawrence's "For the Heroes Are Dipped in Scarlet." Pantertanter was the Swedish
name for the television series *The Golden Girls*. It means Panther Ladies.

"My Daughter La Chola Martina" references Ken Gonzalez-Day's *Lynching in the West:
1850–1935* (Duke). "La Chola Martina" was the derogatory alias bestowed on Mar-
tina Espinoza, a woman believed to be an acquaintance of the bandit Juan Flores. In
1857 Flores and his men killed Sheriff Barton and most of his posse in the countryside
outside Los Angeles. Martina Espinoza was rumored to have tampered with the Barton
posse's guns. This accusation fueled the wave of retaliatory lynching and murders tar-
geting Hispanic men.

ALAKE PILGRIM
Blue Crabs

8. Killing Crabs

Uncle licks his knife under their backs, a gentle slide, jerks up with that same hand (the other holds them down). I hear the *Krak*! I see the blue-black ink flood down their flinching legs like oil on the stone jukking board. Grey ridges cry black tears into the bottom of the sink, flecks of white flesh fly up, the smell a mix of earth, saltwater, blood. I am afraid. Their many-jointed legs still fight against the tethers of green string. Something alive still animates their limbs and whispers: Strike and pinch. They bleed black until he washes them out, white flesh encased in bones, flat and curved shells joined together at the weakest spots. He breaks their bodies open, scrapes the spiky hairs from their legs.

If one is already still, curled up, we do not eat it. I'm not sure why— something about poison, a kamikaze death, the last revenge of crabs.

Sometimes I urge him on, jump up and down, squeal in terrified delight, *Kill them, uncle! Kill them!* Or in a whisper, no less loud, *Uncle, kill them. Kill them now.* Sometimes silence falls and a grassy breeze picks up the call of a lone semp crying for her loved one who just died.

Did I see a bright sliver of regret in his eyes? Or was it just excitement for the cook that he would make—curry coating the slippery taste of my remorse.

24. Tobago Love

We are in his studio high above the bay. His masks devour the walls. His statues wait for me. I turn around, they're always there, eyeless, bigbreasted, longtongued.

We go out again to dinner, his new favorite spot. "Here's my card," he tells the chef-owner when she comes out. They discuss the crab soufflé, Frankfurt, fish broth in Bacolet at dusk. Her hands are small but tough. The blue veins in her temples pulse when he makes her laugh. Loneliness nibbles at the corners of her lips while I listen to the surf break and picture flying just above the sea's dark face, the *shwwwwww* of the wind, the mist of spray.

That night he reaches for me as I search for sleep. I squirm away. He laughs, gets out of bed. The next day I wake up to an ashy aftertaste, more laughter. The downstairs neighbor has come up for their morning smoke. She throws a grin my way. "I hear you paint." They watch me as I hem and haw. "It's been months," I whisper. I don't know why.

A knowing look, she turns away. I hear a giggle, "new protégé," and then she's gone. "I'm making breakfast," he declares, not leaving room for silence. I am thinking of how to ask him. Then I smell them in the sink. They are dead, de-haired, cracked open. I feel the heave surge up before I get away.

That night he's holding me when his cell phone rings. He jumps up, turns it off right away. A pause. I wait. "Love, I have to get back to Trinidad tomorrow to do some work. You can stay. Try to paint. I'll be back in a few days." I say nothing.

"And it's time for you to get over this thing with crabs," a whisper now, knotting his fingers into the roots of my hair. I start to shake. "You're such a child," he says, cradles my face and covers it with slow kisses.

11. Dance doux doux dance

Black skin shivers in the moonlit rain. He pants, "Dance doux doux dance." Spin me stories from under your little dress, from your trembling insides, spin me stories of skirts flying up like wings. Sing for me. *Sing a song of six pence a pocket full of rye, four and twenty black birds baked in pie. When the pie was opened the birds began to sing. Wasn't that a dainty dish to set before the king?*

He catches me while I am sleeping, the wolf. I could not stay awake. He grabs me up in his red red mouth, takes me outside in the rain, to the far end of the yard where no one is listening. I try to dream myself back to sleep, keep my eyes closed to the pain. But he bites down hard. Sing, he tells me. Sing. Sing sixpence while we dance. I feel sick. I cannot remember the song. I cannot remember my name.

"I'm your uncle," he said when he first saw me, his brother's only child. At the funeral everyone stared at him, standing there still as stone, looking down into the hole where my parents had gone. I heard Miss Iva whisper to Miss Elaine, "He loved her too you know." I thought they meant me. But that was strange. He had never visited us before. He just appeared before the funeral and said, "You're my niece. Now your father gone, I will take care of you."

And he did, until something in him grew wild, started watching me from the corners of his eyes, throwing itself against the bars of his mind. "You turnin' more like her every day," he cried, and the rage would boil up in his face like oil, disfigure him. That thing ate my uncle alive. Night after night I could hear it in the room next to mine, snarling and coughing up tears.

Now all of life tastes like the sweat on his lips. He sucks on my eyes when they ask him why - says he will squeeze them out. I scream inside. But no one is listening. Tomorrow morning when the neighbors come to take me to Sunday School, he will pretend that it is all okay. But I know what waits for me inside his smile.

So every night now I sleep up in the pommerac tree, hiding from the moon, praying against rain. I hide and wait: a small body full of darkness, who still dreams of flying away with the sun.

24. The Painting

We met one night at an exhibition, in a gallery made as cold as a freezer, sealed off from the punch-man, rumshop limes, doubles stands and stray dogs just a few streets away in St. James. The evening was all *shoo-shoo* and half-empty wine glasses, and hardly anyone really looked at the art. I stood in a corner pretending to study a painting, the first one I'd ever done—a *lagahoo*, shape-shifter, half wolf half man, red-toothed, clawed and grinning.

When I couldn't take it anymore, I turned around, and there he was, walking toward me across the humming floor.

I learned later that he made love to her on the bed, changed the sheets, but did not move my overnight bag from behind the curtains. She kissed his nipples and behind his ears. He groaned. He whispered her name. He tasted her silky brown skin and thick black hair. He released her soft breasts from their satin bra. He put them in his mouth. She tasted like sea salt. She tasted like hot peppers and sweat. Years later and she's still a guest in his home in Trinidad. A visitor. Whenever she asked if she should bring more clothes, spend more than one night, he never told her "Yes." He never told her "No." With him, it was always "Tomorrow," and she believed him, ate quarter truths. "I am your bright muse," she emailed him once. He never told her otherwise. He never did tell her about the others.

This is what I learned too late. His habit of eating different women begins with a hunger and a gift. The hunger: a spirit that cannot keep still, a whirlwind trying to shake off its loneliness. The gift is more than his quick laughter, more than the power to make each woman feel special, like she is the only one. His gift is the sight. He can see into women's hearts through their eyes, become what they think they want. He feeds them with hope. This is how he makes sure that he will never again be left alone by death, or any goodbye.

At first he is shocked by how easily their limbs bend open wide, how their eyes grow limp as they clasp him between their thighs. It frightens him at first, but then he likes it—the smash, the salty aftertaste. Their cries become a thrill. They want the same thing, he tells himself. After all, they are the ones drawn to the smell of danger rising off his skin, drawn by the red glint behind his eyes.

Now they are something he must have. He searches the many corners of women's eyes, looking for the one who will float to him, unmoored, because she has found herself alone on this island and is hoping that someone will save her.

11. Lagahoo

The bare patch on my uncle's head is hidden beneath a thin grey cloud. His lips are bald and probing, the taste of coins left in my mouth. There is no way out; no sight inside the cave of his chest, my face pressed up against the slimy points of his nipples. I hack for breath. One quick reprieve is all I get before I am pushed back under the line of his lap.

Someone is eating a little girl. Her head is impaled. Up and down and up again. Now he is a *lagahoo*, coughing up rot-scented phlegm.

Who killed the chicken on the side of the road outside our house? Who cracked its neck and left it there for all to see? He is a hunger, a trail of broken body parts nuzzled, gnawed, lured back for the pleasure of sucking life out of holes bit into bone.

I did not recognize him then. He was not my uncle. I thought I could feed him torn off pieces of myself and it would be enough. He dragged me out among the treeshadows releasing their rain in the night and storm. I fought but I could not cry out.... Come close, let me whisper this in your ear. There's choking there, caressing out the air and stabbing lights out. A secret I alone could hear. A child. H-h-h-h-h-h-he said, h-h-h-h-h-h-he said....

I will try to tell you this. A wolf crept up to me at night, left me shredded, bleeding into the ridges of the stone sink at the back of our house: the sink we bluesoaped clothes in, killed crabs in, black ink running out of their cracked skulls. The knife slid gently into their tiny spaces and pried up, while their legs strained frantically against the cords.

My insides leak out and the smell of a swamp rises up, brackish mud, taste of a metallic stream. I hear the break in his voice the snapping cord whipping up the air slaps of spit flying the switch curving up. The spit from his mouth slaps back and forth. The memory of sounds is enough. *Krak!* A bloody tongue wrapped in silence.

24. The Message

I wake up with the memory of him in my mouth, spit him out onto the sheets, stained. I bend down to pick up the covers from the floor. His phone falls out. I hesitate, then look through his missed calls. No numbers at all. I go to his email account, try several passwords with no success. I'm about to give up when I enter "blue crabs," his favorite food, and it works. A stone sinks into my chest. The first message reads, "We need to talk. Katrina." I type "Katrina," click "Search" and read the messages one by one.

"I know about the others," she writes. "The last one you were with called my house. She told me about your "friends," gave me some numbers. I'm going to call them if you don't come."

I search the word "love" and their names appear.

This is what happens when a deep lie finds you: You are bent back; you are splintered open. You crawl on your belly trying to escape the salt trails left by his tongue. You run wall-eyed from side to side, the crooked leg, the cracked back, snap flap flack! *Uurururururrgghghghghg* the slick gurgle slime twitch *mutter utter utter nnno* it's not true. He has never lied to himself or to you. He has never encircled her waiting limbs and whispered sweet things into her wet, opening palms.

If I could have spoken I would have told him this: Before your hands felt like a lie; before the dome of your head came to rest between her longing bones; before you ate my soul and I tried to eat yours, only to find that it was gone; before I began to ask "What's wrong?"; before you, I waited long.

14. The Gift

"Give me those last two bundles you have," my uncle says. Points to the ones he wants. The boy selling them is dark chocolate and thin as a rod. His eyes meet mine. He is beautiful.

This boy hunts blue crabs under the full moon, when they creep cautiously out of their holes, cross the asphalt road, looking for sand, looking again for the sea. He gets the big ones after the rain, braves huge pinchers and cars bearing down in the dark. He dances around the crabs in silver light, knows just how to hover above them with the loop of string, gently lower it and snap! It tightens. He knows just how to hold them. The jagged claw claps closed on empty air. He ties each crab and slips it quickly into his mother's crocus bag. He lets all the little ones go free.

I squirm against the sticky vinyl seat: A forever car-ride. My uncle gets out and goes over to a little girl selling red and green plums across the street. He does not need to tell me to stay put. I am strapped in and burning in the heat. On the floor of the backseat crab eyes twitch from side to side, their joints flinch against tethers of green string. The boy smiles at me with amber eyes. He saunters over and drops a small cloth pouch into my lap. Then he flies away.

I open the pouch with wide eyes. It is full of folded bills—more than enough. My uncle is still haggling with the girl across the street. He is not looking at the car.

I clutch the money with one wet hand and with the other, crack open the door.

24. Swamp and Sea

I am in the mangrove swamp. Something that looks like a wild white dog has a crab on its back, splayed open. I hear the *Krak!*, feel the soft insides sucked out by that devouring spirit. My hands move over my stomach. The swamp smell clings like wet earth and blood. The air is dull. The dog looks up at me with clear red eyes and grins. At first I am afraid, then the rage boils up. A Sunday School verse comes unbidden to mind, up from the mud of fifteen years: *You are not a child of the night or of the darkness. Walk as a child of light.*

I call on the light and it comes down like a cutlass through the hanging mangrove roots. The wild dog cringes back. I smell singed fur. It turns and slinks away slowly, red foam dripping from the corners of its mouth. I turn to go, still looking back, trip over a stone and fall. As soon as my face hits the black water, I wake up.

He is lying next to me, deaf to anything but the reverberation of his snoring. I take care to avoid his wineglass guarding dregs at the side of the bed. I step over his overflowing ashtray. I leave the room. I walk past the masks and statues, still watching me, even now. I gather up my rolls of canvas, brushes, paints, and take them down to my old car. I keep driving until the studio is out of sight.

On my way, I see a young man on the side of the road, selling crabs. His eyes look strangely familiar but I can't be sure. I ask to buy all the bundles he has left. He says, "Take them," and when he smiles, I know.

Minutes later, down by the sea, I cut each crab loose. They crawl away one by one—their escape spilling sweet under my tongue.

TOM BRADLEY
with visuals by Nick Patterson
from *Family Romance*

Now go and smite the Amalekites,
and utterly destroy all that they have,
and spare them not; but slay both
man and woman, infant and suckling,
ox and sheep, camel and ass.
—1 Samuel 15:3

So, have Mom and I instilled an obsessive-compulsive fear of the Sneeze Catastrophic in you yet? Congratulations. Dry-heaving phobias temper the abs and make you more attractive when autopsy time rolls around.

Speaking of which, there is contagion on these pages. There's a flu to make the bubonic plague look like diaper rash, to make Flamma-Manna look like annealing balm for that rash. If I were Bitch Mother, I would have so many warnings for you at this late stage that you might hesitate to turn the page, to peel back the lids on this gawker. I would, for your own good, make you feel like a helpless, repugnant, small creature fastened to an eyeball with a chain more adamantine than those which transfixed the Divine Krystelle Rex's elbows.

Depending on your state of soul-preparedness, this family romance could turn out to be like a spell in the most horrific of all torture chambers. The famous rat cage just might get muzzled to your kisser—except you're the rodent, and you've been hampered with a predisposition to rabies. And a membrane has metastasized along your finger bones where the Mom-

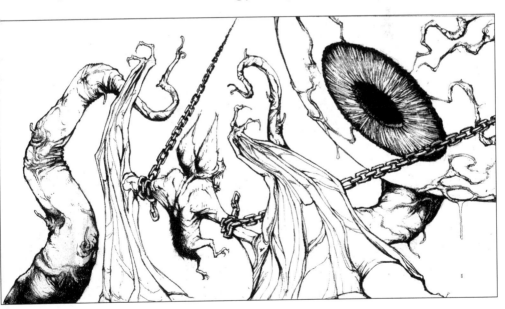

You're the rodent...

Think all the way down to...

pathogens have taken control and secreted sheet tumors.

But this does not mean you need fret about having picked up a pathogen and passing it on. You don't lack permission to commence considering this family romance with a sneeze. Go ahead and hurricane hard enough to blow back this page. Phlegm-paste it flat against the previous. Take a peek through the eyeballs you just atomized in a coarse red shpritz among the tantalizing tints.

An eight- to twelve-hour introspection is indicated at this point. You know, the kind you get sucked into after being sent to your room—not without, but, worse—with your dinner. And you've not been issued the usual personified tallow invigilator to distract the notional flooding that accompanies any unlit bedtime in such a household. It would amount to child abuse if you didn't get there first and prefix the abuse with the self-.

But first, before moving any further into this proposition that is shuffled in so many layers between your fingers, it is recommended that you pause a moment and look inside the stacked deck called yourself. There could be something far worse than a mere prettified Mom-bug mired in the inky condiments of this cellulose sandwich. It could be waiting to be picked up, not by your sinuses or extremities, but by your soul. An immaterial pathogen, so to speak.

When you've been persuaded to eat way too many holy eucharist shaman mush-bowls, prepared by a not so much over-anxious as sadistic mom, a hyper-religiose parent who tries to conceal her perfidy under a veneer of 'shroom piety—you often wind up mired in those hellish eight-to-twelve-hour entheospections, those states of neuro-toxicity that make you understand why your melanin-challenged ancestors were traditional mycophobes, those moods that admit no border between what you see and what you'd give anything to unthink about what you can't bear to look at.

Such is the permanent post-prandial mood at our house—except inside Mom's own head, of course. Her inner pugnacity is such as to render the hugest, most crawling Relic Amalekite turd-growth to nothing more than a dandelion fluff against an eyelid. Her vitality dissolves us, embosoming entheogenicity itself, like vitriol buttering an unleavened wafer, and she's perma-cheery, eyes, mind and, especially, mouth wide open.

Are you ready for that? Stroke your head and think deep into the tentacled core of your subcranial colloids. Are you really prepared to engage your eyeballs so deeply with what you hold in your hands at this moment, until you think all the way down to—

the Relic Amalekites' personal hygiene?

Can it truly be called a crotch?

I don't want this to degenerate into a speciesist tract, but the whisper-snickered tattles about these ethno-types eating with their faces and wiping their assholes with both hands must contain a kernel, or maybe an undigested peanut, of truth.

This idiosyncratic state of personal-hygienic affairs has a direct bearing on why our backyard's mini-ecosystem is peculiarly suited to this relgio-ethnicity, and why they migrated here in such numbers in the first place.

Like the paleolithic-style wretches they were when originally condemned to total species-expungement in splatter-porno-scriptural days, they remain hunter-gatherers at core. (Though, come to think of it, from what position do I condescend, having been reduced to that level myself, or at least the latter half of the job description?) Their proud yet squalidly nomadic culture never invented anything like an alphabet, so paper never entered their so-called "minds." Therefore, neither did that superfluous luxuriance of civilization come near their opposite ends.

So they require handfuls of greenery to be perpetually poised at the ready, tickling up between their struthious legs, to aid in the two-fisted de-chunkification of their uniquely configured fundaments after evacuation of whatever unimaginable bowel apparatus their Jawhey, himself indifferently configured, has bothered to plumb for them by way of a crotch-vent. Sometimes, as I ponder our foreign guests from a few paces off, I wonder if they can truly be said to have crotches any more than oral cavities.

This has resulted in the famously exotic custom, which is known abroad as the—

Middlingly Oriental Grass Wipe

It has come popularly to symbolize their entire presence on the planet, just as kindergartens full of type-two diabetics stereotypify a certain other civilization which will remain nameless.

The on-the-hoof running grass-wipe is doubly piquant as a behavior because, back across the river in the occupied territories of their home-sand, even before we smote them and our Flamma-Manna settled whitely down to liquefy the olive skins of their siblettes, stands of grass were as few and far-flung as oases. Now we have debiologized the place, the above statement can be made even more emphatically.

So, where they've lived for seven thousand years, the chance to wipe one's ass has always been a real treat, the equivalent of stumbling upon a stand of date palms in the middle of a hypoglycemic jag. Finding themselves heli-dumped charitably down to a backyard grassy as ours, our foreign guests

the riverside where they've roamed for seven thousand years...

believe they've been translated whole to their monotheistic heaven and laved in 600 houris' copulation sauces, without even suiciding for the privilege.

This marvelously pullulizing expression of carbon not only promotes the growth of the Flyblown Fruiting Body at home, but it brings forth the occasional marvel of life on the otherwise hermetically sterile sands of the far Judeuphrates bank. The Amalekite ethnicity truly is autochthonous, one with its native soil, for there would literally be no soil without them. To the irreligious, the crypto-Darwinist, it would no doubt reduce to a chicken-egg paradox.

Everyone else will begin to see, on pondering the purity of this symbiosis, the depth and extent of Our Theocracy's crime. We have been destructive to a source of calories as well as clean crotches. We have violated nature, nutrition and hygiene as well. Dad—who, in his youth, helped hawk our weapon in this felony—is attempting to atone by riding at the head of their mounted resistance, doomed as it is.

MATTHEW COOPERMAN & ABY KAUPANG

from NOS

joy is the joy of her indifference   a body   to be lifted   someone to lift her body

is it that others are fathers   mothers   normalcy is tall tall trees

speech something   farther

farther

a hand to be led to the door as an outing-

they that were at the psych-ward   experienced
a type of loss   some types were honored
the loss   some types denied   there were
those that ate the loss   those that planted it
as cardiums   there were those that saw that
life was love and lossy   there were those that
were eaten by loss   they ate it back   they
fertilized the gardens of their abdomen

disability
being an ecological concern
primarily the affordances are
lack
infinite then
without propulsion

| they that were ragged |

this morning having slept alone |the room| then still being mine alone   the light   which died on the other side of the
blinds   was not mine   not *for* me   I being grown and up   a woman   and decipherabley playing into the present history
of baptism

written on my palm   stupid tragic   by my stupid tragic hand I'd
written *love fell*
the grown woman's palm was then *ingrown* or *de-grown*   like the woman
| *I* | is nubile   The Patient _____

_____ shows an interest/puts it down
_____ includes her own speech

_____ heard a word recently
_____ anticipates another event

_____ identifies property as an object
_____ acts out a recently heard ward

_____ distributes objects in a 1:1 manner
_____ creates a collection
_____ chooses to be in a collection

those with low tones and spasticity   those with
damage in their core   those in grey and matter
and low in modeling   in the upper and lower
chambers of ganglia   those centered and dis-
entered   their familial   dysfunctive days

having no discernible disease   the MOC was idiopathic in nature

in the night in our bed   in *our distances*:   lovemaking   talk of tree-cutting   pine beetles   *elsewheres*:   a boy in
the shop slopped it down his descending pants   the mother of child searches   E. Colfax

we   loved by the hour

we unnerved
flew past the coming down

your daughter is not coming out
you daughter will never lose The Diagnoses
we might lose her   *you/your*   daughter   might lose *you/her*

we dis- and -eased

they being drugged were told to stay in
their bed   they being drugged until they
did so   did so   implicitious us wanted
our beds   we wanted everyone to want
to bed   they being drugged were treated
behaviorally   on our sheets   we scored
them

dis-

disturbed she created ADLs   an occupational perspective   someone conjured
nubile in its nature   though   clearly it was diseased

I being scored in bed on sheets acted in a grown behavior
I being the bed and the woman and the falcon am drugged
        you being implicit wanted to want me in bed

I wanted and didn't want this

so it's *nubile*   a proffered and non-proffered
activity

an inning—

its either blues or spectrum or age or implicitous or Ph.D.
funk of the echoes   ricochets   whacking in present tense
all the codes in all the skull   all the meds   all the gloves
can't undo the verdict they said

I'm X Aby Kaupang

I'm X Matthew Cooperman

                    you're

        hearing echoes

EVELYN HAMPTON
My Chute

I would go with my family to the museums and the restaurants, trying to find what I was supposed to love. The nudes were lovely, and I could see how a slab of marble retained the shape of a man, but I would just think how great it would be to have my own chute, a longish tube to push things through—anything, great or trash, it wouldn't matter to me, I would push it all through my chute. It would be easy; my chute would be dark inside at all times of day or night, too dark to see into, so its reality would be mysterious to me—except that I had created it, and knowing this would give me the greatest pleasure because it would be such a relief to look at a thing I had created, which would not have existed if it weren't for me, and to see it only partially. It would make me feel mysterious to me. Then I could relax with my family.

But the inside of my chute is not entirely dark. I am not entirely unable to see that my chute now has teeth, though I never intended it to. I had imagined a sleek, nearly frictionless tube accepting of all I pushed through it. I had foreseen the easy slippage of things out of this world, and the spaces, wide and small gaps, that would appear like cats where things had once been, sometimes curling up and warming them.

I had imagined that in the absence of my family, another room would become open to me—the room I had never known how to get to because my family had always been blocking me. With them removed, I would easily enter an area of high ceilings and intrigue. Then my personality would really be free to scheme. I would attend conventions of influence and prestige, where I would be recognized. I would wear a blazer and jeans.

Except that my chute is not at all how I imagined it would be. I can clearly see that my chute has grown teeth around its opening, a line of incisors and canines the size of mine. What is the purpose of teeth if not to block an entrance? I suppose they are also for ripping and grinding. And they hint at speech—they make little walls for words to hide behind before they venture out.

My chute's teeth are not at all useful to me. Times when I want my chute to chew, it refuses. I haul our hideous loveseat out of our living room to the opening of my chute, and my chute, despite what I think it should do, despite what it has done in the past, does not chew. It does not even move (it used to make a worm-like movement that was so endearing to me) to take the loveseat from me. So I sit on the loveseat beside my chute, bored, barely different from being ordinary.

At these times, the only difference between me and someone who sits on a loveseat in front of a TV is that I fed my TV to my chute. I wanted only my chute—I needed no other images than it. I imagined it and then I made it, and when it was made it was no longer part of me. Yet to see outside of me something that had once been part of me was not as entertaining as I'd thought it would be. In fact it was very lonely. I discovered, once it was made, that my chute had had a hidden use—it had kept me company. Imagined but still unmade, my chute was always with me; I could push anything through it; in fact my chute was the end of all my senses—whatever I heard, felt, saw, touched, tasted, or thought, all could be pushed into my chute, leaving me clean, my senses fresh, as if unaffected by anything. I could push my family through my chute—my chute was very accommodating. Whatever I wanted to lose, there my chute would be, moving like a worm, taking it from my hands, taking it away from me.

During the time when my chute was real only to me, my chute and I shared the same body. Our blood circulated in my veins. What I ate kept us happy and the same.

Then my chute was finished. I had needed to make it in order to feel entirely real. As long as I couldn't see my chute—as long as it was inside of me—I couldn't know for certain that my chute wasn't just a feeling—insubstantial, made of the chemicals of my brain. Even if a doctor could have shown me an image of my chute, still, I would not have been satisfied.

But then to have my chute removed, to have it entirely outside of me—

my family arrives in the Subaru; its windows lower automatically; they look at me; they look at my chute; they look disgusted; they are on their way to the museums; they are condemning me by looking at my chute—

has been my greatest failure and, I realize now that it is real, my greatest fear.

*

How to get my chute back into me? —I write this on a piece of tissue, then push it into my chute.

My chute is suspended at one end from a platform in a tree. My father built the platform for me—I had told him I needed to be able to see (in fact I faked a kind of blindness until he built the platform for me).

My chute angles sharply away from the platform, down through the leaves of the tree, to a place on the ground I prefer not to acknowledge.

I have come to believe that my chute is growing—not *growing away from me*, but growing actually, quantifiably. I have taken a tape measure from my father's hands and I intend to measure my chute. I intend for my measurements to be accurate, exact, but my chute does not make precision easy. By its nature (now that it is out of me, my chute has its own struggles) my chute defies precision and accuracy. It goes off into the trees, suspended every few feet by thick straps tied to branches, toward the source of a river we are forbidden to touch for it has been polluted by us.

My chute does not even move to take the tissue away from me.

My chute is no longer mine.

I would like to convene a meeting concerning my chute; I would like all to be in attendance, especially people with excellent minds; at this meeting the agenda will be *How to get my chute back into me*. I believe this will be a great scientific and philosophical challenge; in fact the greatest of our time, for my chute challenges a duality we have yet to resolve—*thoughts* and *things* are names for two sorts of object, which common sense has always found contrasted.

Now that my chute has become a real chute, how to get it back to being imaginary and mine? It is obvious that this implicates both space and time.

I will need the greatest minds, those that still hoard their excesses, their deepest mines, keeping them unbuilt, undiscoverable—not suspending them stupidly from trees, not exposing them to the eyes of their families.

I shimmy along the outside of the chute, stretching the tape to take measurements I record in a notebook I am quickly filling with questions and observations about the chute. I would record equations, too, except that I don't have any yet—

it is obvious that the chute is growing, perhaps toward a point that is dimensionless—

though I expect to, soon.

JOE MILAZZO

from *A Picture of Bread [Una Imagen del Hostia]*

The Blood Orange

Previously, I'd only known the blood orange as an idea of juice, not a concentration—juice in the most active sense of the word. Almost the verb of it, spilling over the lips in a few delightfully embarrassed drops, a concentrate then of slaver out of control. Slow running not to be caught up to with any inhalation (the lower lip sucked back in, as if ready to plug itself into some brass instrument) however swift, or diverted by any wipe, from palm-heel to elbow's crook. I could not have prepared for the feel of the fruit, the compactness of it. A rind, mottled or mildly unripe, with all the waxy appearance but none of the oiliness of its larger, less baked cousin. (This one I had kept under refrigeration.) Something crumbly in the way the sponge of that rind peeled. How did it yield to the gouge of the thumb, the submarining clench of forefingers? It came away easily, but only in tiny continents, this crust. It came apart rather than off. The white netting underneath, the blind hairs brushing the surface of my palm and protecting rather than complementing the ovoid. White as white can be expected to be, but less fibrous, less prone to commandeer other strands to a general separation, commencing parallel, finishing perpendicular. How could the orange grow heavier once all this was removed? It did. My care, my admirations, hunger to be pleased, all exert their gravities and mock the hollow. So robust, a depth exposed, but, riding my eyes, I do circle around the naked fruit as evidence it is delicate, like the fashion in which the jewel slices the hand into a cradle for glass, a perfect eruption of the sunk. The hand broken by the trepidation, by that which it fears it might break. We are too sympathetic and not greedy enough with our gratitude. The palm and wrist must surrender, or cure the contradiction with a few playful bounces. The individual sections dry, but a dryness undermined by their smoothness, like sardines, puffed smooth from their being packed away in some inimically thick darkness. Their skin slid easily against their neighbors', gave nothing to the fingertips, slightly numb at the breakfast chill of the anticipated flavor. (This one I had kept in the refrigerator.) I mean residue, the feeling that one wanted to shake or rub one's hands free of the resinous cling of whatever it was their scent evoked. Slender in so far as they fit between a pinch, gripped midway down the flank or near the half-moon's end, nothing dares flop, jiggle, they define a useful width. None of those terminal calluses, fat and obdurate. And they tear along the lines of cluster, translucence thus breaking in, not of the sun, trapped from the sun, the eye's own humors streaming down the arm, light caressing itself in the confirmation, the orange is there, the pieces will pass inside where the hands are not useful, the sections to be eaten. A throb paused; this allows me to avoid confronting their hue. Spitting seeds, if not extinguishing them.

LUCY CORIN

Selections from

One Hundred Apocalypses and Other Apocalypses

FRESH

After so many people were washed away by the disasters, there was usually someone outside the grocery store with a collection bucket. On a sunny day I biked over, feeling good. I walked around the grocery store, especially the produce islands, feeling pretty good about my choices and my healthy way of life. Nobody is mentioning how the increasing rate of madness is apocalyptic. It's because we mostly eat corn. There are so many decisions to be made in the grocery, that cold room of consciousness. But tell you the truth, I kept asking for it. I was asking for the apocalypse. I was tired of the way things were going. I was looking forward to fresh everything. With the slate wiped clean, the whole world would be at my beck and call. Anything could be around the corner, I thought, pushing my cart through the grocery air. There was the aisle of condiments. There were the pyramids of newfangled soup. Everything that would have happened in the event could really be a turning point for me.

CAKE

She baked an angel food cake for the dinner party, which means it's as white as is possible in cake except golden on the outside and you have to cut it with a serrated knife. It's funny to eat because you can kind of tear it, unlike most cakes. It stretches a little. It's a little supernatural, like an angel.

I was watching her with her boyfriend because I admire them and am trying to make them an example in my life of good love being possible.

Toward the end of the cake everyone was talking and a couple of people were seeing if they could eat the live edible flowers that she'd put on the cake for decoration. A fairy cake. She told a story about making the cake. There wasn't a lot left. Everyone was eating the ends of their pieces in different ways, and because of the stretchy texture there were more methods than usual, and no crumbs at all.

Really funny cake.

I tried to imagine making the cake, same as I often tried to imagine love. I would never make a cake. So it's down to, say, less than a quarter of the cake and the boyfriend reaches across the table—it's a big table that no one else would be able to reach across, he just has really long arms, and he takes the serrated knife, but when he cuts at the cake he doesn't do the sawing action, he just presses down, which defeats the point of a serrated knife. The cake squishes as he cuts it in half; it was only a piece of itself already, clinging to its imaginary axis, and now it's not even a wedge—it's pushed down like you can push down the nose on your face—and then he takes his piece with his hands and I watch the last piece of cake to see if it'll spring back up but it doesn't, it's just squished on one side like someone stepped on it.

But here's what I don't understand, is how all through it she's just chatting with the dinner guests and it's like he's done nothing at all. She's not looking at him like "You squished the cake!" and she's not looking at him like "He loves the cake so much he couldn't help himself," and he doesn't seem to be thinking "Only I can squish the cake!" Or is he?

I never know how to read people.

But here's what else: watching the round cake disappear, watching the people trying to make the most of their pieces, people coveting the cake on one hand and reminding themselves on the other that this will not be the last cake. But will it be the last? I look at their love and I feel like this could be the very last piece of it on earth, and just look at it.

WANTING

All day he filled his eyes with explosions and commercials. At night he walked through the fanciest part of the neighborhood: blinds crossing vast windows, enormous foyers, each with one shining fixture suspended like the only planet in the universe of one house after another, expanses of plaster, vaulted ceilings, the geometries of staircases, rugs on walls. Automatically his mind unified with want. More flowers, more pottery, better furniture, less dirt, excellent collections of film through history, tailored clothing, quality craftsmanship, the cutting edge, caring so much, the fluffy covers, the beauty, the rich. No wonder televisions hunched behind louvered cabinet doors, sniffing through the slats, their pissed mouths shut. He walked to get his head out of the war, and walking worked. Why, why, why? One day he'd been wondering, and then, walking, wanting everything he saw is what explained it all. Then he was back where he started, in the cul de sac in the cosmos between the news and the body. Next door, his neighbor's silver rowboat was beached in the cactus garden. It gleamed in the street-lit night, appearing as shards. Like anything else, the thing about an apocalypse is it can't go on forever, and this is what saves it and saves us in the end. Sure, not everyone, but I mean us in general.

For some months nothing would do to eat except bread, any kind, including biscuits, croissants, dinner buns, hoagie rolls, Irish soda, artisan peasant, challah, brioche, lavash, pugliese, baguette full, demi, sweet, sour, marble, pita, vegan, Wonder or whatever grain, any of a zillion crackers, which sounds like a decent amount to eat except that bread was it, and it was nothing but bread. She tried to find other things to eat. She searched her cookbooks and then the last of the phone books, imagining meals. Woe on the sofa, woe on the stairs. She went out and walked around town, reading menus, her pockets heavy with cash. She took the train into the city where guys in red jackets or bowties stood in the street outside their restaurants, took her by the elbow, and described the food they could give her. Her head, like someone else's stomach, filled with meals. She let the ideas of them accumulate in piles before her, multicolored, glistening, weighting her utensils, stopping at her teeth. Then she went home and ate bread, hating it, and hating ending up with one and then another piece of Christ, slice of life, hunk of flesh, daily shut the fuck up about bread. Bread, the least common denominator of food. The earth carried everything else like condiments, like lace, like prefixes and suffixes. Then one day. Then one day. Then one day.

OPTIONS

A. MANY

A little man with enormous glasses in a floppy green hat and a blue rain slicker has placed himself on an orange stepladder eye-to-knots with a dormant tree in front of the arched entrance to his mouse-colored house, raising a yellow hacksaw, sizing it up for pruning, which he's clearly always doing; it's pared to the shape of a candelabra, bare knuckles, he has made its history. The bones of a cathedral, the inside of a whale, architectures of bodies, buildings, heavens enclosing earth, some god on a stepladder, composing, friendly, the sky one density of gray, his foggy, neighborly smile among colors, as if nothing else in the world matters.

B. HALF

Or a drawing I remember from an exhibit of the works of madmen: the pencil lines of half a city, one line for the sidewalk extending horizontally, like a sidewalk or a plank from the truncated SkYlInE _____, a line moving rightward into the blank page, like time.

THREAT

For years, a telephone pole leaned, a fear at the back of the neighborhood. That evening they went home and poured several very even trays of ice cubes. I was dressed for the apocalypse. I was depressed for the apocalypse. I carried a bundle of dust like a nest. My heart beat in its fleshy pocket. Girls sketched one another in an auditorium. Worms had tried to make it across our porch overnight and now they lay like something shredded, like shredded bark, but deader. My friends, looking ashen, kept waiting for the telephone. An iris wilted into a claw. A bathtub sunk in our vast yard. New birds gathered like, I don't know, a lack of entropy?

PUPPET

When she speaks to me in the voice of her dog, do I answer the dog? A guy who worked with me at the store was tryping to make it as a puppeteer. We had a party at his house for our manager, Linda, who was leaving, and she brought two white terriers with her for beer and cake. We gathered as if for a group photo, facing the empty sofa. Eric got out his puppets and crouched behind it. These were hand-puppets in the shapes of a donkey and a fish. Then the donkey and the fish came up from behind it. Eric was a good puppeteer, and the donkey and fish were funny, but what was funniest was Linda's puppet-sized dogs, who sat in the front row and were completely taken in by the magic. They followed with their heads like in tennis. You could see how excited they were to find out what would happen next. After all, I want to know what will happen next. I want to know what will happen if I look at you while you're talking as if you are your dog and talk back to you as if I'm—I don't know, what could I talk to you like? Anything?

THE CYCLE OF LIFE

She really needed some time off work so she took maternity leave, but the baby was so much work it was like she wasn't getting any time off at all, so she killed the baby (hold on, hold on...) and that gave her time off for grieving, a whole other hell of work plus the guilt, and by the time she started to recover she had to go back to work, but pretty soon the future seemed so stupid she started wanting a baby again. When she looked into her options, one that apparently a zillion people had chosen and she hadn't even known about was a move to the trash-heaps of Navarro. That put things in perspective. No, she thought, my options are way more limited than that, thank the good lord above. She felt her back against the warm wall of her office. She felt her cells battling it out below-deck. She ate a stale pastry. She had one more idea. It was like an egg in her brain waiting to go off.

JULY FOURTH

Got there and the ground was covered with bodies. Lay down with everyone and looked at the sky, bracing for the explosions.

CECILIA CORRIGAN

Winner of the 2013 Margaret P. Plonsker
Emerging Writer's Residency Prize

about *Titanic*

From my place as a reader—secluded, rural and solitary—reading this wild
text of Cecilia's inserted extra screens, jittery and scathingly brilliant and
very funny, into my readerly cognition. She reminded me that indeed it is
a world of screens now, even or especially off at the edge of things—the
screens of our communications devices of course, such as this one, where
I am writing now, the screens of the entertainment media that slide with
such phantom immediacy into our affective lives and our memories, per-
meable decorative surfaces that obscure as they animate what they shelter,
and the presciently named screen memories of Dr. Freud, where images,
events, fantasies and errors combine to produce the wildly variable and
shifting synthetic representations we call memory. In the screen structure,
in the *Titanic*, representation and subjectivity are straddled by the erot-
ics of a joyous doubt.

—*Lisa Robertson, judge, 2013-2014 Plonsker Prize*

The most important thing that I think television and poetry have in com-
mon is that they're regulated by set, discrete time limits, which break down
the larger whole into small parts. I'm saying episode is to season as poem is
to poetry book. To respond to your question about training, I'd say I aspire
to imitate television in my poetry, or, to be less cute, to plunder the tactics
television uses to control and compel its viewer.

—*Cecilia Corrigan*

Cecilia Corrigan's first book, *Titanic*, is an epic love poem depicting the eternal
gothic romance between man and machine.
    Alan Turing, cracker of the Nazis' Engima code during World War II, and the
father of artificial intelligence, is the protagonist of this savagely witty and performa-
tive work of hybrid poetry. Turing escapes his frustrated love life and tragic death
into the safe haven of virtual reality. The setting shifts from Snow White's forest,
to Ludwig Wittgenstein's seminar at Cambridge, amid various iMessage chats and
appearances by a variety of exciting guest stars, from Frank O'Hara and Judith Butler
to Katy Perry and Julianne Moore's BMW.
    Fearless, feminist, and outrageous, this book will infect its readers with its desper-
ate irony and tragic flipness. *Titanic*: collide with destiny!

from *Titanic*

was never very confident in my voice, you see.

So I thought, rather than just sing them, which would probably bore the pants off everybody, I would uhm, I'd like to kind of *portray* the songs.

In rendering the book for you the somewhat unusual course has been adopted of printing the original side by side with the translation. Such a method of presentation seemed desirable both on account of the obvious difficulties raised by the vocabulary and in view of the peculiar literary character of the whole. As a result, a certain latitude has been possible in passages to which objection might otherwise be taken as over-literal.

This is a book for people who are interested in getting involved with the real world. If that doesn't suit you well, the door's right back where you came in.

No ?

Before we get started I'd like to tell you a little bit about me and where I'm "at" right now in my life. First off, I'm just come out and say that for about eight years now I've been a daily user of a .05 microgram compound of (S)-2-amino-3-[4-(4-hydroxy-3,5-diiodophenoxyl)-3,5-diiodophenyl] propanoic acid, which is being metabolized as we speak in my liver, kidneys, brain, and muscles.

A game is an activity defined by rules in which players try to reach some sort of goal. Games can be whimsical and playful, or highly serious. They can be played alone or in complex social scenarios. Think about all the games you know you guys. Who did you play them with? That's right: your family!

Wait. Ok. I know I'm avoiding the topic. I also use, more or less every day, 0.15 mg of levonorgestrel, ($\underline{d}$(-)-13 beta-ethyl-17-alpha-ethinyl-17-beta-hydroxygon-4-en-3-one), a totally synthetic progestogen, and 0.03 mg of ethinyl estradiol, (19-nor-17α-pregna-1,3,5 (10)-trien-20-yne-3,17-diol), cellulose, D&C Red 30, FD&C Yellow 6, lactose, magnesium stearate, and polacrilin potassium to suppress my gonadotropins, inhibit my ovulation, thicken my cervical mucus and change my endometrium.

Now, about 27 years and 35 weeks ago, the development of my external genitalia would have been fully differentiated in my mom's uterus. My genitals would have started forming weeks before that. Now, let's say instead of the tiny cells of my clitoris and labia majora, a little penis had formed on me, around week 11 of my mom's pregnancy in the spring of 1986.

In this case I'd be a male baby, a man now. Let's call me David. Let's say I was taking a similar compound of synthetic estrogen, like maybe an extremely high-dosage daily injection of stilboestrol. I'd experience a reduction in libido, reduced testicular size, impotence, and probably I'd begin to grow breasts and put on weight. It's likely I'd become depressed due to my hormonal imbalance, and become extremely lethargic, as the lack of testosterone would affect my mental acuity.

Before the symptoms became too brutal, I'd carry on with my television show, up until my first birthday in October 1987.

My television show has a live audience. They're responsive, engaged, and affectionate. Occasionally one of them will come up to me after the show, explain they have a fatal disease of some kind, say how much my show has helped them. We'll hug and I'll give them some merch. Sometimes I wonder what else I could have done, till I remember the substantial yearly donations to various "Cure for" charities.

I'm gonna tell you a love story.

                    CECILIA
        Thank you! Th-thanks, thank you. Thank you very
        much, good evening welcome to the program! I'm your
        host Cecilia Corrigan, there's this guy, what's his name
        again, it's your musical host Paul Shaffer.

                    PAUL
        Cecilia, nice to see you.

                    CECILIA
        Paul, did you see the TV movie the Renee Richards
        story?

                    PAUL
        I didn't catch the Renee Richards story.

                    CECILIA
        (To audience)
        What was that movie called, that Renee Richards
        movie? Second Serve? Second Serve all about Renee
        Richards who was a —

PAUL

—Second Wha?

CECILIA

Second *serve*, a professional tennis player who formerly was a man, an opt, uh thamolic, uh surgeon an eye surgeon, yeah—

PAUL

—Yeah, yeah—

CECILIA

—and uh then became female and played tennis for a number of years. You know I found, the most interesting thing was, the hardest part about becoming a woman for ah, Dr. Richards, was learning to like Tom Jones so—!

PAUL
(Cracks up, claps, playfully boos)

CECILIA

Aw stop it c'mon, hey! I'm just a kid trying to make a living, leave me alone, will ya! Uh.. what else, oh! This is exciting, the Pope is coming to visit the United States in the spring of 1987 he's going to visit Florida, he's gonna visit Texas, and he's also going to visit California and the purpose of his visit, he says, is to find the best damn chili dog in the United States.

Laughter

Also, Soviet dissident Anatole Shiranski met with Ronald Reagan yesterday and he asked him for—the president—and he asked him for his help getting Jews out of the Soviet Union. And, oddly enough this morning, Ronald Reagan also got a call from Kurt Waldheim asking for his help in getting the Jews out of Austria, so, it's a very——

Laughter/Boos

CECILIA
(Nodding)
are you fans of Kurt Waldheim, is that it? Uh... What are we doin'? Oh what a show folks Trisha Low is

here, Marv Albert is here, and another edition of
stupid pet tricks. Here we go again folks here's what's
his name, here's Paul.

PAUL

Thanks, thank you, etc. Long night ahead, Cecilia?

CECILIA

No! does it, does it seem like it's gonna be a long
night? What are we doin' first, hate mail?

PAUL

Yeah hate mail.

CECILIA

Ok. Let's see here.

Opens a letter from a viewer, reads

"Your discovery of the contradiction caused me the
greatest surprise and, I would almost say, consterna-
tion, since it has shaken the basis on which I intended
to build arithmetic.... It is all the more serious since,
with the loss of my Rule V, not only the foundations
of my arithmetic, but also the sole possible founda-
tions of arithmetic, seem to vanish."

*

"for English, press one. Para Espanol, oprima el dos. Pour le français, appuyez
trois. Für Deutsch, Drücken Sie viermal."
     Beep
"You have selected English. Welcome to the Guggenheim Museum. Thank you for
joining us for our Spring 2003 exhibition season. If at any time you wish to hear a
section repeated, just click the back button on your audio device. You can also skip to
the next section by clicking the forward button.
     "The Guggenheim Museum is at once a vital cultural center, an educational
institution, and the heart of an international network of museums. Visitors can
experience special exhibitions of modern and contemporary art, lectures by artists
and critics, performances and film screenings, classes for teens and adults, and daily
tours of the galleries led by experienced docents. Founded on a collection of early
modern masterpieces, the Guggenheim Museum today is an ever-growing institu-
tion devoted to the art of the 20th century and beyond.
     "Please select from the following exhibit features: Press one for an introduction to
The Cremaster Cycle. Press two for Matthew Barney's Cremaster sculptures. Press

three for Matthew Barney's Cremaster photographs. Press four for—"

Beep

"Matthew Barney's Cremaster Cycle sculptures share a common link in that they are derived from the multi-layered narratives of the project as a whole. The sculptures on view here are constructed from the artist's signature materials, including plastic, metal, and Vaseline. These sculptures function as three-dimensional incarnations of the characters and settings. They exist independently from the films, but embody the same content—now expressed in space rather than time. The sculptures you'll see here are largely sourced from the third film in the cycle, combined with works from the other parts of The Cremaster Cycle. The sculptures are displayed on the museum's ramp, paced in alignment with their order according to the cycle itself.

"To hear information about specific sculptures in the show, enter the first four letters of the sculpture's title."

Beep beep beep beep.

"You have selected *The Ehric Weiss Suite*. This piece, constructed with black acrylic, stainless steel, Vaseline, and live pigeon, is located on the museum's fifth floor, in a small room adjacent to the main gallery, visible through a transparent door. Truly one of the most melancholic and affecting works in the exhibit, the piece is constructed as a tribute to the death of Erich Weiss. The pigeons included in the installation are professionally rented from a carrier pigeon stable in Queens, New York. You'll notice that the coffin and the floor are encrusted with the shit of the pigeons and their feed. This is because they are there all the time. They are wearing black coats, because they are in mourning for Harry Houdini. Take care to stand clear of the unsealing door, please.

"Thank you. Please enter the installation through the now-opened Plexiglass door. The pigeons are well-trained and friendly. Simply remove your shoes if you are concerned about the ruination of their high quality due to the artwork's materials, i.e. pigeon guano. Please approach the coffin with care in order to affect a minimal amount of physical influence on the installation's composition, and on the psychological state of the pigeons.

"Stand aside for the opening coffin. Thank you. If you have any extra materials such as purses or sketchpads, please place them on the ground next to the coffin. Thank you. Please step up into the coffin to enjoy the full virtual reality design of the installation.

"Please step into the coffin.

"Please step into the coffin. Thank you. Please mount the Plexiglass and acrylic headset over your forehead with the viewing screen positioned to encompass your entire line of vision. Press four once you have mounted the headset.

"Press four once you have mounted the headset.

"Press four once y—"

Beep

"Thank you. Please lie back in the sculpture to begin the presentation.

Please lie back.

Please lie back in the—

THE MADELEINE P. PLONSKER
EMERGING WRITER'S RESIDENCY PRIZE

www.lakeforest.edu/plonsker

Yearly deadline: March 1

Previous Publication Credits

Gina Abelkop
Selections from "Greta" from *Darling Beastlettes* (Apostrophe Books, 2012).
Selections originally appeared as "Excerpts from Greta," *42Opus* (2007).

James Tadd Adcox
"Viola Is Sitting on the Examination Table," from *The Collagist* (2012): http://
thecollagist.com/the-collagist/2012/2/8/viola-is-sitting-on-the-examination-table.html.

Luis Aguilar translated by Lawrence Schimel
"Death Certificate" from *Ground Glass* (Mantis Editores/BookThug, 2012)

Aaron Apps
"Barbecue Catharsis" originally appeared in *Carolina Quarterly* (2013) and is
forthcoming in *Intersex: A Memoir* from Tarpaulin Sky Press (2014).

E.R. Baxter III
from *Niagara Digressions* (Starcherone Books, 2012).

Matt Bell
from *In the House upon the Dirt between the Lake and the Woods* (Soho Press, 2013).

Margo Berdeshevsky
"Square Black Key" originally appeared in *Kenyon Review Online*, winter 2012: http://
www.kenyonreview.org/kr-online-issue/winter-2012-2/selections/square-black-key/.

Shanita Bigelow
"Meditations on Meaning" originally appeared as "line: all else and more," *Drunken
Boat*, No. 16 (2013): http://www.drunkenboat.com/db16/shanita-bigelow.

Marina Blitshteyn
"Kaddish" originally appeared in *No, Dear Magazine*, Issue 10, Eds. Emily Brandt
and Alex Cuff (2012).

Katy Bohinc
"Selections from Dear Alain" originally appeared in *Armed Cell* Issue V, August 2013.

Amaranth Borsuk & Kate Durbin
from *Abra* (1913 Editions, forthcoming). "whirling capital embarking" was originally
published in *Lit* 22 (September, 2012): 84-85; "embarking embellishment waves" in
Action, Yes! (Summer 2010); and "embarking stretching arcane" in *Spoon River Poetry
Review* 38.1 (June 2013): 32-33.

Tom Bradley & Nick Patterson
from *Family Romance*, illustrated novel (Jaded Ibis Press, 2012). Previously published as "Tom Bradley's Family Romance" in *The Drill Press,* August 2012.

Alexandra Chasin
"J. Wanton Vandal, Won't You Guess My Name?" from *Brief* (Jaded Ibis, 2012).

Elizabeth J. Colen
Five Fictions from *What Weaponry* originally appeared in *Spork Press* (2012): http://sporkpress.com/?p=951.

Dennis Cooper
from *The Marbled Swarm* (Harper Perennial, 2011).

Lucy Corin
Selections from *One Hundred Apocalypses and Other Apocalypses* (McSweeney's, 2013). "Fresh" (appeared as "Groceries"), part of "Want" (appeared as "Wanting"), and "Puppet" originally appeared in *Gulf Coast* 20.2 (2008): 81-87; "Bread" (part of "Want") in *Sou'wester* 38.2: 38 (2010). "Cake," "July Fourth," and "Threat" in *The Apocalypse Reader*, ed. Justin Taylor (Thunder's Mouth Press, 2007); "Options" in *Rampike* 20.1 (2011): 66; and "Cycle of Life" in *Caliban Online* issue 5: 21.

Cecilia Corrigan
from *Titanic* (Lake Forest College Press, 2014).

T. Zachary Cotler
from *Sonnets to the Humans* (Ahsahta Press, 2013).

Marisa Crawford
from *8th Grade Hippie Chic* (Immaculate Disciples Press, 2013).

LaTasha N. Nevada Diggs
"April 18th," "daggering kanji," "blind date," and "symphony para ko'ko i gamson (symphony for a octopus harvest)" from *TwERK* (Belladonna, 2013).

Stacy Doris
from *Fledge: A Phenomenology of Spirit* (Nightboat Books, 2012).

Carina Finn & Stephanie Berger
"The Rouging Heart and Other Sundance Films" and "Three Balls in My Court and One in the Hole" originally appeared in *Smoking Glue Gun*, Volume 6.

Angela Genusa
from *Tender Buttons* (Gauss PDF, 2013): http://www.gauss-pdf.com/post/41911267120/gpdf062-angela-genusa-tender-buttons.

Diana George
"*Imperator,*" *Birkensnake* 5 (2012): http://birkensnake.com/imperator.php.

Eckhard Gerdes
from *Hugh Moore* (Civil Coping Mechanisms, 2010).

Carmen Giménez Smith
"In-Between Elegy," "The If of Omission," and "Let Down My Bucket" from *The City She Was* (Center for Literary Publishing, 2011).

Lara Glenum
"[This Poem Is My Vocal Prosthesis]" from *POP CORPSE!* (Action Books, 2013).

Karen Green
from *Bough Down* (Siglio Press, 2013).

Kate Greenstreet
"Forbidden" from *Young Tambling* (Ahsahta Press, 2013).

Christopher Grimes
from *The Pornographers* (Jaded Ibis Press, 2011).

Carol Guess & Kelly Magee
"With Human" from *Juked* (March 2013): http://www.juked.com/2013/03/carol-guess-kelly-magee-with-human.asp.

Evelyn Hampton
"My Chute" from *LIT* 23, vol. 13, no. 1 (2013): 44-47.

Tytti Heikkinen translated by Niina Pollari
from *The Warmth of the Taxidermied Animal* (Action Books, 2013).

Johannes Heldén
"Elect" from *Spring Gun Press* # 8 (2013, English version, http://www.springgunpress.com/johanneshelden/elect_en.html) and previously published as "Väljarna" in *Bonnier Lyrik* (2008, Swedish version, URL now dead) and "Väljarna" in *ELMCIP Anthology of European Electronic Literature* (2012, Swedish version, http://anthology.elmcip.net/works/valjarna.html).

Christopher Higgs, Blake Butler, & Vanessa Place
from *ONE* (Roof Books, 2012).

Janis Butler Holm
"Sound Poems: From *Rabelaisian Play Station*," *The Journal (*2013): http://thejournalmag.org/archives/3738.

Jayson Iwen
"Death Style" and "Making Up Time in Indiana" originally appeared in *The Nemadji Review* (2012): 9. "Things This Thing Called I Loved" originally appeared in *Express Milwaukee* (Feb. 2012): http://expressmilwaukee.com/article-permalink-17689.html.

Michael Joyce
from *Disappearance* (Steerage Press, 2012).

Aby Kaupang & Matthew Cooperman
"Joy is the Joy of her Indifference" (excerpted from *Disorder, Not Otherwise Specified*), originally published in *Interim Magazine*, 2012.

Erin Kautza
"Hour of the Star" originally published in *Projecttile Lit*, Volume 1, February 2013.

Becca Klaver
"More Lyrics for My Favorite Band" and "The Superlatively Derogatory Colloquial Epithet, *Shammy*" from *Nonstop Pop* (Bloof Books, 2013).

Richard Kostelanetz
from *A Book of Eyes* (Archae Editions, 2013), by permission of the author/artist. Copyright 2013 by Richard Kostelanetz.

Hank Lazer
"N18P54," "N18P58" originally appeared in *Fence* Vol. 15, No. 1 (Summer 2012).

Janice Lee
"The Horse," "The Lovers" from *Damnation* (Penny-Ante Editions 2013), originally published in *The Collagist* (Issue 50, September 2013): http://thecollagist.com/the-collagist/2013/8/25/damnation-by-janice-lee-penny-ante.html.

Ji Yoon Lee
from *IMMA* (Radioactive Moat, 2012).

Lucas de Lima
"MARIAS," "KILLSPOT," "GHOSTLINES" from *Wet Land* (Action Books, 2014). All poems previously published in *Gobbet*.

Ella Longpre
"Hotel Problem" originally appeared in *elimae* (November/December 2012): http://cooprenner.com/2012/11/Hotel.html.

Erin Kautza
"Hour of the Star" originally appeared in *Projecttile*, Volume 1 (February 2013).

Farid Matuk
"Pantertanter," "Shake the Bear Funny Name," "My Daughter La Chola Martina" from *My Daughter La Chola* (Ahsahta, 2013).

James McGirk
"The Op in the Expanded Field" from *NNATAN* 0 (0.nnatan.org, 2012).

Joe Milazzo
"The Blood Orange," *summer stock* 6 (2012): http://www.summerstockjournal.com/2012/09/joe-milazzo.html.

Brian Oliu
"Boss Battle: The One With the Long Neck," "Boss Battle: A Woman Made of Feathers," "Save Point: Inn," from *Level End* (Origami Zoo Press, 2012).

Daniela Olszewska
Selections from *Citizen J* (Artifice Books, 2013).

Aimee Parkison
"Dirty-Dirty Shorts" from *Dirty: Dirty*, edited by Debra Di Blasi (Jaded Ibis, 2013).

Ted Pelton
"Columbine" appeared in *Crossborder*, vol. 1, no. 2 (Fall 2013).

Justin Petropoulos and Carla Gannis
"excavations of the body politic or terra infirma" from *<legend> </legend>* (Jaded Ibis Press, 2013).

Alake Pilgrim
"Blue Crabs" was first published in *The Literarian*, Issue 13 (2013): 81-91 and online at www.centerforfiction.org/magazine/issue-13/.

Laura Relyea
"Ke$ha Is As Ke$ha Does," "Ke$ha and I Frolic In The Backyards Of Our Neighbors," "Ke$ha and I Never Play The Victim," and "Ke$ha Alights!" originally appeared in *Coconut* 17, and are from *All Glitter, Everything* (Safety Third Enterprises, 2013).

Kim Rosenfield
from *USO: I'll Be Seeing You* (Ugly Duckling Presse, 2013).

Tracy Jeanne Rosenthal
"we will always be /kwir/," originally appeared as "/kwir/ an introduction," *PANK Magazine* (2011, 6.13): http://pankmagazine.com/piece/queer-two-from-the-special-issue-editor/.

Joanna Ruocco
from *Another Governess/The Least Blacksmith* (FC2, 2012).

Suzanne Scanlon
"Girls With Problems" from *Promising Young Women* (Dorothy, 2012).

Joseph Scapellato
"James Monroe" originally appeared as part of "James Madison, James Monroe, John Quincy Adams," *Heavy Feather Review* 2.2 (2013).

Kim Gek Lin Short
from *China Cowboy* (Tarpaulin Sky Press, 2012).

Amber Sparks & Robert Kloss
from *The Desert Places* (Curbside Splendor, 2013). Originally appeared as "The Birth of the Monster," *Vinyl Poetry* (2012): http://vinylpoetry.com/volume-6/page-35/.

Anna Joy Springer
"Variations on a (Fucked) Theme: The Ruling Class Rules for Realism" originally published in *Eleven Eleven* 12 (Winter, 2012): https://elevenelevenjournal.com/2012/01/25/anna-springer/.

Stephanie Strickland & Nick Montfort
"Duels—Duets" was published online in Python and JavaScript versions by New

Binary Press, 2013: http://duels-duets.newbinarypress.com/.

Dennis James Sweeney
"A Series of Sketches of Things Happening on Jalan Legian in Kuta Beach, Bali on Thursday, September 8, 2011, Rearranged in Such a Way as to Give Not Details But an Impression," originally appeared in *DIAGRAM* 12.2 (May 2012): http://thediagram.com/12_2/sweeney.html.

Troubling the Line: Writing from the First Anthology of Trans & Genderqueer Poetry
from *Troubling the Line: Trans & Genderqueer Poetry & Poetics*, edited by TC Tolbert and Tim Trace Peterson. Nightboat Books, 2013.

Jeff VanderMeer
"No Breather in the World But Thee" originally appeared in longer form in *Nightmare Magazine* (2013).

Various Authors
from *I'll Drown My Book: Conceptual Writing by Women*, edited by Caroline Bergvall, Laynie Browne, Teresa Carmody, and Vanessa Place (Les Figues Press, 2012).
 Jen Bervin, untitled excerpt from *Draft Notation* (Granary Books, 2014).
 Angela Carr, "Of the still middle" from *The Rose Concordance* (BookThug, 2009).
 Mette Moestrup, "Hairtypes" from *kingsize* (Gyldendal, 2006), translation *kingsize* (subpress, 2014).
 Yedda Morrison, "Darkness all that / the remains" originally appeared in *Darkness* (Make Now Press, 2012); and *Little Red Leaves* (LRL e-editions, 2009): http://littleredleaves.com/ebooks/.
 Harryette Mullen, "Aren't you glad you use petroleum..." originally appeared in *S*PeRM**K*T* (Singing Horse, 1992) and was collected and reprinted in *Recyclopedia* (Graywolf, 2006).
 Frances Richard, "The Separatrix" from *Anarch.* (Futurepoem, 2012).
 Cia Rinne, "o sole mio," from *milano notes*, in: *notes for soloists* (OEI Editör 2009).
 Kim Rosenfield, from *Lividity* (Les Figues Press, 2012).
 Rosmarie Waldrop, "Kind Regards" from *Streets Enough to Welcome Snow* (Station Hill Press, 1986).

Brooke Wonders
"What We Can't Reach" from *Monkeybicycle* (2012).

Amy Wright
"Excerpt from *The Butterfly Nail: Prose Translations of Emily Dickinson*" originally appeared in *Sleeping Fish* (2012) Series XI: http://sleepingfish.net/Xi/Wright.htm.

Kate Zambreno
from *Heroines* (Semiotext(e), 2012).

Laura Zaylea
"Using Basic Conjunctions: And, But, So, Or" from *Speak2MeInCode: A Guide to Effective Writing*, featured in Avenues of Access: An Exhibit & Online Archive of New 'Born Digital' Literature. January 2013: speak2meincode.com and dtc-wsuv.org/elit/mla2013.

Contributor Notes

Aaron Apps is currently a PhD student in English Literature at Brown University where he studies poetry and poetics, sexual somatechnics, animacy, and the history of intersex literature. His manuscript *Dear Herculine* won the 2014 Sawtooth Poetry Prize and is forthcoming from Ahsahta Press. His other collections include *Compos(t) Mentis* (BlazeVox, 2012) and *Intersex: A Memoir* (Tarpaulin Sky, 2014). His writing has appeared in numerous journals, including *Pleiades, LIT, Washington Square Review, Puerto del Sol, Los Angeles Review,* and *Carolina Quarterly*.

Gina Abelkop is the author of *I Eat Cannibals* (coimpress, 2014), *Darling Beastlettes* (Apostrophe Books, 2012), and *Trollops in Love* (dancing girl press, 2011). She lives in Athens, GA, where she runs the DIY feminist press Birds of Lace and curates the Avid Poetry Series.

James Tadd Adcox is the author of *The Map of the System of Human Knowledge* (Tiny Hardcore Press 2012), and *Does Not Love*, a novel (Curbside Splendor Publications 2014). He lives in Chicago.

Luis Aguilar's numerous collections of poetry include *Los Ojos Ya Deshechos* (2007) and *Fruta de Temporada* (2011). He has won the Fernando Benítez Cultural Journalism Award and the Nicolás Guillén International Literature Award, among many other honors. He is a professor at the Autonomous University of Nuevo León.

E.R. Baxter III, Niagara County Community College Professor Emeritus of English, has been a fellow of New York State Creative Service Award for fiction and a recipient of a Just Buffalo Award for Fiction. Publications include *Looking for Niagara* (poetry, Slipstream Press); *Niagara Digressions* (creative non-fiction, Starcherone Books); *Niagara Lost and Found: New and Selected Poems* (Abyss Publications); and the chapbooks *And Other Poems; A Good War; Hunger;* and *What I Want*. He is a founding member of Niagara Heritage Partnership. His website is www.erbaxteriii.com.

Matt Bell is the author of the novel *In the House upon the Dirt Between the Lake and the Woods*, a finalist for the Young Lions Fiction Award, a Michigan Notable Book, and an Indies Choice Adult Debut Book of the Year Honor Recipient. He is also the author of two previous books, *How They Were Found* and *Cataclysm Baby*, and his next novel *Scrapper* will be published in late 2015. His stories have appeared in *Best American Mystery Stories, Best American Fantasy, Conjunctions, Gulf Coast, The American Reader,* and many other publications. He teaches creative writing at Arizona State University.

Margo Berdeshevsky currently live in Paris. Her poetry collections, *Between Soul and Stone* and *But a Passage in Wilderness* were published by Sheep Meadow Press (2007+2011). Her *Beautiful Soon Enough* received FC2's Ronald Sukenick Award for Innovative Fiction (University of Alabama Press, 2009.) Other honors include the

Robert H. Winner Award from the Poetry Society of America, and eight Pushcart Prize nominations. A new poetry manuscript titled *Square Black Key* is at the next gate, while a cross-genre novel, *Vagrant*, is forthcoming from Jaded Ibis Press. Please see: http://margoberdeshevsky.blogspot.com.

Stephanie Berger is the creator and Madame of The Poetry Brothel. Her collections of poetry include *In The Madame's Hat Box* from Dancing Girl Press and a collaborative chapbook *The Grey Bird: thirteen emoji poems in translation* from Coconut Books. Her poetry has appeared or is forthcoming in *Fence, Bat City Review, Styleite, Similar:Peaks, Smoking Glue Gun, H_NGM_N, Coconut,* and other publications. Stephanie works as the Director of The Poetry Society of New York, producers of the New York City Poetry Festival and The Typewriter Project. Occasionally she tumbles at stephani-berger.tumblr.com.

Caroline Bergvall is a writer and artist based in London. Co-editor of *I'll Drown My Book*. Most recent project, *Drift* (out with Nightboat Books, June 2014).

Jen Bervin's work brings together text and textile in a practice that encompasses poetry, archival research, artist books, and large-scale art works. Her work was included by curators Nora Burnett Abrams and Andrea Andersson in *Postscript: Writing After Conceptual Art*, "the first exhibition to examine the work of conceptual writing, investigating the roots of the movement in the art of the 1960s and 70s and presenting contemporary examples of text-based art practices." Bervin received a 2013 Creative Capital Grant in Literature for *The Silk Poems*, an experimental book nanoimprinted on silk film and read with light as a projection.

Born and raised in North Carolina, **Shanita Bigelow** now resides in Chicago where she works and writes. Her work can be found in *African American Review, North American Review, Drunken Boat, NAP,* and *Chorus: A Literary Mixtape*, among others. *Wherever Clarity is Necessary,* her first chapbook, was published by dancing girl press.

Marina Blitshteyn was born in the Former Soviet Union and came to the US as a refugee in 1991. She studied English at SUNY Buffalo and creative writing at Columbia University. Her chapbook, *Russian for Lovers,* was published by Argos Books in 2011. She is a Contributing Editor for *Apogee Journal* and curates the la perruque performance series in Brooklyn, NY.

Katy Bohinc: "I am no one, I am free." Slavoj Zizek said of *Dear Alain*, "This Book Should be Banished!"

Amaranth Borsuk is the author of *Handiwork* (Slope, 2012), and, with Brad Bouse, *Between Page and Screen* (Siglio, 2012). **Kate Durbin**'s most recent books are *E! Entertainment* (Wonder, 2014) and *The Ravenous Audience* (Akashic, 2009). Their collaboration *Abra* (forthcoming, 1913 Editions) received an NEA-funded Expanded Artists' Books grant from the Center for Book and Paper Arts at Columbia College, Chicago. As part of that grant, the book will be published as an artist's book and iPad app, created in collaboration with artist Ian Hatcher, in 2014. Track the project at a-b-r-a.com.

Tom Bradley has published twenty-five volumes of fiction, essays, screenplays and poetry with houses in the USA, England and Canada. His other ventures with visual artists include *Felicia's Nose* (MadHat), *We'll See Who Seduces Whom: a graphic ekphrasis in verse* (Unlikely Books) and *Elmer Crowley: a katabasic nekyia* (Mandrake of Oxford). His latest book is *This Wasted Land and Its Chymical Illuminations* (Lavender Ink/ Dialogos), a poem of 900 lines by Marc Vincenz with 200 footnotes by Tom, all built upon a 300-item bibliography. Further curiosity can be indulged at tombradley.org.

Laynie Browne is the author of ten collections of poetry and two novels. Her work appears in the second edition of *The Norton Anthology of Postmodern American Poetry*. Her newest collection *Lost Parkour Ps(alm)s* was just published in France, in both French and English editions by Presses Universitaires de Rouen et Du Havre. Her honors include: a Pew Fellowship in 2014, a National Poetry Series selection, a Contemporary Poetry Series selection and the Gertrude Stein Award of Innovative Writing. Two collections are forthcoming, *Scorpyn Odes* (Kore Press) and *P R A C T I C E* (SplitLevel).

Blake Butler is the author of *Nothing*, and several other works. He lives in Atlanta.

micha cárdenas is a performer, writer, student, educator, mixed-race trans femme latina who works with movement as a technology of change. micha is a Provost Fellow and PhD candidate in Media Arts + Practice (iMAP) at University of Southern California and a member of the art collective Electronic Disturbance Theater 2.0. Her co-authored book *The Transreal: Political Aesthetics of Crossing Realities* was published by Atropos Press in 2012. In 2014 micha is a visiting scholar in the Faculty of Information at the University of Toronto.

Angela Carr's most recent book of poetry is *Here in There* (BookThug 2014). Her other poetry books are *Ropewalk* (2006) and *The Rose Concordance* (2009). Currently, she teaches creative writing and poetry at The New School for Liberal Arts. In addition, she is a translator. Her translation of Québécoise poet Chantal Neveu's *Coït* was also published by BookThug (2012). Originally from Montréal, Carr now lives in New York City.

Alexandra Chasin is the author of *Selling Out*, *Kissed By*, *Brief*, and the forthcoming *Anslinger Nation*, a speculative, partial, and documentary history of prohibitionist drug policy, starring Harry J. Anslinger, first Commissioner of the Federal Bureau of Narcotics (University of Chicago Press, 2015). She writes fiction and nonfiction neverminding the difference. Chasin directs Writing On It All, a public participatory writing project that takes place on Governors Island in New York Harbor every June. She teaches writing at Lang College, The New School.

Ching-In Chen is author of *The Heart's Traffic* and co-editor of *The Revolution Starts at Home: Confronting Intimate Violence Within Activist Communities*. A

Kundiman, Lambda and Callaloo Fellow, they are part of the Macondo, Voices of Our Nations Arts Foundation and theatrical jazz writing communities, and have worked in the Asian American communities of San Francisco, Oakland, Riverside and Boston. They have been awarded fellowships from Soul Mountain Retreat, Virginia Center for the Creative Arts, Millay Colony, and the Norman Mailer Center. In Milwaukee, they are *cream city review*'s editor-in-chief and senior editor at *The Conversant*. www.chinginchen.com.

Elizabeth J. Colen is the author of poetry collections *Money for Sunsets* (Steel Toe Books, 2010; 2011 finalist for the Lambda Literary Award and Audre Lorde Prize in Poetry) and *Waiting Up for the World: Conspiracies* (Jaded Ibis Press, 2012), as well as flash fiction collection *Dear Mother Monster, Dear Daughter Mistake* (Rose Metal Press, 2011) and hybrid long poem / lyric essay *The Green Condition* (Ricochet Editions, 2014). She lives and works in the Pacific Northwest.

Dennis Cooper is the author of nine novels, including the five-novel sequence *The George Miles Cycle, My Loose Thread, God Jr., The Sluts,* and *The Marbled Swarm.* He is a frequent collaborator with the French theater director Gisele Vienne and the French/American visual artist Zac Farley. He lives in Paris and Los Angeles.

Matthew Cooperman is the author of numerous books, most recently *Imago for a Fallen World* (Jaded Ibis, 2013) and *Still: of the Earth as the Ark which Does Not Move* (Counterpath Press, 2011). A founding editor of Quarter After Eight, and current poetry editor of Colorado Review, he teaches at Colorado State University in Fort Collins, where he lives with the poet Aby Kaupang and his two children. More information can be found at www.matthewcooperman.com.

Lucy Corin is the author of the short story collections *One Hundred Apocalypses and Other Apocalypses* (McSweeney's Books) and *The Entire Predicament* (Tin House Books) and the novel *Everyday Psychokillers: A History for Girls* (FC2). She spent 2012-13 at the American Academy in Rome as the John Guare Fellow in Literature.

Cecilia Corrigan's writing has appeared in *n+1, The Capilano Review, LUMINA Journal, The Claudius App, The Journal,* and *The Henry Review,* among others. Her chapbook *True Beige* was published in 2013 by Trafficker Press. Various performances have been exhibited in a variety of media at MOMA, The New Museum, CAGE Gallery, as well as Brown, Yale, and the University of Iowa. She is also a comedian and screenwriter, having previously written for HBO. She lives in New York City.

T. Zachary Cotler is the author of a novel, *Ghost at the Loom,* a book of criticism, *Elegies for Humanism,* and three books of poetry, *House with a Dark Sky Roof, Supplice,* and *Sonnets to the Humans.* His awards include the Colorado Prize, the Sawtooth Prize, the Amy Clampitt Residency, and the Ruth Lilly Fellowship. He is a founding editor of *The Winter Anthology.*

Marisa Crawford is the author of the poetry collection *The Haunted House*

(Switchback Books, 2010), which was the winner of the 2008 Gatewood Prize, and the chapbook *8th Grade Hippie Chic* (Immaculate Disciples Press, 2013). Her poems, essays and articles have appeared in *EOAGH*, *Black Clock*, *Fanzine*, *Delirious Hem*, *The Hairpin* and the *Bitch Media* blog. Find her online at marisacrawford.net.

LaTasha N. Nevada Diggs is the author of *TwERK* (Belladonna* 2013). She has been published widely and her performance work has been featured at The Kitchen, Exit Art, Brooklyn Museum, The Whitney, MoMa, Queens Museum and The Walker Center. As a curator/director, she has staged events at El Museo del Barrio, Lincoln Center Out of Doors, The David Rubenstein Atrium, Dixon Place, Symphony Space and BAM Café. A recipient of several awards, residencies and fellowships, LaTasha, along with Greg Tate, are the founders and editors of Coon Bidness/yoYo and *SO4* magazine.

Stacy Doris was a poet who created a new world of connections with each book. Always desire always how who we are and what we want and how we want and how existence is mediated but mediation as part and parcel plays a part. Through the great differences among the 6 books in English and 4 books written in French her writing always voices a most concrete immediacy while she works through layers of traditions. Light and depth. Born in Connecticut (1962). The year she died (2012, San Francisco) several of her former students won prestigious poetry prizes.

Carina Finn is the author of *Invisible Reveille, Lemonworld & Other Poems, The Grey Bird: Thirteen Emoji Poems in Translation, MY LIFE IS A MOVIE*, and *I HEART MARLON BRANDO*. She is also a playwright and multimedia artist, and works as a pastry chef in New York City.

Carla Gannis is an interdisciplinary artist who lives and works in Brooklyn, New York. Gannis is the recipient of several awards, including a 2005 New York Foundation for the Arts (NYFA) Grant in Computer Arts, an Emerge 7 Fellowship from the Aljira Art Center, and a Chashama AREA Visual Arts Studio Award in New York, NY. She has exhibited in solo and group exhibitions nationally and internationally. Her solo exhibitions include "The Multiversal Hippozoonomadon & Prismenagerie" at Pablo's Birthday Gallery, New York, NY; "The Non-Facial Recognition Project" at Edelman Gallery, New York NY; and "Jezebel" at The Boulder Museum of Art, Boulder, CO.

Angela Genusa is a writer and artist. She is the author of *Composition* (Gauss PDF, 2014), *Twentysix Wikipedia Articles* (PediaPress, 2103), *Musée du Service des Objets Trouvés* (PediaPress, 2013), *Spam Bibliography* (Troll Thread, 2013); *Tender Buttons* and *Jane Doe* (Gauss PDF, 2013); *Highlights for Ren* (Lulu, 2013), *onlinedating. teenadultdating/Adult-Dating* (Lulu, 2012) and *The Package Insert of Sorrows* (Lulu, 2011). Her book *Simone's Embassy* is forthcoming from Truck Books.

Diana George's fiction has appeared in *Birkensnake, Third Bed, Chicago Review*, and elsewhere. An essay of George's appeared in *The Collagist* under the name "Collective in Support of the Imprisoned Grand-Jury Resisters Matt Duran, KteeO Olejnik, and Maddy Pfeiffer." George lives in Seattle, works as a technical editor, writes for the port-trucker's newsletter *Solidarity*, and is the proofreader of *Asymptote*, a magazine of literary translation.

Eckhard Gerdes has published books of poetry, drama, and ten novels, including *Hugh Moore* and *My Landlady the Lobotomist* (a top five finisher in the 2009 Preditors and Editors Readers Poll and nominated for the 2009 Wonderland Book Award for Best Novel of the Year). He has won the Bissell Award, been a finalist for the Starcherone and the Blatt awards, and was nominated for Georgia Author of the Year. He has a book of literary theory, *How to Read*, due in October 2014 from Guide Dog Books. He lives near Chicago and has three sons.

Carmen Giménez Smith is the author of a memoir, *Bring Down the Little Birds*, and four poetry collections—*Milk and Filth*, *Goodbye, Flicker*, *The City She Was*, and *Odalisque in Pieces*. *Milk and Filth* was a finalist for the NBCC Award in Poetry. She is the recipient of a 2011 American Book Award, the 2011 Juniper Prize for Poetry, and a 2011-2012 fellowship in creative nonfiction from the Howard Foundation. She recently co-edited the anthology *Angels of the Americlpyse: New Latin@ Writing* (Counterpath, 2014). A CantoMundo Fellow and formerly a Teaching-Writing Fellow at the Iowa Writers' Workshop, she is the publisher of Noemi Press.

Lara Glenum is the author of four books of poetry, including *The Hounds of No*, *Maximum Gaga*, *POP CORPSE!* and *All Hopped Up On Fleshy Dumdums*. She is also the co-editor, with Arielle Greenberg, of *Gurlesque: the new grrrly, grotesque, burlesque poetics*. She teaches in the MFA program at LSU.

Karen Green is an artist and writer whose *Bough Down* (Siglio, 2013) has been called "the most moving, strange, original, harrowing, and beautiful document of grief and reckoning I've read," by Maggie Nelson (Los Angeles Review of Books). Her work has also been published in Open City and anthologized in *Bound to Last: 30 Writers on Their Most Cherished Book*. Her visual work is collected by individuals and institutions including the Yale Beinecke Library and the Whitney Museum of American Art special collections. She exhibits with the Space gallery in Los Angeles and the Calabi gallery in Northern California.

Kate Greenstreet's books are *Young Tambling*, *The Last 4 Things*, and *case sensitive*, all from Ahsahta Press. For more information, visit kickingwind.com.

Christopher Grimes is the author of *Public Works: Short Fiction and a Novella* (FC2, 2005) and *The Pornographers* (Jaded Ibis, 2011). His stories have appeared in *Western Humanities Review*, *Beloit Fiction Journal*, *Reed*, *Cream City Review*, *First Intensity*, *KNOCK*, and elsewhere. He teaches literature and fiction writing at the University of Illinois at Chicago.

Carol Guess is the author of fourteen books of poetry and prose, including *Darling Endangered*, *Doll Studies: Forensics*, and *Tinderbox Lawn*. She teaches Creative Writing and Queer Studies at Western Washington University, where she is Professor of English.

Evelyn Hampton is the author of *Discomfort* (Ellipsis Press 2014) and *WE WERE ETERNAL AND GIGANTIC* (Magic Helicopter Press 2009).

Duriel E. Harris is the author of two print collections: *Drag* and *Amnesiac* and *Speleology*, a video collaboration with artist Scott Rankin. A co-founder of The Black Took Collective and Editor for *Obsidian: Literature in the African Diaspora*, Harris holds degrees from Yale and NYU, and a PhD from the University of Illinois. A MacDowell and Millay Colony fellow, Harris has been awarded grants from the Illinois Arts Council, the Cave Canem Foundation, and the Rockefeller Brothers Fund. Current projects include the sound compilation "Black Magic" and *Thingification*—a one-woman show. Harris is an associate professor of English at Illinois State University. (www.thingification.org).

Tytti Heikkinen is a Finnish poet and the author of *The Warmth of the Taxidermied Animal*. She has studied comparative literature and Finnish literature at the University of Helsinki, and her poems have been translated to Russian, French, and Italian.

Johannes Heldén is an author, visual artist, musician. He is the author of eleven books, most recently *Evolution print* and *Terraforming* (OEI); five digital works, most recently *The Factory* (Möllebyen Literature) and *Evolution digital* (w/H. Jonson, premiered at the Centre Pompidou, 2013); three music albums, most recently *System* (Irrlicht, 2013). Solo exhibitions include: the Media Archaelogy Lab in Boulder, Bonniers Konsthall in Stockholm, Gothenburg Museum of Art amongst others. Group exhibitions include Remediating the Social at Inspace, Edinburgh, Against Time at Bonniers Konsthall, and Chercher le texte at Centre Pompidou. Grants and awards: the N. Katherine Hayles award, The Kalleberger Grant, Hawthornden amongst others.

Christopher Higgs wrote *The Complete Works of Marvin K. Mooney*, a novel. He is also a literary critic, independent curator, and educator.

Janis Butler Holm lives in Athens, Ohio, where she has served as Associate Editor for *Wide Angle*, the film journal. Her prose, poems, and performance pieces have appeared in small-press, national, and international magazines. Her plays have been produced in the U.S., Canada, and England.

Jayson Iwen is a poet, novelist, translator, teacher, editor, and technical writer. He is the author of *Six Trips in Two Directions*, *A Momentary Jokebook*, and *Gnarly Wounds*, among other publications. He has won the Emergency Press International Book Award, the Cleveland State University Ruthanne Wiley Memorial Novella Award, and the Academy of American Poets Award. He currently dwells in the Twin Ports with his wife and two children.

Michael Joyce's eleven books include seven novels, most recently *Foucault, in Winter, in the Linnaeus Garden* (Starcherone, 2015) and *Twentieth Century Man* (Seismicity, 2014) as well as a book-length sequence of poems, *Paris Views* (Blazevox, 2012). *afternoon, a story* (Eastgate, 1987), was followed by other electronic works on disk and online. Ongoing digital work includes *The Surface of Water*, an augmented reality, blended panoramic narrative project with Jay David Bolter and Maria Engberg, and *Fictional Encounters*, a project combining aspects of collaborative drawing, film-making, locative fiction, with Alexandra Grant, Robert Nashak, and Lucas Kazansky.

Originally from the hinterland, **Erin Kautza** now lives and works in Philadelphia.

Becca Klaver is the author of the poetry collection *LA Liminal* (Kore Press, 2010) and several chapbooks, including *Nonstop Pop* (Bloof Books, 2013) and *Merrily, Merrily* (Lame House Press, 2013). She attended the University of Southern California and Columbia College Chicago, and is a PhD candidate at Rutgers University, writing a dissertation on contemporary women's poetry and the everyday. Becca co-founded Switchback Books and is co-editing the second edition of *Gurlesque*. Recently, she curated the What's So Hot salon series and Women Poets Wearing Sweatpants website. Becca grew up in Milwaukee and now lives in Brooklyn.

Hank Lazer's seventeen books of poetry include *Portions* (Lavender Ink, 2009), *The New Spirit* (Singing Horse, 2005), *Elegies & Vacations* (Salt, 2004), and *Days* (Lavender Ink, 2002). In 2008, *Lyric & Spirit: Selected Essays, 1996-2008* was published by Omnidawn. *N18*, a handwritten book, is available from Singing Horse Press. Pages from the notebooks have been performed with soprano saxophonist Andrew Raffo Dewar at the University of Georgia and in Havana, Cuba.

Aby Kaupang's most recent poetry collection is *Little "g" God Grows Tired of Me* (SpringGun Press, 2013). She has had poems appear in *FENCE, La Petite Zine, Dusie, Verse, DQ*, & others. She holds master's degrees in both Creative Writing and Occupational Therapy from Colorado State University. She lives in Fort Collins with the poet, Matthew Cooperman. More info at http://www.abykaupang.com.

Robert Kloss is the author of *The Alligators of Abraham* and the co-author (with Amber Sparks and Matt Kish) of *The Desert Places*.

Individual entries on **Richard Kostelanetz**'s work in several fields appear in various editions of *Readers Guide to Twentieth-Century Writers, Merriam-Webster Encyclopedia of Literature, Contemporary Poets, Contemporary Novelists, Postmodern Fiction, Webster's Dictionary of American Writers, The HarperCollins Reader's Encyclopedia of American Literature, Baker's Biographical Dictionary of Musicians, Directory of American Scholars, Who's Who in America, Who's Who in the World, Who's Who in American Art, NNDB. com, Wikipedia.com*, and *Britannica.com*, among other distinguished directories. Otherwise, he survives in New York, where he was born, unemployed and thus overworked.

Janice Lee is the author of *KEROTAKIS* (Dog Horn Press, 2010), *Daughter* (Jaded Ibis, 2011), and *Damnation* (Penny-Ante Editions, 2013). She currently lives in Los Angeles where she is Co-Editor of *[out of nothing]*, Reviews Editor at *HTMLGIANT*, Editor of the new #RECURRENT Novel Series for Jaded Ibis Press, Executive Editor at *Entropy*, and Founder/CEO of POTG Design. She currently teaches at CalArts and can be found online at http://janicel.com.

Ji Yoon Lee was born and raised in Korea and came to the United States with purpose unknown. Her poems have appeared in *Karlie Kloss, Bambi Muse, NAP,* and *Seven Corners*. Her first chapbook *IMMA* was published by Radioactive Moat Press. Her second chapbook *Funsize/Bitesize* is forthcoming from Birds of Lace. Her manuscript was one of the finalists of 1913 First Book Prize 2012. *Foreigner's Folly: A Tale of Attempted Project* (Coconut Books, 2014) is her first full-length collection.

Lucas de Lima was born in southeastern Brazil. He is the author of *Wet Land* (Action Books, 2014) as well as the chapbooks *Terraputa* (Birds of Lace) and *Ghostlines* (Radioactive Moat). A contributing writer at Montevidayo.com, he pursues doctoral studies in Comparative Literature at the University of Pennsylvania.

Ella Longpre is the author of the chapbook, *The Odor of the Hoax Was Gone* (Monkey Puzzle Press 2013). Her work has appeared in *elimae, Summer Stock, Dinosaur Bees, NOÖ Journal,* and *Everyday Genius*. Longpre is the 2013-14 Anne Waldman Fellow at the Jack Kerouac School of Disembodied Poetics. She has served as Poetry Editor at *Fanzine* and is currently Senior Editor of the *Bombay Gin Literary Journal*.

Kelly Magee's first collection of stories, *Body Language* (University of North Texas Press), won the Katherine Ann Porter Prize for Short Fiction. Her writing has appeared in *The Kenyon Review, The Tampa Review, Diagram, Ninth Letter, Black Warrior Review, Colorado Review,* and others. She is an Assistant Professor of Creative Writing at Western Washington University.

Farid Matuk is the author of *This Isa Nice Neighborhood* (Letter Machine, 2010) and *My Daughter La Chola* (Ahsahta, 2013). His work has appeared in *Poetry, The Baffler, Denver Quarterly, Flag & Void,* and *The Iowa Review,* among others. Matuk teaches in the MFA program at the University of Arizona.

James McGirk is a writer and adjunct professor based in the Cherokee Nation of Oklahoma. For more information please visit: jamesmcgirk.com.

Joe Milazzo is the author of *Crepuscule W/ Nellie* (Jaded Ibis) and *The Habiliments* (Apostrophe Books). He co-edits the online interdisciplinary arts journal *[out of nothing]* and is also the proprietor of Imipolex Press. Joe lives and works in Dallas, TX, and his virtual location is http://www.slowstudies.net/jmilazzo/.

Nick Montfort wrote #! (pronounced "Shebang" and published by Counterpath in 2014) and *Riddle & Bind*; he co-wrote *2002: A Palindrome Story* with William Gillespie. He has participated in dozens of literary and academic collaborations, including *The Deletionist* (with Amaranth Borsuk and Jesper Juul) and *Implementation* (with Scott Rettberg). He is associate professor of digital media at MIT and faculty advisor for the Electronic Literature Organization. The MIT Press has published four of Montfort's collaborative and individually-authored books, most recently *10 PRINT CHR$(205.5+RND(1)); : GOTO 10*, a collaboration with nine other authors that Montfort organized. His site is http://nickm.com.

Tracie Morris is a poet who works in multiple media. Her sound poetry has been presented at the Whitney Biennial, MoMA, The Silent Barn, Jamaica Center for Arts and Learning, The Gramsci Monument with Thomas Hirshhorn for DIA. She's the author-vocalist of the collection *Rhyme Scheme* (Zasterle Press, 2012). She's completing "Eyes Wide Shut: A not-neo-Benshi Read" (Kore Press). Tracie has a poetry MFA from Hunter College, CUNY and a Performance Studies PhD from NYU. She is a former CPCW Fellow of the University of Pennsylvania. She's Professor & Coordinator of Performance + Performance Studies at Pratt Institute.

Yedda Morrison is the author of several books of poetry, including *Darkness* (Make Now Press, 2012), *Girl Scout Nation* (Displaced Press, 2008) and *Crop* (Kelsey Street Press, 2003). Her work has been included in the anthologies *Kindergarde* (Black Radish Press), *Against Expression* (Northwestern University Press), *I'll Drown My Book* (Les Figues Press) and *Bay Poetics* (Faux Press). From 1998-2002 she co-edited *Tripwire, A journal of Poetics*. She is part of the artist/writer's collaborative The Collective Task (www.collectivetask.com). Yedda is currently represented by Republic Gallery in Vancouver, BC. She lives and works in San Francisco.

Harryette Mullen is the author of several poetry collections, including *Recyclopedia*, winner of a PEN Beyond Margins Award, and *Sleeping with the Dictionary*, a finalist for a National Book Award, National Book Critics Circle Award, and Los Angeles Times Book Prize. Her poems have been translated into Spanish, Portuguese, French, Italian, Polish, German, Swedish, Danish, Turkish, Bulgarian, and Kyrgyz. A collection of her essays and interviews, *The Cracks Between*, was published in 2012 by University of Alabama Press. Her new poetry collection from Graywolf Press is *Urban Tumbleweed: Notes from a Tanka Diary*.

Sawako Nakayasu's newest book is *The Ants* (Les Figues Press, 2014). Her translation of *The Collected Poems of Sagawa Chika* is forthcoming soon from Canarium Books.

Brian Oliu is originally from New Jersey and currently teaches at the University of Alabama, where he is the Associate Director of the Slash Pine Press internship. He is the author of *So You Know It's Me* (Tiny Hardcore Press, 2011) a series of Craigslist Missed Connections, *Level End* (Origami Zoo Press, 2012), a chapbook based on videogame boss battles, *Leave Luck to Heaven*, an ode to 8-bit videogames, and *i/o* (Civil Coping Mechanisms, 2015), a memoir in the form of a computer virus.

Daniela Olszewska is the author of four collections of poetry, including *cloudfang: : cakedirt* (Horse Less Press, 2012) and *Citizen J* (Artifice Books, 2013). She was born in Poland and received her MFA from University of Alabama, but she self-identifies as a Chicagoan.

Aimee Parkison is an Assistant Professor teaching in the Creative Writing Program at Oklahoma State University. She has received a William Randolph Hearst Creative Artist Fellowship from the American Antiquarian Society, a North Carolina Arts Council Fellowship, a Christopher Isherwood Fellowship, a Writers at Work Fellowship, and a Kurt Vonnegut Fiction Prize from North American Review. Parkison's books are *The Innocent Party* (BOA Editions' American Reader Series 2012), *Woman with Dark Horses* (Starcherone 2004), and *The Petals of Your Eyes* (Starcherone 2014). Her work has appeared in numerous literary magazines and anthologies. More information can be found at www.aimeeparkison.com

Ted Pelton is the author of five published books, all fiction, including *Bartleby, the Sportscaster* (Subito, 2010) and *Malcolm & Jack (and Other Famous American Criminals)* (Spuyten Duyvil, 2006; eBook, Dzanc, 2013). He is also the Founder and Emeritus Publisher of Starcherone Books, as well as the Chair of English at Tennessee Tech University. He has received National Endowment for the Arts and Isherwood Foundation fellowships for Fiction. "Columbine" is from his newest work, a novel-in-stories called *The Trickster Woodchuck.*

Justin Petropoulos is the author of *Eminent Domain* (Marsh Hawk Press 2011), selected by Anne Waldman for the 2010 Marsh Hawk Press Poetry Prize & *<legend> </legend>* (Jaded Ibis Press 2013) with Carla Gannis. He is currently an adjunct faculty member at New Jersey City University. (justin@entropymag.org)

Alake Pilgrim is a fiction writer from Trinidad & Tobago in the Caribbean. She has had residencies at the Community of Writers at Squaw Valley and the Cropper Foundation Writers Workshop. Her stories have twice been awarded the Regional Prize for Fiction in the Commonwealth Short Story Competition, as well as a Small Axe Literary Prize. In 2014, she participated in the Callaloo Creative Writing Workshop in Barbados. She is currently a student in the MFA Creative Writing program at Louisiana State University and is completing her first short story collection.

Vanessa Place writes poetry, prose, and art criticism; she is also a criminal lawyer and co-director of Les Figues Press.

Niina Pollari is a poet and translator in Brooklyn. Her first full-length, *Dead Horse*, is out in 2014 from Birds, LLC.

Laura Relyea is a writer and the Editor and Chief of Vouched Books. Her fiction has appeared in *NAP, Necessary Fiction, Thought Catalog, Coconut Poetry* and elsewhere. Her chapbook, *All Glitter Everything*, was published by Safety Third Enterprises in October 2013. She both fears and respects glitter.

Frances Richard is the author of *Anarch.* (Futurepoem, 2012), *The Phonemes* (Les Figues Press, 2012) and *See Through* (Four Way Books, 2003). She writes frequently about contemporary art and is co-author, with Jeffrey Kastner and Sina Najafi, of *Odd Lots: Revisiting Gordon Matta-Clark's "Fake Estates"* (Cabinet Books, 2005). Currently she teaches at the California College of the Arts in San Francisco.

Cia Rinne is a poet and artist based in Berlin. Publications of visual, acoustic and conceptual poetry in different languages, a.o. *zaroum* (2001), *notes for soloists* (OEI Editör 2009), and *should we blind ourselves and leave thebes* (H//O//F 2013), sound works and exhibitions, a.o. at the Grimmuseum Berlin, Signal in Malmö, and at the Kumu Art Museum in Tallinn. She has also worked on documentary projects, most recently on a book on the Roma of seven different countries (*The Roma Journeys*, 2007).

Kim Rosenfield is the author of several books of poetry, including *Good Morning—Midnight—* (Roof Books 2001), *Tràma* (Krupskaya 2004), *re:evolution* (Les Figues Press 2009) *Lividity* (Les Figues Press, 2012) and *USO: I'll Be Seeing You* (Ugly Duckling Presse 2013). Her work has been included in the anthologies *Against Expression* (Northwestern University Press), *Bowery Women* (YBK Publishers, Inc.), *Gurlesque* (Saturnalia), *I'll Drown My Book* (Les Figues Press), and *The Unexpected Guest: Art, writing and thinking on hospitality* (Liverpool Biennial, ART/BOOKS). She is a recipient of a Fund For Poetry grant and is a founding member of the international artist's collective, Collective Task. Rosenfield lives and works in NYC.

Tracy Jeanne Rosenthal's experiments in scholarship have been performed in art, literary, and academic contexts including The New Museum, Machine Project, The Poetry Center of Chicago, Rutgers University, and USC. She is the author of three chapbooks, *Ri Ri (Re)Vision* (Publication Studio), *This Is The ENDD* (Wilner Books), and *Close* (Sibling Rivalry Press), and is a regular contributor at *Rhizome.org*. Her favorite crystal is angelite.

Joanna Ruocco co-edits *Birkensnake*, a fiction journal, with Brian Conn. She is the author of *The Mothering Coven* (Ellipsis Press), *Man's Companions* (Tarpaulin Sky Press), *A Compendium of Domestic Incidents* (Noemi Press), *Another Governess / The Least Blacksmith: A Diptych* (FC2), and *Dan*, forthcoming from Dorothy, a publishing project. Toni Jones, her more athletic alter ego, just released her first novel, *No Secrets in Spandex*, from Crimson Romance.

Suzanne Scanlon is the author of a novel, *Promising Young Women* (Dorothy, 2012), and a forthcoming work of creative nonfiction titled, *Her 37th Year, An Index* (Noemi Press, 2015). New fiction has appeared in *Spolia* and *MAKE Literary Magazine*. She lives in Chicago and teaches creative writing at Columbia College and in the MFA program at Roosevelt University.

Joseph Scapellato was born in the suburbs of Chicago and earned his MFA in Fiction at New Mexico State University. His work appears in *Kenyon Review Online*, *Post Road*, *PANK*, *Unsaid*, and other places.

Lawrence Schimel writes in both Spanish & English and has published over 100 books as author or anthologist, most-recently the poetry collection *Deleted Names* (A Midsummer Night's Press). He lives in Madrid, Spain where he works as a Spanish—>English translator.

Kim Gek Lin Short was born in Singapore and spent her childhood in places like Manila, Jakarta, and Calgary. She moved to the States during the wonderful terrible 80s and lived in Denver, San Francisco, and Brooklyn before settling in Philly where she lives with her husband and daughter. Kim's work has been nominated for a Pushcart Prize and has appeared in numerous publications such as *Absent*, *Caketrain*, and *No Tell Motel*, and anthologies like *Narrative (Dis)Continuities: Prose Experiments by Younger American Writers*. She is the author of two lyric novels *The Bugging Watch & Other Exhibits* and *China Cowboy*, both from Tarpaulin Sky, and the chapbooks *The Residents* (dancing girl press) and *Run (Rope-a-Dope)*, a Golden Gloves winner.

Amber Sparks is the author of *May We Shed These Human Bodies*, and the co-author (with Robert Kloss and illustrator Matt Kish) of *The Desert Places*.

Anna Joy Springer is a writer and visual artist who lives in Los Angeles and teaches at UC San Diego, where she directs the MFA Program in Writing. Her books are *The Birdwisher* (Birds of Lace, 2009) and *The Vicious Red Relic, Love* (Jaded Ibis, 2011). She sang in the bands Blatz, The Gr'ups, and Cypher in the snow.

Stephanie Strickland's 7th book of poems, *Dragon Logic*, was published by Ahsahta in 2013. Her 8th, *V : WaveTercets / Losing L'una*, was published by SpringGun in 2014, accompanied by the Vniverse app for iPad, created with Ian Hatcher. She has collaborated on nine electronic poems, most recently "Sea and Spar Between" and "Duels—Duets" with Nick Montfort and "House of Trust" with Ian Hatcher. She is a member of the Board of Directors of the Electronic Literature Organization. For more information on her work, go to http://stephaniestrickland.com.

Dennis James Sweeney's writing has appeared in places like *DIAGRAM*, *Indiana Review*, *Mid-American Review*, and *Unstuck*. He is the author of *What They Took Away*, winner of the 2013 CutBank Chapbook Contest, and *THREATS*, a chapbook of poems forthcoming from alice blue books. Originally from Cincinnati, he lives in Corvallis, Oregon.

Zoe Tuck, and her love of poetry and magic, were born in Texas. Since relocating to the SF Bay Area, she has been an active member of the local literary community, working at Small Press Distribution and co-curating Condensery Reading Series. She is the author of *Terror Matrix* (Timeless, Infinite Light). Other work appears in *Troubling the Line* and *It's night in San Francisco but it's sunny in Oakland*. She currently blogs about writing by queer and trans folks and Bay Area literary culture for the *Michigan Quarterly Review*. She is a poetry reader for *HOLD: a journal*.

Jeff VanderMeer's most recent fiction is the NYT-bestselling Southern Reach trilogy (*Annihilation*, *Authority*, and *Acceptance*), all released in 2014. The series has been acquired by publishers in 16 other countries and Paramount Pictures/ Scott Rudin Productions have acquired the movie rights. His *Wonderbook* (Abrams Image), the world's first fully illustrated, full-color creative writing guide, won the BSFA Award for best nonfiction and has been nominated for a Hugo Award and a Locus Award. A three-time World Fantasy Award winner and 13-time nominee, VanderMeer has been a finalist for the Nebula, Philip K. Dick, and Shirley Jackson Awards, among others.

Rosmarie Waldrop's recent poetry books are *Driven to Abstraction, Curves to the Apple, Blindsight* (New Directions), and *Love, Like Pronouns* (Omnidawn). University of Alabama Press published her collected essays, Dissonance (if you are interested). Two novels, *The Hanky of Pippin's Daughter* and *A Form/of Taking/It*. All are available in one paperback (Northwestern UP). She has translated Edmond Jabès's work (her *Lavish Absence: Recalling and Rereading Edmond Jabès*, is out from Wesleyan UP) as well as Emmanuel Hocquard, Jacques Roubaud, and, from the German, Friederike Mayröcker, Elke Erb, Oskar Pastior, Gerhard Rühm, Ulf Stolterfoht. She lives in Providence, RI and co-edits with Keith Waldrop Burning Deck books.

Emerson Whitney is a writer and artist based in Los Angeles. Emerson's writing has appeared in CA Conrad's *Jupiter 88, Bombay Gin, Work Magazine, Troubling the Line: Anthology of Trans and Genderqueer Poetry*, NPR, the Huffington Post, the New York Observer, and elsewhere. Emerson co-edits *THEM* literary journal, is a 2013 kari edwards fellow, and a Teaching Artist in Residence on behalf of California Institute of the Arts.

Brooke Wonders' fiction has appeared in *Clarkesworld, Electric Velocipede*, and the *Year's Best Dark Fantasy and Horror 2013*, among others. Her nonfiction has appeared in or is forthcoming from *Brevity, The Collagist, DIAGRAM*, and elsewhere. She reviews for *American Book Review, Entropy Magazine*, and *Essay Daily*, and she serves as nonfiction editor at online literary magazine *The Account*. She joined the Languages and Literatures faculty at the University of Northern Iowa in August of 2014.

Amy Wright is the Nonfiction Editor of Zone 3 Press, and the author of four chapbooks. Her work can also be found in *Bellingham Review, Brevity, Denver Quarterly, Drunken Boat, Quarterly West, Southern Poetry Anthology* (Volumes III and VI), *Tupelo Quarterly*, and is forthcoming in *POOL* and *Kenyon Review*.

Kate Zambreno is the author of two novels, *O Fallen Angel* (Chiasmus Press) and *Green Girl* (Harper Perennial). She is also the author of two works of innovative nonfiction, *Heroines* (Semiotext(e)'s Active Agents) and *Book of Mutter* (forthcoming from Wesleyan University Press in October 2015). A novel, *Drifts*, is forthcoming from Harper in 2017. She teaches in the creative writing programs at Columbia University and Sarah Lawrence College.

Laura Zaylea is a filmmaker and new media artist whose work centers around queer identities and experimental storytelling. Her feature film *Hold The Sun* (2009) was awarded Best Avant-garde Film at the Amsterdam Film Festival and her queer-themed shorts *Camouflage Pink* (2002) and *Lydia Li* (2004-2006) were supported by a grant from the Open Meadows Foundation. Her screenplays have won awards at the University Film and Video Association and the Atlanta International Film Festival. Zaylea is an Asst. Professor at Temple University. More about her work can be found at www.LauraZaylea.com.

Editor Notes

Volume editor **Megan Milks** is the author of *Kill Marguerite and Other Stories* (Emergency Press, 2014) and the chapbook *Twins* (Birds of Lace, 2012). Her fiction has been published in three volumes of innovative writing as well as many journals. Her editing history includes co-editing the arts/culture magazine *Mildred Pierce* (2005-2010) and the scholarly volume *Asexualities: Feminist and Queer Perspectives* (Routledge, 2014), as well as guest co-editing one of seven issues of *Birkensnake 6* (2013). She is also an editor at *Entropy* and has written criticism for the *Los Angeles Review of Books*, *The New Inquiry*, *Hyperallergic*, and *Fanzine*, among others.

Series editor **Davis Schneiderman**'s recent novels include the DEAD/BOOKS trilogy (Jaded Ibis), including the blank novel *BLANK*, the plagiarized novel *[SIC]* (Fall 2013), and the ink-smeared novel *INK* (forthcoming); along with the novel *Drain* (Northwestern 2010). He co-edited the collections *Retaking the Universe: Williams S. Burroughs in the Age of Globalization* (Pluto 2004, RealityStudio.com 2014), *The Exquisite Corpse: Chance and Collaboration in Surrealism's Parlor Game* (Nebraska, 2009); and *The &NOW AWARDS: The Best Innovative Writing* (vols. 1 and 2). He is Associate Dean of the Faculty and Director of the Center for Chicago Programs, as well as Professor of English and Director of Lake Forest College Press/ &NOW Books at Lake Forest College.

Joshua Corey is co-director of &NOW Books and the Plonsker Series Editor. His own works include four poetry collections, the most recent of which is *The Barons* (Omnidawn Publishing, 2014), and a novel, *Beautiful Soul: An American Elegy* (Spuyten Duyvil Press, 2014). With G.C Waldrep he edited *The Arcadia Project: North American Postmodern Pastoral* (Ahsahta Press, 2012), an anthology of innovative nature poems. He lives in Evanston and is an associate professor of English at Lake Forest College

Cover designer **Jessica Berger** is a fiction writer and, on occasion, a visual artist. She is an editor for *The Account* magazine and her work has appeared in *PANK*, *The &Now Awards: The Best Innovative Writing*, *Metazen*, and elsewhere.

the turn became a calling

she took a sudden turn for worse

"wandering in the house of the voice is"

is turning

he had become a public person

the call the turning this is

the call the call could be

as taking a turn

. the call

as turning

the case

then one way you

could be called to

as having as